Alone on the Great Wall

Alone on the Great Wall

William Lindesay

Fulcrum Publishing
Golden, Colorado

Cover Calligraphy by Beth Marcue
Cover Photographs by William Lindesay
Book Design by Patty Maher

First published by Hodder & Stoughton in Great Britian, 1989

Library of Congress Cataloging-in-Publication Data

Lindesay, William.
    Alone on the Great Wall / William Lindesay.
        p.   cm.
    ISBN 1-55591-079-3 (pbk.)
        1. Great Wall of China (China) 2. China—Description and travel—
1976– 3. Lindesay, William—Journeys—China. I. Title.
DS793.G67L565 1991   91–71367
915.1—dc20   CIP

Printed in the United States of America

0   9   8   7   6   5   4   3   2   1

Fulcrum Publishing
350 Indiana Street
Golden, Colorado 80401

To Wu Qi

CONTENTS

PART FOUR—REFORMS

Calligraphy by Feng Jin Hai of Hao Tan, Dingbian County, Shaanxi Province, which reads "English friend traveling the Great Wall."

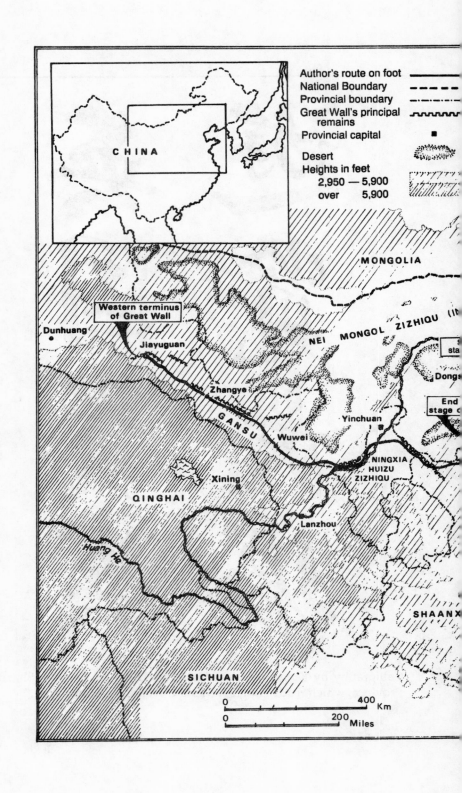

Author's route on foot ———

National Boundary ———

Provincial boundary —·—·—

Great Wall's principal remains ⌐⌐⌐⌐

Provincial capital ■

Desert

Heights in feet

2,950 — 5,900

over 5,900

CHINA

MONGOLIA

NEI MONGOL ZIZHIQU (I

Western terminus of Great Wall

Dunhuang

Jiayuguan

Zhangye

GANSU

Wuwei

Yinchuan

NINGXIA HUIZU ZIZHIQU

Xining

QINGHAI

Lanzhou

Huang He

SICHUAN

SHAANX

Dongs

End stage o

sta

0   400 Km
0   200 Miles

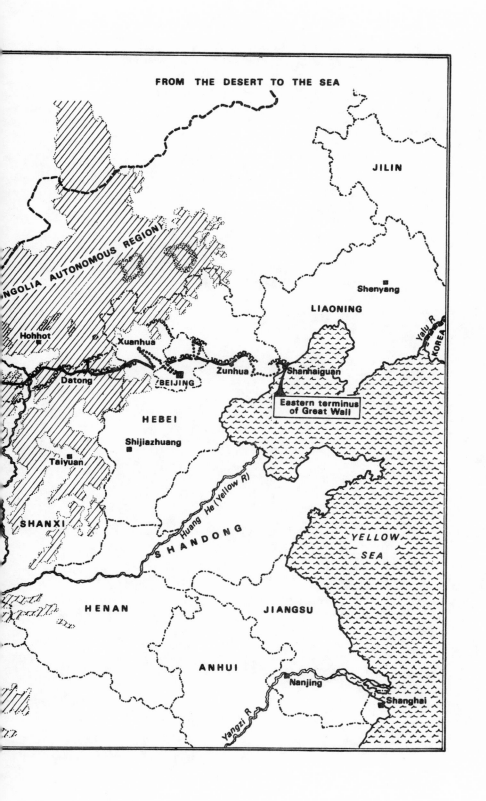
FROM THE DESERT TO THE SEA

FOREWORD

by Dr. Han Suyin

Three years ago, fortuitously, William Lindesay and I were together in Manchester—or was it Birmingham?—waiting to appear on a television program. As usual we, the consenting sheep, huddled in rubbery armchairs, waiting while the media lords were preparing to praise or to maul us. William and I talked. I found him an alert young man of disarming simplicity, full of wonder for the earth, our planet, his spirit's surge the stuff which drove explorers and adventurers to cross the oceans, reach the North Pole, wade through unknown jungles, one of those whose endeavors brighten and enlarge our lives. He wanted to run the Great Wall of China.

"How are you going to explain to the people you meet in China what you are doing?"

He showed me a little pocket book on which he had scribbled, in his own not too legible writing, that he was William Lindesay, and that he was running the Great Wall.

"This will never do," I told him, full of my knowledge of how the simplest things can become awkward when meeting with unbudging officials. "No one reads English very much in China's hinterland, which is where the wall begins, 3,100 miles or more from the Pacific Ocean. You will be in the desert lands of Central Asia, with many national minorities, Kurds and Tajiks and Huis and Uighurs, as well as Han Chinese. You should have a letter in both Chinese and English, stating that you are running the Great Wall for fun and friendship. You may meet bureaucrats. Bureaucrats I know well, having had to deal with them in many countries all my life. They are there to obstruct, deny, suspect, retard, interrogate, never to encourage something they cannot understand. You need a nice letter for bureaucrats."

"Who's going to do *that*?" said William, a bit puzzled.

"Me. I know how to deal with them. I'll write a nice letter, and I have a friend who will do it on his computer typewriter, so that it is easily read and looks more important. In both English and Chinese."

So it was done. My friend Ye Nienlung, the son of eminent writer Ye Junjian, well known in both England and in China, produced a perfect letter, suave, bland, speckled with the appropriate cliches. Off went William Lindesay, and ran the Great Wall.

But it was not the letter, it was William's wonderful candor, that purity of mind and aim, which brought him success. He met affectionate care all the way, and this book is not only his own odyssey but the great story of the people of the Wall. A bright child of the cosmos, William ran for all of us who in our hearts dream that each day of our lives might be a step of love.

Dr. Han Suyin
Lausanne, 1989

ACKNOWLEDGMENTS

Thomas Cook Traveller's Cheques Ltd. was the sole sponsor of my journey, and it was largely through the enthusiasm and loyalty of Neil Pirie that I was given the financial opportunity to achieve my ambitious goal. Thanks also to Roger Taylor, Regional Director of TCTC, and Claudia Cheung of the Hong Kong office. Thomas Cook's parent organization, the Midland Group, provided my foothold in Beijing. Considerable assistance was given by the Group's representative, Lance Browne, and his staff, Jennifer Yang, Stephanie Chien, Zhang Ling, Jimmy Liu; and at the London end of Global Banking operations thanks to the "Asia Region" at Cannon Street, especially Roger Stebbing.

Out on the Great Wall I could rely on the highest quality equipment. Inside a rucksack designed by Dave Allport at Troll I carried a Lightline sleeping bag, Gore-tex sleeping bag, and an Ultrafleece suit, all of which were provided by Bob Newey of Mountain Equipment. Helly Hansen Lifa wear and Polisox were worn continually. Then it was all up to my feet. They were cushioned with Gel technology shoes developed by the Asics Tiger Corporation of Japan. Particular thanks are due to Yutaka Sasai, Mr. Kitimura, Tom Haddley, and Eddie Allen. Any foot problems were dealt with using Scholl footcare products. Photographic services and expenses were provided by Max Spielmann of Merseyside, while Sony UK supplied a Video 8 camera on which to shoot library film. I am also indebted to Kevin Steele of British Airways in Beijing for his assistance with travel services.

Underlying all this support was the firm foundation of family. My mother and father, Dorothy and Hamilton Lindesay, have given me a home base for researching, reorganizing and recording my exploits. David, whose athleticism has always been an inspiration, has given much brotherly advice and practical assistance. My brother Nicholas has endured a Wall fever similar to my own in his role as UK coordinator. I owe him the greatest of thanks for ceaseless encouragement, from the idea on Hadrian's Wall to the reading of my manuscript, and everything in between. This supporting fabric of the Lindesay family was mirrored in China by the many families in Gansu, Ningxia, Shaanxi, Nei Mongol, Shanxi, Hebei and Beijing who received me with warmth and kindness. A letter of introduction prepared with the assistance of Dr. Han Suyin and printed by Mr. Ye of Sinolink was invaluable for communication.

On my return to the UK, the Chinese Ambassador to London, Ji Chao Zhu, and his staff welcomed me, my family and my sponsor to the Embassy, thus providing the occasion for me to thank the Chinese people for the infrastructure that they spontaneously offered. The product of all those individuals is recorded here. Thanks to Wu Qi for being historical adviser and translator.

WL

A Note on Transcription

The Pinyin method of transcription, as used in the People's Republic, is used in this book. The principal pronunciation equivalents are as follows:

Chinese letter	English sound
c	ts
q	ch
x	sh
z	dz
zh	j

PART ONE

Open?

He who contemplates a pilgrimage *per lineam valli*, if he has a thorough love of antiquity, and duly appreciates the importance of the great structure he is to see, will not enter upon the enterprise lightly.

—*J. Collingwood Bruce,*
Handbook to The Roman Wall, 1863

1

One Wall Leads to Another

There is an affliction known as wall fever. . . . This is a healthy and rewarding pursuit.

—*Alfred Wainwright*

When some people see a mountain they have to climb it. When some see a wall their curiosity asks what is on the other side. But if you see a long wall, an old wall, and you're a runner, then you want to run along it. My brother Nicholas had his eye on Hadrian's Wall in Northumbria and when he made his intentions known, with more than a hint of invitation in his voice, I accepted the challenge, insisting we set a date in the near future. My experience is that unless you make a commitment opportunities pass by. Life seemed full of people who talked about achievement yet never did anything more adventurous than watch television.

Three months later we sheltered from a strong wind in the lee of the Roman Wall near Housesteads. In just a day and a half we were having a brief taste of escapism. We talked about self-reliance and how we were concerned only with our stomachs, our feet and knowing our location. Nicholas thought of a distant relative of Hadrian's Wall. A very distant relative indeed.

"What do you know about the Great Wall?"

"China, you mean? Not much; all I know about China is the Great Wall, Chairman Mao and chopsticks."

3

"But just imagine a journey along the Great Wall."

"Near impossible I should think. It's at least 1,000 miles long and it crosses deserts and mountains."

At the time I was more concerned with treating a couple of incipient blisters. Moreover, we were forty miles from our goal. The following morning we did reach Bowness on Solway. Walls are barriers that runners take great pride in overcoming. The concept of the wall in the Marathon, where the mind battles against the body's willingness to concede defeat, is entirely appropriate. Our success in following this eighty-mile Wall was put into perspective as Nick photographed me holding the OS map unfurled as if it were a flag of victory. A postmark to verify our arrival seemed appropriate. On the map ideally. The postmaster obliged and joked, "Land's End to John o' Groats next?"

"More like the Great Wall of China," I quipped back.

Hadrian's Wall to the Great Wall was an ambitious graduation. But I had been trying to conceive a purposeful adventure for the past decade. Everything seemed to have been done before. Now, not only did I have the idea, I also had opportunity, for at the age of twenty-eight I was single with no ties. To the envy of many of my contemporaries, I could change the direction of my life with a letter of resignation.

It had all been just words until I inspected the China section in Manchester's Central Library. To my surprise there wasn't a book solely about the Wall, though many described it in passing or offered the well-worn image of rebuilt Wall near Peking, covered with tourists. Superficial though the statistics were, it was obvious that Hadrian's Wall was a child's toy in comparison. The materials from which the Great Wall was built could encircle the globe at the equator with a barrier almost eight feet high and over three feet thick. The scale of the structure impressed a member of Lord McCartney's British Legation in 1790 who estimated that there was more stone and rubble in the Wall than in all of the United Kingdom's buildings of the day. However, it was the more poetic description by a French traveller, the Count de Beauvoir, that seized my imagination.

It is a supremely wonderful sight!
To think that these walls,
built in apparently inaccessible places,
as though to balance the milky way in the sky, a walled way
over the mountain tops,
are the work of men makes it seem like a dream . . .
This fantastic serpent of stone, its
battlements devoid of cannons, its
loopholes empty of rifles . . .
Will be stored in my mind like a magic
vision forever.

If anything, the lack of detailed information encouraged me, as I realized I could be working on a unique idea.

On to the map room. I have always had a passion for maps, dating back to prep school days when my headmaster, the Rev. John Patrick MacMillan, felt so strongly about their worth that he preached "by your bedside you should have a Bible, a prayer book and an atlas." My father's family had been travellers. He had docked in Shanghai and been impressed by the beauty of the women. His Aunt Gertrude, known to me as Great Auntie Gertie, was a Norland nanny who had worked for Tsar Nicholas II and survived the Russian Revolution to lead a nomadic life, Baedeker in hand. I can still see her huge leather suitcases, their corners sheathed in metal, standing in our hallway awaiting her departure. She even made a reservation for herself on the first commercial trip to the moon.

In Manchester's Central Library China seemed as distant as the moon if the available chartage was anything to go on. There was, however, the double spread in the *Times Atlas of the World*. Among the menacing brown hues of desert, mountain and plateau I found the castellated symbol for the Wall, and traced it from China's heartland, negotiating gaps, overlaps and loops to the coast on the Yellow Sea near Peking—which had now become Beijing to conform with the Pinyin transcription of Chinese characters as adopted by the People's Republic of China (to be used from now in this book). Although this map gave me some basic information, it failed to throw any light on the possibility of a traverse on foot. It was like navigating the Pennine Way with a map out of the back of a pocket diary. So I tracked down the more elucidating, but out of print, *Times Atlas of China* to Bartholomew, its Edinburgh cartographers. Now I was convinced of the journey's feasibility because, although the majority of the route crossed desert, there appeared to be scattered settlements near the Wall. My outbreak of Wall fever was growing severe. I kept a photocopied map of north China in the credit card compartment of my wallet. The only possible cure was a journey along the entire length of the Wall. I handed in my notice to the polytechnic in Manchester and committed myself to attempting the traverse in the following spring.

The reaction of people to my ambitious plan was varied. My mother and father immediately pledged their support and gave me a base from which to work. Nicholas (whom I could always blame for the idea) was enthusiastic and highlighted things in my favor. And there were many: China was the fascinating country of the moment, and my proposed journey had never been attempted before. My eldest brother David tended to be more cautious and emphasized some likely problems: where would the money come from, and how would I cope physically and mentally with such a long journey on foot alone? My roommate, Simon, who had witnessed one of my most fanatical periods of training, thought the actual running would present the least of my difficulties, and it would be the bureaucracy that would be the main problem.

I was surprised and encouraged to discover that previous journeys along the Great Wall had not been complete, even on horseback. However, considering China's isolated and turbulent history since 1949, when the People's Republic was founded, maybe I should not have been too surprised. The Cultural Revolution had been a decade of almost zero contact with the outside world. But following the death of Mao Zedong in 1976 an open-door policy has made some progress, and tourism has risen steadily in the wake of renewed diplomatic relations and trading. Undoubtedly now was the time to put all my resources into making the journey before anyone else did. I felt fortunate that China had been preserved as possibly the last great adventure opportunity. I recalled my student days, when I was hungry for knowledge, and how little news ever came out of China. Such ignorance yearned to be educated. Everyone wanted to know more about the country that constituted nearly one quarter of the world's population.

Earlier travellers' tales allowed me to form some impression of what my own journey would entail. Mildred Cable and Francesca French, two missionaries of the 1930s, described their life in northwest Gansu Province in their classic, *The Gobi Desert*. They wrote of their caravan's approach to the Jiayuguan fortress, at the very west end of the Wall:

> *The cart bumped mercilessly over the loose stones of the dismal plain, and each slow mile brought the outline of the fort into clear relief. It was an impressive structure. To the north of the central arch was a turreted watch-tower, and from it the long line of the Wall dipped into a valley, climbed a hill and vanished over the summit. Then a few poplar trees came into sight, and it was evident from the shade of green at the foot of the Wall that here was grass and water.*
>
> *The massive monument now towered overhead, and impressive though it was by its own dignity, it made a yet further appeal to the imagination, for this was Kiayukuan (Barrier of the Pleasant Valley), the barrier which marks the western end of that amazing and absurd structure known as The Great Wall of China, dating back to 214 BC, and built as a protection against enemy Tartar tribes. The length of Wall, which outlined the crest of hill to the north, would continue irrespective of difficulties caused by mountains and valleys, rivers and deserts until it reached the sea 1,400 miles away.*

It was not until 1905 that an American attempted to travel along the whole length of the Wall. William Edgar Geil described his journey, rather lightheartedly, in *The Great Wall of China*, which became a bestseller of the day. His obsession was clear as he described his feeling on sailing across the Pacific to make the journey with a caravan of horses and local guides.

"We ate with the Wall, slept with the Wall, thought Wall." Geil's adventures motivated other travellers to explore the regions he was unable to penetrate. In particular, Clark and Sowerby restricted their investigations to the Ordos region where they were puzzled by the presence of many mud walls. In modern times there has been only one significant journey. A retired US Air Force general succeeded in walking the main remains of the Wall in 1980. The aerial view of the Wall snaking over the mountains in Hebei Province was a sight that haunted General

Scott into his retirement, and cutting loose from one of the few package tours to China during that time, he dressed up as a Chinese and satisfied his ambition.

My aim was to eclipse all these previous journeys. I would run carrying the absolute minimum gear and depend largely on the hospitality of local people for my basic needs of water, shelter and food. For all that, I still needed a sponsor and that meant producing an expedition prospectus. It was not a modest document. The introduction stated that the aim of the journey was to travel on foot from Jiayuguan in Gansu Province to Shanhaiguan on the Yellow Sea coast. This distance was approximately 1,800 miles, and was defined as being the length of a route between the accepted start and finish of the Great Wall, travelling in a predominantly west to east direction, and without making any detours along spurs of the Wall to the north or south.

No publication seemed to be able to agree on the length of the Wall or, more precisely, they neglected to state their method of evaluating this. Some Sinologists point out that walls as such have continued beyond both Jiayuguan and Shanhaiguan. It is upon the older maps especially that remnants of Wall are shown to reach Yumen (in the west) and the Yalu River (in the east), which marks the present national boundary between the PRC and North Korea. These walls, being composed of mud and willow branches, have disappeared completely from the landscape as a result of weathering.

The main confusion over length arises from the fact that the Great Wall is essentially a linkup and extension of previously existing walls. During the so-called Warring States period of Chinese history (c. 475–221 BC), when China was not a single unified empire, the individual kingdoms constructed walls as defensive structures. Eventually China became unified under Emperor Qin (221 BC), and after he identified the common enemy as the barbarians to the north, a Great Wall was joined up making use of existing walls.

Throughout the history of the wall, the border position between the Chinese and nomadic peoples altered as each party infringed upon the other's territory and built new walls in advanced or retreated positions. A route through all the remains would be in the order of 4,225 miles and involve much doubling back.

If I was confident and positive on the surface about my journey's prospects, inside I felt increasingly cautious and fearful. I only needed to scan my maps to be confronted with place names which were difficult to pronounce. I pictured myself lost or frustrated at my inability to communicate. When I looked at the ochre shading which represented desert I saw myself sheltering from dust storms and searching for water. And when I reached rivers I envisaged no bridges and trouble in finding a crossing. I could not conquer these images; I could only strive to control and limit the fear they imbued in me. To this end I made a start at learning the language of mainland China, Mandarin, or *Putonghua*, and embarked on a program of survival practice and bushcraft. Learning how to collect water from condensation on pebbles in the desert did seem farfetched and ridiculous in Britain during December, but it might save my life the following year in the Gobi.

Physically I was well prepared, since for the three previous years I had logged my training miles down in a diary with the same enthusiasm that a miser displays in counting his money. Having older brothers and sisters has been on the whole an advantage. I had bagged my first 3,000-foot summit at the age of eight with Nicholas when we climbed Snowdon clad in tweed jackets, shirts and ties, short trousers and leather-soled crocodile shoes. Real Mallory and Irvine stuff! Any unsuspecting hiker must have thought we had lost our way to church. My eldest brother, David, taught me at a tender age to run long and fast. The fruit of his coaching, a clean sweep at St. Aidan's sports day, is immortalized in a photograph of me grappling with all the silverware that still rests on the piano in my parents' home. Early fell-running prowess was shown by winning a race to the top of Moel Fammau and receiving five shillings from headmaster Mackie as the prize. I bought a map with my winnings.

So the maxim of the Lindesay brothers has always been "don't walk if you can run," and consequently the decision to run the Great Wall, rather than merely walk it, was not a perverse intention on my part but a natural form of locomotion—one which I understood. It is told that the Red Army often astounded the Nationalists by their ability to trek eighty kilometers in a day on the Long March at what these days would be called "yomping" pace. Their determination would be an inspiration as I tackled my own Long March on the Wall and tried to emulate their spirit, speed—and stealth. I had decided to train daily unless serious injury or illness prevented me from doing so. Running in all weathers at all times of the day, I sometimes "morning, noon, and nighted": three runs in twenty-four hours. All in all I had reason to be confident about my ability to cope with a big run since my preparation had topped the 10,800-mile mark. Nevertheless, some specific training ensued that included longer runs in the adverse weather and rough terrain of the Peak District.

With every stride of my training China was on my mind. It was New Year 1986 and the prospectus for the expedition was being circulated to potential suppliers of equipment and providers of finance. The *Liverpool Daily Post and Echo* printed a picture of me studying the *Times Atlas of China*. The response from manufacturers was encouraging, and the search for a single company to underwrite costs gained a swift response in a telephone call from Neil Pirie, marketing controller of Thomas Cook Traveller's Cheques Ltd. He said that they received many sponsorship requests, most of which were rejected, but my idea seemed well presented and could be a potential winner. When could I come to Peterborough to discuss the plan further?

It turned out that Thomas Cook had recently introduced a traveller's cheque in collaboration with the Bank of China which depicted the Great Wall. Neil Pirie himself had lived in Hong Kong for three years, during which time he had made numerous visits to the People's Republic. He understood the extreme difficulties of attempting something quite unprecedented in China. It struck me that he was genuinely interested in the company being involved in a good adventure, and the following day he phoned to confirm that Thomas Cook Traveller's Cheques would finance my journey.

With seven weeks to go before departure, I had yet one lingering worry. My approaches to authorities had been of a one-way nature. Direct requests for information, even advice, had been unanswered. My suggested point of contact in China was the China Sports Services Company (CSSC), but an application to them on my behalf by the British Amateur Athletics Board drew no response. The general consensus of opinion by recent China travellers was that large portions of the Wall are in areas normally closed to foreigners. Access in China is divided into three categories: open, closed and forbidden. Until the very recent past forbidden was a synonym for all travel in China. But even with the cautious opening up of certain areas in the 1980s, the free movement of travellers "without let or hindrance," as requested in the British passport, is something still unknown in the Middle Kingdom. It was becoming increasingly clear that the hierarchy of authorities in China was either unwilling or incapable of providing me with a magic piece of paper that would ensure an entirely smooth journey. Moreover, the information I had on the CSSC suggested it was a commercial company that sold support services to expeditions of various kinds. I regarded any such support with skepticism, as it would diminish or even extinguish the adventure of the journey. I was now convinced that the first man along the Wall would be the one willing to take a gamble, maybe setting a precedent in the process. And my bags were packed full of the gear for doing just that.

2

Bound in
Red Tape

"Viewing flowers from horseback."
—*Proverb of poet Mary Jiao from*
Tang Dynasty c. AD 796

I had now been living and dreaming Wall for six months, so I was reasonably able to take in my stride the publicity I owed my sponsors. The eve of departure saw me jogging, albeit cautiously, on the Thames Embankment wall near Lambeth Bridge with Big Ben in the background. The resulting photograph appeared in *The Times*. Now the news was out—I really did have to do it!

Hong Kong was my stepping-stone to China, and waiting for my flight on to Beijing, I decided to use up my last small coins on some Strepsils (advice of a *Mail* reporter: "Terrible air out there, they're still burning coal"), some postcards and the last English-language newspaper I'd see for months. Waiting to pick up a *South China Morning Post* from the pile at the kiosk till, I could not believe my eyes. The words Great Wall leapt out at me from a front-page headline which ran, "Griffiths May be Beaten to Great Wall." I lunged for a copy and scanned the opening paragraphs. They spelled trouble.

Never in all my months of meticulous training and planning had I entertained the possibility that somebody else might have had the same idea as me at the same time. Superficially at least, this was the case. For here was someone called David Griffiths who was all set to travel the Wall with a support vehicle, guide-interpreter and personal physician. A totally unappealing method and not my style of doing things at all, but it did explain the resounding silence from the China Sports Services Company (CSSC), who were all too clearly enjoying relieving David Griffiths of a ridiculously large quantity of US dollars for their services and, if the paper was to be believed, assuring him of the privilege of being the first to run the Wall.

Could they do this? I would find out at first hand in a few hours' time. I boarded the Beijing flight, my mind in turmoil, ready for a fight.

"*Ni hao.*" I uttered my first timid words of Mandarin at the immigration desk.

The woman officer in green uniform returned my greeting. "You are English?"

"Englishman, yes. I've come to see the Great Wall."

Carefully stamping my visa, she smiled and handed me back my passport. I was in China at last.

A driver was waiting to take me to the office of Midland Bank Group, the parent of Thomas Cook, who applied themselves straight away in trying to arrange an appointment with the CSSC. But all was in vain. They flatly refused to see me and denied having received my letter or the one written on my behalf by the British Amateur Athletics Board. Already I realized those approaches had been mistakes. I was a talented marathon runner, yet merely planned to use that endurance quality as a means to an end in conquering the Great Wall adventurously. I was planning a journey, not a sports event.

I retreated to my hotel room and a welcoming glass of jasmine tea, my luggage piled around me in silent reproach. Packed in those bags was exactly what I needed to help me through every eventuality once on the Wall. But with my path blocked by bureaucracy and my actions scrutinized by the press, who continued to highlight a completely fabricated rivalry story, I wondered when I would ever have the opportunity to be alone on the Great Wall.

My main problem was that I did not know what power the CSSC actually possessed. Were they solely a commercial organization, simply protecting their own financial interest? If they could grant special permission with the one hand, could they ban people with the other? Were there any other authorities I could appeal to? The trouble with my plans was that they were totally alien to the Chinese way of thinking. Independent thought and the philosophy of going it alone are rare characteristics in the collectively minded Chinese. For them individuality is a synonym for strangeness and unreliability. Only group achievement is desirable.

We made one more attempt to have a showdown with the CSSC, but camping in their foyer next morning produced only the stonewalling request for a written proposal from Britain. I was beaten into a tactical retreat. But before I left China I treated myself to the psychological torture of visiting the Great Wall as a tourist along with everyone else at Badaling, just thirty-seven miles north of Beijing. Walking off as far as possible to escape the crowds, I reached a place that commanded a stunning vista. Now I realized why the Chinese liken the Wall to a dragon with its slender body dipping in and out of view to distant horizons. The sight of it impressed me with awe, fear, excitement and above all an absolute conviction that I should return.

Back home in England I had to shake myself out of my depression and apathy and patiently await the next seasonal opportunity. As I had suspected many months before, the clandestine approach was going to be necessary. Five months later, in total secrecy, I was once again back in Beijing—and on my way to the Great Wall.

▪▪▪ 3 ▪▪▪

China
Apprenticeship

For me there are three species of human
beings: Chinese, non-Chinese who have
been to China, and others.
— *Dr. Han Suyin*

The pagoda-style roof and clock towers of Beijing railway station were silhouetted against the dawn sky. An amber glow filled the eastern horizon and was reflected off the glazed tiles. As I approached the station along Zhan kou lu, a steady stream of cyclists was already beginning to flow down the city's wide avenues. Many other people, also heading for early departures, took a final opportunity to stock up with food from the multitude of stalls just opening for the day's business. Some were clearly supplying themselves with rations for several days. China is a big country, and travelling from Beijing railway station, you can reach any of its now thirty provinces and regions, except Tibet.

Directly outside the station hall things became more hectic. Exhausted travellers, just arrived from far-flung corners of the country, emerged to be confronted by a sea of people who had bedded down for the night, barricaded by their luggage and carpeted by the *Renmin Ribao* (the *People's Daily*). My immediate concern was boarding the right train. The day before I had purchased my soft-seat ticket at a special desk that serves only "foreign guests" and "compatriots" from Hong Kong and Macao. For the privilege of obtaining a ticket at such short notice on a grossly overcrowded railway system, the "guest" is subjected to an idiosyncrasy that most find hard to accept: namely paying for the ticket at three times the usual price in foreign exchange certificates. These necessary certificates are only obtained by encashment of hard currency in China. Chinese people use renminbi, literally "people's money," officially of the same value but really worth about sixty-five percent of the value of FECs. Hence a black market exists where 100 FEC = 160 renminbi.

Inside the huge station I proffered my ticket towards a well-dressed bespectacled young man: always a good bet for directions as spectacles are usually indicative of education and therefore the possible knowledge of English. He directed me up an escalator, a modern contraption that amused the locals as they stumbled on and off it in a nervous or thrilled fashion, depending upon their age. Above me on a map of China's railways on the tiled wall, I traced my intended route eastward, from the red star that marked Beijing to the Yellow Sea coast. Down on the platform, those travelling hard-seat class were already overfilling the carriages. Soft-seat class was at the front of the train. Outside car number three stood the guard inspecting tickets, immaculate in her crisp white shirt with epaulettes, a navy blue skirt and peaked cap.

"Shanhaiguan?" I muttered in my foreign monotone. She repeated it back with rising and falling tones of pronunciation, using exaggerated lip movements to produce the quite musical sound. Exactly on time, the quarter-mile-long monster pulled out of the murky railyards into the brightness of a promising day.

Once on the move, the humidity became a little more tolerable as the air of the carriage was kept in constant motion. We were well catered for, as each group of seats had access to a large thermos of boiling water for making tea. Porcelain mugs, complete with lids to keep out the flies, were provided. The piped music was interrupted for an announcement of our route. This train would terminate in Shenyang, Liaoning Province and would pass up the Yellow Sea coast through the resort of Beidaihe. That, I imagined, was the likely destination of many of my fellow passengers, following the example of China's ruling class in visiting the much-admired seaside resort. "Comrade Chen" (China's equivalent of the Joneses) had in recent years taken quite readily to having a vacation, an activity previously regarded as bourgeois. Purges and revolutions come and go, and now just a decade after the Cultural Revolution ended, money can buy choice, privilege and comfort, as exemplified by the three classes of accommodation on this train. We, the fortunate ones, were shaded by lace curtains and sipped our jasmine tea in cool spacious comfort, while our "comrades" suffered the overcrowding and heat of the hard-seat compartments.

At Beidaihe the train emptied considerably, and the solitude of the final stretch of the journey to Shanhaiguan gave me time to run the gamut of emotions from apprehension to relief to excitement at reaching the place that had been the focus of my attention for so long.

This was small-town China, with interest, surprise and fascination in every glance. The main street, between station and hotel, had all but lost its status as an efficient thoroughfare. The wares of curbside traders encroached on the road; people abandoned their bicycles to haggle a fair price. There were cobblers, bicycle repairers, barbers and ratcatchers. At the height of summer, this was the season of plenty: mounds of melons, pyramids of pears, cartloads of cucumbers and trays of tomatoes. Much of the street food on offer looked appetizing, so after watching the routine of ordering and method of eating, I took a seat under a canopy. The food was best described as a fritter containing pork, corn and chives. Meanwhile I engaged in banter with the locals who derived much entertainment in watching me struggle with chopsticks, which I abandoned for my second helping, preferring to use fingers that were considerably cleaner.

In the early afternoon the skies darkened and the air became incredibly humid. First the raindrops made a pitter-patter on the large-leafed plane trees shading the street. Within minutes it became a torrential downpour which created pandemonium as shoppers sped off and peddlers rushed to salvage their goods from the storm. The deluge lasted only until early evening, though my clothes had little chance of drying in the moist atmosphere of my room. It was a very drab and basic hotel. The Chinese talked in loud voices, whole families of them in the small rooms. Men cleared their throats and hawked raucously into the spittoons outside every door. The lack of any floor coverings in the rooms or corridor only served to amplify the sound of this revolting habit.

My task on this eve of departure was a final examination of the contents of my rucksack and a repeated questioning of the necessity of every single item contained therein. The bulk of my equipment was taken up by my bivouac system, consisting of a thin foil-covered insulating mat, a Gore-tex (breathable fabric) sleeping bag and finally a down sleeping bag. The sole change of clothing I possessed was socks and briefs. I had sacrificed the familiarity of my many-tooled Swiss army knife for its simpler two-bladed cousin. Once under way, I hoped that some items would prove surplus to requirements. I would certainly have no qualms about leaving behind things of value for I knew that from now on the only fortune of the journey was survival itself. When I turned in for the night, I was kept awake by the buzzing of mosquitoes, the howling of steam engines from the nearby railyard, and the loud talking of my neighbors, who continued until the early hours. I am told that Mandarin Chinese has to be spoken loudly so that intonation can be inferred.

At first sight it appeared like any other beach on a summer's day, evoking some childhood memories of seaside holidays. Photographers would take a snap for a fee, swimming suits were lined up on rails for hire, the frilly variety that my sister wore as a child. But this was no ordinary beach to me, for around the headland slabs of stone lay in ruins in the sand and on the adjacent cliff. Here is the site known as Old Dragon's Head. The very end—or beginning—of the Great Wall, not ravaged by waves or Mongols but by an airborne attack during the Sino-Japanese War. For me this place was both the start and the finish. It was the finish of anticipating and planning and the start of the odyssey. With a departing ritual of walking in the wash of the waves and touching the sands, I looked out to sea at the ships plying their way towards the port of Qinhuangdao and then set off up the cliff and on to the Wall. Standing high above the surrounding fields, the path on the Wall was well worn and obviously used regularly. The sides were stripped of their stone casing as they had presented a convenient and valuable source of building material. After just half an hour I gulped lukewarm water from my flask on the edge of the town and cursed the brutal humidity. Passing through Shanhaiguan, a long stretch of the Wall had been renovated, huge clean-cut blocks and white mortar sitting atop the old and decaying stone.

Hundreds of Chinese tourists piled out of small buses on day trips up from Beidaihe and the snap photographers did a roaring trade in front of the main gate on the Wall, the First Pass under Heaven. This was the last opportunity to obtain provisions. From now on I would employ the "camel principle": eating when food was available rather than when specifically hungry. As the Wall continued through fields of ripening maize, I considered the palatability of raw corn cobs should the need arise. Topping up my water supply at a little farm caused another worry: the water was boiling, so the bottles had to be well separated from my back and my film supplies when I repacked the sack. Besides this, the prospect of drinking hot water when suffering from a raging thirst was not a pleasant one. Ahead, the Wall's easy path across the coastal plain was brought to an abrupt end. A reconstructed section, with its new stone bright in the sunlight, scaled the mountains, then continued in dereliction, deteriorating with height into a barely discernible linearity, and finally climbing out of sight.

The climb was steeper than it looked from afar. Some steps were a yard high and the rampart became defensively narrow. Halfway up the mountain, perched on the most precipitous of slopes, stood a watchtower, only accessible by way of a long metal ladder. Beyond this, the Wall lay in dilapidation, its pavement rough with crumbling bricks and mortar. Now out of sight and earshot of inquisitive visitors I bivouacked. The sun went down behind the mountain and a full moon rose against a deep blue sky, giving the sentinel watchtower an eerie outline. On the foothills below echoed the cries of a shepherd gathering in his flock for the night. Then all was quiet, save for the whistle of the wind through the empty cannon loopholes.

I was glad to see the sky lighten. Managing a couple of hours of solid sleep before midnight, I had been awakened by rustling in the vegetation. After that I was not confident enough to relax, and only managed short naps until daybreak. Looking to the Yellow Sea coast, I watched the sun's disc edge above the horizon and the slow trading of color between the fading orange sky and the brightening green and yellow hues of the plain. Gradually my route of the previous day clarified, from the sea to the town, over which now hung a patch of dawn smog caused by the coal-burning stoves of townsfolk. Between town and mountains, the low angle of sunlight gave the Wall a shadowed edge, underlining the strategic importance of Shanhaiguan—"mountain-seapass." I thought of soldiers from centuries ago billeted in this very watchtower, waking up and pausing to witness this morning ritual of the sun.

It took just minutes to pack up the bivouac. Breakfast was a few gulps of water, nicely chilled in the night air, and a bread roll, hard and dry. Ascending the mountain, the Wall narrowed with the severity of the slope. Irregular-shaped blocks, rather than cut stones or "mortar" bricks were used, reminiscent of Hadrian's Wall in both the scale and quality of the remains. Approaching the summit, gaps began to appear and the rubble was covered in vegetation. Within just an hour of sunrise the sweat poured off me, and I became perturbed about the prospects of penetrating the remote country ahead in such temperatures.

The scale and detail of the maps I had did not exactly inspire me with confidence. Attempts to procure good scale chartage of the route were met with the familiar "*mei you*" (have not any) syndrome. Only wall maps of the whole country and city plans seemed available. This I could only conclude was a security-based strategy of Chinese officialdom to keep their geography as little known as possible. Without doubt a civilization as ancient as China would have had the main regions of its territory well mapped. However, I had to use the tools I had, which were a Chinese character wall map, scale 1:1.6 million, and photocopied maps from the *Times Atlas of China* which I had sprayed with waterproofing solution. Behind me to the south lay a huge lake, and yes, the Wall now beat a path to the north, parallel to the distant coast. Increasingly my progress seemed barred in following the Wall directly. It plunged into a ravine and then out again by the most precipitous of paths. At times I was a single slip from broken bones, yet I still marvelled at and questioned the engineering and reasoning in building such ramparts on these rugged peaks.

The hours sped past if the miles did not. The familiarity and security of the view to the coast, and with it the benefit of checking my position, had now disappeared. At the same time the scanty remains degenerated into nothing, after which I could only guess its route before choosing a long descent westwards towards a valley in the hope of finding water. Fighting through waist-high scrub and clambering over man-sized boulders, I reached the valley scraped and scratched. The stream was dry. Despite better intentions, I was not disciplined enough to prevent myself from further reducing my canteen. Now my water supply was less than half a quart.

Checking the position of the sun seemed futile for it was directly overhead. The continuation of my journey seemed foolhardy in such awful heat, yet I plodded on up the valley. All thoughts of where the Wall was had vanished, being replaced by the optimism that soon I would stumble upon a mountain community. But there seemed little sign of man's activity. As minutes passed into hours, my optimism waned, and here on only my second day the nightmare of a frantic search for water was a reality. Nausea and weakness now added to the problem. But worst was the onset of panic and delirium induced by the sight of jagged peaks, thickets and screes in every direction. There was no option but to stop and rest in the shade.

I slept for over four hours. The sun had thankfully dipped below the peaks and so another night out was inevitable. As the cool air of the valley descended my raging thirst moderated only slightly. My skin and face were burning. My head split with pain and once inside the sleeping bag I shivered and sweated. The day had seemed an unfair battle, with the Wall cowardly soliciting its allies of heat and humidity to warn me that this journey was to be no easy contest. And now as the dark fell, creatures of the night emerged, and wolves howled in the distance with the echo of the valley confusing me as to their position. Collecting a pile of throwable-size stones by the head of my sleeping bag, I kept my torch to hand and prayed. This was going to take some getting out of; the only decision to make was made. I had to retrace my route to safety. This time the Wall had won; my only consolation was survival.

* * *

Back in Beijing I accepted that I had paid the price for a major logistical error. Impatience to start the journey in totally unsuitable weather had resulted in a baptism of fire. No one could have continued; few would have survived. On the telephone, Nicholas and David reiterated these truisms. My choice was now simple: either to wait for cooler weather in the east, or to start out afresh from the western terminus where the high plateau was more temperate. There was no time to waste. My healing process was complete.

Jiayuguan, in the province of Gansu, is served by rail from Beijing, one of the many long-established oasis towns of the Hexi corridor which have been rejuvenated since the building of the line to Urumchi in China's most westerly region, Xinjiang. My ticket, a large piece of paper, looked more like a restaurant bill where the cost of three dishes was added up to give the final total. These items were the normal price to

Chinese, a hard-sleeper supplement and a foreigner surcharge. It also stated the distance as being 1,430 miles from Beijing. More remarkable was the journey in time. Hauled out of the capital by diesel, we chugged out of Xi'an by steam, through a pitted loess landscape where people dig their homes into the hillsides to survive the summer's heat. Winding through remote river valleys, we passed labor gangs thankful for the short respite that our passage provided; they wore looks of hopelessness on their faces. When we stopped at stations, which were often without platforms, women jostled to sell eggs and apples to us, while urchins tried to dispose of a less sought-after commodity: hedgehogs and squirrels tethered by string. Finally, the long climb out of Lanzhou on to the plateau corridor of Gansu gave me a preview of the first 370 miles of my proposed route.

After some fifty-five hours it was a relief to leave the smoky carriage at Jiayuguan. My expectations about the prevailing weather on the 5,900-foot plateau were well founded, for it was both cool and windy. Leaving the station, I was asked to show my passport, presumably in order that my visa could be checked. Jiayuguan, after all, was an "open" town which the foreigner is allowed to visit without any additional documents.[1] Walking from the railhead into the town, I was surprised by the total absence of vernacular architecture. Take away the people, and these stark concrete blocks could have been anywhere. Men wore the favored blue or green tunic suits with "Mao" caps, while the women only differed from them in the brightness of their jackets and headscarves. They seemed to like reds, pinks and purples. Many wore their scarves wrapped across their faces, for the wind was cold and laden with dust.

The sighting of the fortress at Jiayuguan immediately prompts one to inquire why it was constructed at such a remote and far-flung outpost of the Chinese Empire. At a place where the climate is so inhospitable, and the landscape so forbidding, there stands this citadel, the scale of its ramparts accentuated by its elevated position on the desert terrain.

---

[1] With a valid visa the foreigner has access to a list of open towns/cities as published by the Ministry of Public Security Division of the Entry and Exit of Aliens. To be granted access to visit closed places requires additional documentation, in particular the possession of the Alien's Travel Permit. These, however, are seemingly only issued for "economic purposes," e.g. businessmen visiting factories, or "educational purposes."

Under the wide and empty skies of Central Asia it appears pedestalled, and surely it must have been a vision of disbelief to travellers of long ago as their caravans approached it. But this was no trick of the mind, for ahead lay the entrance to the Walled Kingdom, and to pass eastwards through its portal was a passage from the unknown to the civilized.

Emperor Taizu of the Ming Dynasty chose to terminate the Great Wall at Jiayuguan, though older walls had continued further west towards the Lop Nur area. It was a strategic decision, for when the high mud wall was supplemented by nature's own defenses, a formidable stronghold was created. Above the western gate of the fortress, a large plaque inscribed with calligraphy reminded travellers of their entrance through the "First Fortified Pass on Earth." There was no alternative. To the north and west nothing but desert and mountain could be seen. The southward panorama was even more formidable with the snowy peaks of the Qilian Mountains, and the desert in between was sealed off by the very last few miles of mud wall. Since the first caravans of merchants trekked across Asia from Europe along the route which became known as the Silk Road, this site at the end of the Great Wall was regarded as China's mouth. On the day I was to start my own journey, I could identify closely with the hardships and challenges that faced those Silk Road travellers. Although today mankind has the technology to see behind his neighbor's frontiers and above the barriers of nature with aerial intelligence, a country can surely only reveal its true character and heart gradually to a traveller on foot, progressing at the right receptive pace.

Theater could not have created a finer setting. The Wall ends where the stony desert plain grades towards a slope before the foothills of the Qilian Mountains. It is here, completely hidden and unnoticeable from afar, that nature lends an insurmountable hindrance, a secret weapon as an obstacle to potential invaders. At first one hears a hiss, and then a roar, before the turbulent torrent of muddy water is seen. For here is a cliff, below which the Taolai River has cut a deep ravine in the loose and uncemented desert sands and gravels.

4

Comrade Chen

Friendship is a necessity.

—*Aristotle*
The Ethics

Voices echoed in the streets. Then there was music of a marching tempo. The public address system of Jiayuguan, the town's alarm clock, was awakening the town; it was only 6:30 a.m. and still dark. Dawn broke at a later hour in these regions, for the whole of China adheres to a common time zone, when more aptly its longitudinal extent of over sixty degrees would be better accommodated by four distinct zones. This means that toward the west the mornings are darker and the evenings lighter. That might appear of little consequence, but if the Beijing cadres had to do their *tai-ji* exercises in total darkness, no doubt things would change.

In the chill of my room I donned all the clothing I possessed, gulped down some jasmine tea and hurried outside, eager to take advantage of the veil of darkness which hung over the town. Today I would sacrifice following the Wall directly since its line ran too close to the Long March rocket launching center in the north of Jiuquan County. This would be a forbidden area, as opposed to a closed one, and I had no wish to aggravate the authorities by going anywhere near this sensitive region.

At the edge of town I left the road, took a compass bearing and negotiated the open desert. Without the railway line, navigation would have been almost impossible with the map I possessed: its scale was twenty-eight miles to the inch! The general trend of the Hexi corridor, being a northwest to southeast orientation, did help my sense of direction, though my most valuable pathfinding asset was a list of towns along the line of the Wall that I had persuaded a Chinese friend to copy out in my notebook in both character and Pinyin forms.

The hours passed slowly, though my morale was high because I felt strong and happy in the cool but bright weather. Every couple of hours I was able to have a drink of water at a farm and douse my dusty legs in an oasis irrigation channel. But I had to remind myself that this was the desert, my maps were inadequate, and therefore I should, like all other people of the desert, treat water as the most valuable commodity.

By late afternoon I judged myself to be east of Jiuquan town[1] and therefore well into "closed territory." From now on I would have to employ my own rules and regulations in order to improve my chances of negotiating the route along the Wall to the next "open" town. For a start, I could not stay the night anywhere that would entail registration and reporting to the Public Security Bureau (PSB). This meant that I did not expect to sleep in a hotel bed until the town of Zhongwei in Ningxia— some 430 miles away.

Now, with an empty stomach, weary limbs and a burning face, I set my hopes on the hospitality of the local people. The oasis fields were full of family groups harvesting together, children at play while their parents toiled. Then they saw me. The reaping, threshing and plucking stopped. Their gaze stayed with me until I had passed safely by. To alleviate their suspicions I would give a smile and a wave, or just "*Ni hao*," which always met with a similar gesture.

I picked an isolated farm on the edge of a village. Smoke and a bicycle parked outside indicated someone was at home. Entering through an archway into a courtyard, I found a woman washing clothes in a large enamel basin.

"*Ni hao. Ying guo ren. He shui?*'" (Hello. I'm English. Water to drink?), cupping my hands to mime the drinking.

---

[1]Jiuquan—"Wine-Cup Spring." Known as Soochow in old accounts of the region.

Author's route on foot ————
Connecting route ----
Great Wall's principal remains 〰〰〰
Provincial boundary —·—·—

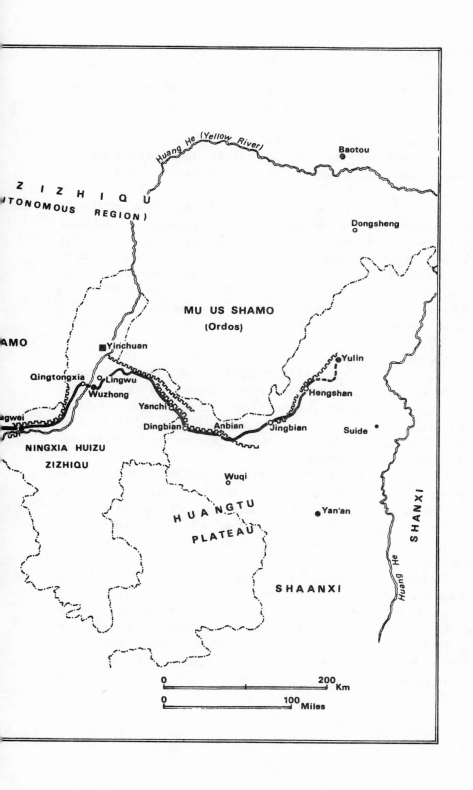

Wearing the largest of smiles, she wiped her hands on the back of her trousers and approached me as I took off my rucksack.

"*Ying guo ren!*" (Englishman.)

"*Dui, ying guo ren!*" (Correct, English.)

We crossed the threshold through a bead curtain. The room was cool and dark, and it took a short while for my eyes to adjust. I took a seat on the raised sleeping area called the *kang* and watched the woman scald out a jar with boiling water poured from a huge thermos flask. "*He shui, he shui*" (Drink it up!), she said. The water, piping hot, made my lips sting as I slurped at it. She was a woman of gentle nature and wore a pretty yet shy smile. Aged about thirty, she was clad in the ubiquitous green tunic, trousers, and a white shirt. Her long hair was tightly plaited and secured by a rubber band. Standing across the room with evident wariness, she likewise assessed my own appearance. When she had contemplated possible reasons for my coming to the village, she decided to tell others and left the room.

The room was sparse in its decoration and furnishing. The mud wall showed where paint had flaked, and a film of dust covered everything. A mirror, edged with painted flowers, was flanked by a stately portrait of Mao Zedong on the one side and a photo-montage of men in military uniforms, women too, school classes, couples, children and babies on the other. This frame of family history, the centerpiece of the room, was adorned with a red tasselled cord.

The young woman returned with her parents and children. I stood up immediately and smiled, but the old man beckoned me to sit down. He crouched on his haunches, produced a crumpled packet of cigarettes from his breast pocket and offered me one. He persisted, so in the end I accepted and put it in the pocket of my shorts. The women were dispatched out on his instruction.

Opening my rucksack, I delved inside to find my notebook. The eldest boy peered over my shoulder, eager to learn what I carried. As soon as he saw the Chinese characters on the front page, he muttered excitedly and the others gathered around. The boy handed the old man the book, but he was unable to read. He called the women, who arrived carrying two watermelons. They all gathered round the young woman who took the book and read aloud to the others the introductory lines of my diary.

"*Wei Zhong guo de peng you men. Wo shi ying guo ren. . . . Wo jiao Wei lian lin sai . . .*" (Hello, Chinese friends! I'm English. My name is William Lindesay.)

They listened in silence, captivated by the oration, then raised voices of delight, beamed and gestured approval. To seal our friendship, two huge and succulent melons were cut up. The little boy proudly handed me a chunk under his mother's direction and encouragement. It was wonderful refreshment, the solid fleshy red chunks crushing into cool juice against the roof of my mouth. Collecting the black seeds in hand, I approached the door to throw them outside, but they all laughed and advised me to spit them out on the floor as they did, which was admirably demonstrated by the old man in a comic fashion. More melon was offered and other fruits brought in from the outside store. It certainly looked as if I had been accepted, and with introductions and their assessment of my character now complete, they returned to their chores.

The boys stayed, and fetched a basin of well water for washing. My face had burned, for I had no allowance in my equipment for protective cream, but the cool water soothed the skin. Not wanting to waste it, I then washed my socks and hung them to dry outside. Meanwhile the women were preparing food. They mixed a huge lump of dough and appeared flattered that I found interest in their chores. "*Shen me?*" (What?) "*Mian bao*" (bread) was the answer. The dough was placed in a large round covered tin and thrust into hot embers in the courtyard. Within minutes it produced a wonderful aroma.

We ate our fill during the evening, each consuming several bowls of *mian tiao tang* (noodle soup). There was a continuous flow of visitors as news of my presence spread. People were content to come for half an hour to stare at me, my size thirteen shoes and notebook. In the chill of the night we huddled around the oil lamp, wrapped in blankets and talking as best we could. Finally, we bedded down for the night, all of us side by side on the *kang*, which would be heated from below when the weather got colder.

Their first job of the morning was starting a fire. A breakfast of as much rice as I could eat would, I hoped, sustain me until the evening. When I offered the old man some money, he was insistent he would accept nothing. Ten yuan would have been a considerable sum to him, yet it appeared he did not wish to tarnish our friendship. So with a departing gesture of *"hao peng you"* (good friend), I walked off, back through the green fields to the open desert. The whole family stood at their door to wave goodbye.

When the village had faded into the distance, and the fields of the oasis had yielded to the barrenness of the desert, I was more aware of my solitude. Yet I was accompanied by the journey itself; it was exhibiting a character of its own to become a likeable person, a friend. To develop our relationship required input, and so I feared to do anything that would jeopardize our joint success; similarly I would do anything to increase our chances of success. As with any new friendship, we needed to show trust and commitment to one another. My journey had already comforted me with the warmth and kindness of a Chinese family. My belief that we could succeed together was heightened. Our challenge was to follow the Wall, whose appearance, behavior and traits were as deceptive and fickle as any human being. The Wall had already punished us at its eastern end, but we had surprised it by mounting a challenge on its western flank. I hoped that our promising new friendship would develop over the coming weeks.

It was a rough track which crossed the undulating desert ridges and edged closer to the Qilian Mountains. The desert was stony, strewn with red jaspers, green olivines, and multicolored quartz. Vegetation was limited to scrub thorn bushes, often detached and blowing over the ground like a ball. Birds were totally absent, and the only animal life was the small lizards skidding across the ground and the desert rats that retreated to their burrows on any disturbance. Apart from these creatures, no life prospered.

Distance was deceptive. The faint outline of a building which I estimated would take about twenty minutes to reach eventually took a full hour. What I had hoped would be a refuge from the burning sun turned out to be an abandoned lime kiln, now used as a shelter for animals. Travellers had passed along this track for many years, furrowing it with cart ruts. Today carts are still used, pulled by donkeys or camels, though now the wheels have rubber tires. Drivers sit cross-legged, wrapped in a blanket or goatskin to block out the wind and sun, sometimes dozing off and trusting their beasts to maintain a steady course. Some encounters might involve an exchange.

"Qu na er? Na guo ren?" (To where? Which country?)

"*Qingshui*," I would reply, pointing whence they came to ensure my route was correct.

Qingshui lies under the towering Mount Qilian (18,200 feet), the peak that gives its name to the whole range fringing the southern edge of Gansu Province. Emerging on tarmacadam road, I followed it to the village center where several trucks were parked. Old men sat on the steps of the general store, while traders watched over their vegetables laid out on sackcloth upon the dusty ground. Black piglets with curly tails grovelled in the dirt, gobbling up rotting cabbage leaves and melon skins. Although wary about lingering in the village I was ravenous. I satisfied my hunger on a huge plate of noodles and green peppers in a *fandian* (literally, a rice house) that served the truck drivers. This feast cost eight mao (about twenty cents).

With over sixty miles of the route covered, I felt in high spirits. Once again my journey was to be good to me that evening. I sighted a solitary farm, well off the road in the shade of tall poplar trees, and was received with copious amounts of jasmine tea and bread. The family elder was the grandmother, in blue tunic and skullcap; she had tiny feet, no bigger than those of her granddaughter. The binding of feet to limit their growth has been carried out for over 1,000 years and was intended to signify freedom from manual labour. The peculiar habit, originally restricted to the households of the ruling class, the Empress and concubines, later became fashionable and percolated all strata of society. The foot's growth was stunted by binding the toes under the foot and was borne with "pain and pleasure." Women with bound feet became desirable as wives and were regarded as good bearers of children. Because of the class association, foot binding became frowned upon after the downfall of the Qing Dynasty in 1911, and therefore it was fair to assume this old lady was an octogenarian. She was greatly amused by my attention to the size of her feet; it was only later I learned that for a woman to display her feet is considered erotic and looking at a woman's feet is synonymous with having desires towards her!

The rest of the family was composed of mother, father and one child, a daughter, which was in keeping with the population control policy of one child per family. As their guest, I was treated with the utmost cordiality and served first with a bowl of noodles. Then the man of the house was served, followed by the women. The child was served last of all from her mother's bowl. When it came to second helpings the same rule applied, the women only eating if there was anything left in the pot. To end the meal, the woman climbed up to the roof store and brought down a Hami melon of a succulence that I had never before enjoyed. Its name derives from the town of Hami in neighbouring Xinjiang. The family also grew the larger *xi gua* or watermelon.

The women cleared away the bowls and chopsticks, and the man watched me produce my romanized script as I wrote my diary by the light of a flickering candle, no doubt as fascinated as I myself when observing the Chinese pen characters. Recollecting the events of the day, I gained a feeling of satisfaction: a routine seemed to be developing, my body was hardening to the task and my mind was willing to be adaptable. I had always felt happiest when making progress towards somewhere or something. Now, examining my map, despite its quite unsatisfactory scale, I could trace the progress I had made towards my goal.

With the onset of darkness the family readied itself for bed. The woman brushed the *kang* free of dust and grit with a small besom. Then, after unfolding the cotton wadded quilts with silken covers and covering the hard bead pillows with small towels, we proceeded to sleep. The peasant farmers possess little to divert them in the way of radio or books, and any newspapers were several weeks old. Their whole life is directed towards producing their own food, building their farms, fuelling their cookers, clothing their children and caring for the elders. To succeed in this entails spending all hours of light in the fields, and any distraction from this is superfluous and counterproductive to the basic task of self-sufficiency.

When my eyes opened it was already full daylight. The peaks of the Qilian Shan loomed magnificently in the clear autumn sunshine, a new horizon of ridges having come to light since the previous day. Rice left over from our dinner was used to brew a porridge that I found more palatable with the addition of cane sugar. The peasants preferred to eat theirs with dried beef and pickled vegetables. They persuaded me to taste this, but the salty flavor and pungent odor were too much for first thing.

Before I left, the couple presented me with a small snapshot of themselves. I, in turn, gathered the family outside and prepared to frame a photograph using the self-timer mechanism. They all appeared puzzled as to who would take the picture! Suddenly, on recognition of this unique occasion, the mother ran off with her daughter—returning minutes later with the little girl's dusty blue tunic replaced with a pink dress!

The kindness of such people fortified me against the lonely hours of running in the empty landscape. My brothers and I had identified the psychological problems of isolation, but we knew that the longer I could contain the stress, the stronger in mind I would become. One game was to subtract eight hours, and contemplate what my family back in England might be doing. It was a comforting thought that the hospitality that supported me out here in China was an extension of my own family's support back home.

The brightness of the dawn subsided into an overcast day. As the color of the desert merged with the sky, no oases appeared within sight, and apart from a scanty cover of thorn bush or fleshy-leaved succulents, no life flourished. A group of workers in the distance held promise of a short rest and the opportunity to top up my water canteen. I was soon to realize that this was no ordinary workforce. Smashing rocks with hammers, they were a head-shaven labor gang, their torsos gleaming with sweat and motions leaden with fatigue. Immediately I became worried, not for my safe passage but for fear of questioning by their guards. With the glares of fifty or more men fixed upon my every stride, I continued along my way, merely uttering an indistinguishable acknowledgment to a guard who looked just as dumbfounded as the men themselves. I wondered what crimes these men had committed to deserve such punishment. In China, executions for murder, robbery and crimes against the state are carried out quite regularly. Perhaps they were being imprisoned for political offenses.

The character of the desert was quite different from what I had imagined. The terrain was largely flat, occasionally undulating with the presence of ridges. The surface was firm, the top encrustation the result of sand and gravel being bound together with continuous nighttime condensation. Small stones scattered the surface. This type of desert, which is common in Central Asia, is the 'gobi.' The term is derived from Gansu and Turkestan and is often misused as the name of the desert rather than a description of it. According to my map, I was now traversing the southern edge of the Badain Jaran Shamo (literally, sand waves)—which was gobi in character.

For the first time since I left Jiayuguan signs of the Wall reappeared. There were huge beacon towers, several miles apart, though the Wall between them had been weathered away. In the shadow of one such mighty structure lay a lonely grave; never was a more desolate location chosen as a place of rest for the dead. It was a conical mound of gravel, in which were pressed several sticks. These had strands of colored crepe paper attached, white being in prominence for this is the color of mourning. How recent the burial was I could not detect, for the dry climate tends to make things look new whatever the age. Paying my respects to the unfortunate soul I wondered what tales this person could have told of China's turbulent recent history.

Gaotai was the next town marked on my map. I estimated it to be twenty miles away. Making good daily progress in terms of mileage was important, for it was now mid-September and, even thinking positively, I estimated the remaining route would take me until December to complete, providing there were no delays or problems. In the village of Jianshanshi I asked an old man, "*Qu Gaotai, san shi gongli?*" (Gaotai, twenty miles?)

"*Gaotai . . . bas shi li,*" (eighty li) was the reply. The *li* is the old Chinese unit of distance, and approximately one-third of a mile. The Chinese refer to the Great Wall as "*Wan li Chang Cheng'an li Chang Cheng*" (the Great Wall of ten thousand li). Well, it's about twenty-five miles, I figured, and thought of halving the distance by sunset. "*E le,*" (hungry) I said, but they could not understand. This was simple to mime, merely by rubbing my stomach. Out of the cupboard came rock-hard bread; with water, however, it was quite edible and filling.

The line of towers continued across a small range of hills which appeared to be an arm of the Qilian Shan reaching out into the desert corridor. Their red-gravel slopes were deeply gouged with wadis, the fossil-river result of former catastrophic flooding. As a light evening breeze crossed the plain, I was to witness a strange phenomenon. Occasional dust devils spiralled across the desert surface, and one passing within yards of my path was strong enough to ruffle my hair, shorts and shirt, its dust clogging my eyes and its chill cooling my sweaty brow. Like ghosts of Silk Road travellers of old, the eddies marched across the empty plain.

Now feeling exhausted and grimy, I resigned myself to sleeping under the stars. Though aware of breaking one of the golden rules of desert bushcraft, I bivouacked out of sight in a wadi. The time between dusk and darkness seemed interminably long without the company of the peasants and stunningly quiet. I was miles from anywhere. All was very silent indeed that night, apart from my rather poor humming of hymns.

Daybreak is no time to linger in the desert. The lack of any cloud cover to insulate the earth during the night results in the loss of heat and freezing conditions. Putting on my full Ultrafleece suit, I remembered to shake my shoes to rid them of any creatures which had taken refuge in them during the night (a tip recollected from Spike Milligan—and also my father who served in the North African campaigns). Stiff, tired, cold and dusty, I drank a little icy water and hobbled away. Even the prospect of a Chinese breakfast seemed enticing. The track led towards the railway line. A train labored along like an enormous black snake, its plume of smoke hanging in the dawn sky. Never being the sort of person to work well without breakfast, I felt my morale perk up as the track crossed a sealed road. Here, in a small brick building at the barrier, a railway worker was just brewing some tea and rice porridge. He seemed as pleased with his breakfast company as I was. Moreover, he was able to direct me towards the Wall, which I understood to lie close to the railway line at the foot of the Qilian Shan.

How good it was to be directly on the line of the Wall once again. The first remains since Jiayuguan! My heart lifted, even though I felt rather tired and weak. My thirst seemed unquenchable despite three mugs of tea drunk with the railway man. Was this just exhaustion or the onset of illness? Whatever the cause, running, even slow jogging, was beyond my capability, for it was all I could do to walk slowly.

Slowly the landscape was changing. Between ridges and in hollows lay pockets of windblown sand, like remnant patches of snow. The sand patches swamped out what little vegetation the stony terrain had managed to foster. Gradually, the sands became a sea of sand dunes, the very desert image one associates with cartographers' yellow on the maps. The stony track had long since been drowned by their waves. Looking almost manmade in their symmetry, without a grain of sand out of place, barkhan dunes filled the view in all directions. Wave upon wave, a stationary sea, its motion frozen until the next winds rearranged the sands. Here was nature at her most design-conscious, shaped in perfect crescent moons.

My progress was pitifully slow, with each planted step sinking into the loose sand, each stride sliding apart. The sand filling all the space in my shoes reactivated old sores and initiated new ones. Wading through this sea sapped my energy completely. The dunes convected hot air on to my face, and I needed to cover my eyes against the intense glare.

In desperation, I headed north and eventually reached a sealed road. Tall poplars, planted each side of the road, provided good shade. A couple of trucks laden with watermelons sped past blasting their horns, and several cyclists twisted their necks and strayed all over the road to ensure their eyes had not deceived them. A boy at the wayside was selling Hami melons amid a litter of rinds and seeds. I bought two from him and marched on.

I managed to mime my state of distress at a farm with golden corn cobs ripening on the roof and was invited in to rest. The old lady of the household brought out her entire pill collection, wrapped in twists of newspaper, and selecting two different kinds of tablets, gave me four to take. God only knew for what malady they were originally intended. I did not wish to offend her by openly casting doubts on her diagnostic powers, so I palmed them with all the skill I had developed as an awkward small boy who had been the despair of our family doctor.

I forced down a few strands of noodles to please the family at the evening meal, but feeling dreadfully weak and hot, I was thankful when the predictable flow of inspecting visitors departed and I was able to take to my bed.

I took a turn for the worse during the night and succumbed to the final nightmare of being caught short with diarrhea and not managing to find the way out in time because the door had been bolted. Now I felt demoralized and embarrassed, not to mention filthy and stinking. In the moonlight outside it was all I could do to wipe my legs with sunflower leaves, then return to bed. At daybreak, I discovered the woman had washed my soiled Ultrafleece trousers and underpants; they were hanging on the line to dry. In some respects the Chinese are the most humane people in the world.

My temperature continued to rage as I lay prostrate with a damp towel on my brow. The old woman persisted in her role as dispensing pharmacist, giving me yet different colored tablets, but I steadfastly maintained my childish deceit, just as I had when my aunt would give me money to take an aspirin. I began to think of the Wall as an enemy who had cast a spell of disease upon me. I kept on visualizing the gloomy memories of the previous days: the miserable faces of the labor gang, the lonely grave and the mysterious winds eddying across the desert. Were these three bad omens? My medical supplies were basic. I carried Streptotriad for dysentery, but rather foolishly I was unsure of the symptoms.

Despite the obvious discomfort I was suffering, the family continued to show me off to visitors. This I regarded as exemplifying a callous trait in the Chinese character. On specific occasions, they had shown themselves as deriving interest from others' misfortune. I had seen several traffic accidents where grown men shrieked with delight at the sight of a mangled bicycle. Admittedly, I was in an area where few foreigners strayed, but I was hard put to respond civilly when the daughter of the house arrived, accompanied by twenty or so of her excited pigtailed, bright-jacketed schoolmates, grinning, giggling and saying "gooder morning"—in the late afternoon.

A decision appeared to have been taken. Ushering me to collect my things, the woman returned my clean clothes. Was this to be the end of the journey? Were they handing me over to the Public Security Bureau? We walked outside into the brilliant sunshine. My feet were very sore, my legs weak and I felt lightheaded as I was led up a narrow lane to a huge archway whose pillars were inscribed with a red character slogan punctuated by exclamation marks. At the apex of the arch was a large red star. This was the Linze commune. Passing through the entrance where children milled round yelling "*Wai guo ren*" and "*Lao wai*" (foreign person, old foreigner), I was conducted to the sick bay. A formal delegation soon mustered and sat themselves down on the empty beds, while the interpreter among them flexed his English on me.

"How are you today?" he said loudly.

"I am sick."

"Rest in our new hospital." Then, pointing towards his comrades, "He is doctor. She is waitress. They are leaders."

The doctor, cigarette in hand, came over to examine me. The rest of the delegation closed in with the attentiveness of medical students on their morning round. The windows shutters vibrated as the peasants clamored for a view. I was told I had a temperature of 101. The doctor, with the help of the "waitress," proceeded to inject me in the backside with the audience continuing to view. I felt sick and dizzy.

"Our leaders are very worried," he emphasized with a pained facial expression. "They will decide." And off they all went, with the exception of the doctor and waitress who rested on the spare beds. They provided enamel basins, ubiquitous in China, for my toileting. As my diarrhea gave little or no warning of its approach, I quickly had to rid myself of inhibition to squat over the basin, splurting and farting, as the faces at the windows struggled to catch a glimpse of me. It was wishful thinking that they would give me any privacy. How could they be so inconsiderate; had they no pity?

Hiding beneath a sheet, lying close to the wall, or squatting in the corner, I could not escape the shaven-headed, Mao-capped faces leering in at the shutters, climbing upon each other's backs and straining their necks for a better view. It was a nightmare which only ended two days later when my kind friends organized transport to take me to hospital in the next town. As I climbed shakily into the jeep, the sound of the firing engine was like a nail in my journey's coffin. For Zhangye was at that time a closed town and I knew my evasive tactics had come to an end.

The men's ward at Zhangye's hospital was full of dismal cases, many of whom looked to be "waiting to see Marx," so I was allowed to stay in the hotel, as long as I did not leave the compound except for my daily visits to the hospital for injections.

My fragile condition was now complicated by a badly swollen toe and the ball of my foot was tender to touch. But the *coup de grace* was delivered by the inevitable visit from the man from the PSB (Public Security Bureau), brandishing his book of rules. He wanted to know where I had come from. I told him Jiuquan, which was the nearest place from the nationwide listing of 350 open cities.

"Jiuquan is open place, 125 miles away," he protested. "How did you come here?"

"Running and walking. I'm interested in the Great Wall."

"You cannot come here. You can see Great Wall at Beijing. To see a not-open place must have a travel permit."

"Can you give me one?"

"Our capital city, Lanzhou, give."

"So will they give me one?"

"Only for business. You have broken the law of People's Republic of China—this book says we will punish you."

"I am sorry."

"As a foreigner you have suffered with illness, so we will not punish you." He continued to tell me that I was welcome to stay until I felt fully recovered, then they would arrange my train ticket to an open place. "Then you can enjoy sightseeing."

Barely able to walk, and with my health on a downward spiral, I faced no alternative but return to Beijing. As the huge steam engine hauled in the train to Zhangye station, I wondered whether the journey had come to its end, with the Wall having the victory.

*　*　*

I arrived back in Beijing on October 1st, China's National Day, and stood in Tiananmen Square where Chairman Mao proclaimed the founding of the People's Republic in 1949. The square, flanked by the monumental socialist architecture and the starkly contrasting Ming-style Gate of Heavenly Peace, was the focus of celebration as the Chinese people gathered for their thirty-seventh birthday. Red flags were hoisted from every building. Large white character slogans on red backgrounds pronounced the way forward: "On with the reforms"; "Work to achieve the four modernizations." With these guiding maxims, China looked to the future while not being allowed to forget her struggles in the past. Huge portraits of Lenin, Stalin, Engels, Marx and Dr. Sun Yat Sen joined the embalmed Mao Zedong to observe the reforming nation.

Just as China looked both backward and forward, I was likewise considering my own fascination with and ambition in the country. The attraction of my goal was clearer than ever before. The Communist forefathers, the slogans, the red flags and the goose-stepping troops, and with them the superstition and wariness of any alien who tried to see behind the curtain, made the country such a citadel. All the mystique and the obstacles China put in my way made the task more worthwhile. Over the past weeks I had covered just a small proportion of the journey but had already exploded many of China's myths and misconceptions. I would return to China in 1987 for a final attempt.

Limping home with the unwanted souvenirs of an injured foot and a bad stomach would have been depressing on its own, but with the plan of returning to the Wall the following spring already made, licking my wounds was made bearable. Dysentery, which I had been too inexperienced to recognize, was eventually cured. The stress-fractured toe took a little longer. The Casualty Department records of Wirral's Arrowe Park Hospital now have an entry under "Nature and cause of injury" which reads, "Running along the Great Wall of China." Nobody turned a hair at the time. They were probably all too overworked to notice. But rest and therapy during the winter restored me and gave me time to think.

David Griffiths, I heard, had lost his sponsors and postponed his attempt. My sponsors at Thomas Cook remained loyal and, what is more, Neil Pirie did not embarrass me by demanding any written evidence of official Chinese permission. It was entirely fortunate that such a Sinophile was responsible for my funding, a man who appreciated that, superficially at least, the mechanics needed to achieve our ambitious project were essentially "China by storm." I now felt able to defend my blatant intention to trespass. Admittedly, just to ignore any statute laws pertaining to foreigners' movements would be unacceptable, a criminal action. However, I held the belief that the Chinese people wanted me to succeed. The peasant farmers who had been so warm and friendly and provided the infrastructure for my journey were a testimony to that belief. The law serves the people, so, I argued, it was acceptable for me to engineer my own exceptions to the rule and display a revolutionary spirit to overcome the barriers put before me. Even the Great Leader himself might have agreed with that reasoning. Ingenuity and imagination, begging and bribery are the arms of the revolutionary. But the strongest weapon is belief. I would leave nothing but friendship and footprints, and take nothing but notes, names and photographs.

Allowing for bureaucratic delays and the inevitable injury, I had to face the fact that the journey was going to take longer than originally estimated. Moreover, the extreme climate meant that only the spring and autumn were suitable. So I would divide my journey into two stages, and remain in China during the intervening hot summer. With my dearly won knowledge, I was now ideally equipped to make a clandestine journey. I had served my China apprenticeship. Now it was time to return and remain there for however long it took to succeed.

PART TWO

Closed

There are numerous walls within the Chinese world; the Great Wall merely protects the Chinese against devils from without.

—*Sun Longji*

From the top, postmarks from Jiayuguan and Shandan, Gansu Province; the China Railway stamp at Changliushui; and the People's Government of Yanchi County, Ningxia.

5

Along the Silk Road

A journey of a thousand miles begins
with a single step.
                  —*An early Chinese proverb,*
                  adapted by Mao Zedong

Spring had not yet succeeded in relieving the city from the north
China winter. When I left Beijing five months ago at the height of the
golden season, the streets were lined with tens of thousands of potted
chrysanthemums. Without these splashes of color, and the camouflage of
well-clothed trees, the dismal grey tenement blocks were all too starkly
apparent. Now the dry and icy wind, holding all the venom of a Central
Asian crossing within it, unleashed a vengeance with every gusty breath,
driving all color into hibernation. The clothes-consciousness of the new
generation was temporarily shelved in preference for comfort from the
intense cold. Now the population was painted with military hues. The
clothing, green greatcoats and beagle-eared hats, made small people look
big. Beijingers actually classify the winter weather according to the
number of insulating layers necessary for protection, with limbs assuming a hideous chubbiness from the heavy lagging. The worst days are
"fifteeners."

As the reality of facing "the Dragon" again drew near, all my self-
doubts returned. Potential problems that were solved or dismissed quite
easily at home were more daunting than ever. The objective in sheer

distance seemed impossible to attain. My emotions were landsliding towards submitting to the Wall without any further physical encounters.

Somehow I coaxed myself into reserving a rail ticket to Jiayuguan. Just five days then remained in which to administer psychological first aid and be on that train. Running was the only medicine known to me.

By seven o' clock the *tai-ji* classes were in full swing. Septuagenarians shuffled along with small transistors in hand. At the lakeside men bellowed loudly, ridding their bodies of anger and frustration. It was quite clear that the concept of exercise, for the Chinese elders at least, was centered as much on the mind as the body. The sight of a bare-chested man punching the trunk of a tree was an illustration of what a man could do with his head separated from his heart.

One morning at breakfast in my hotel I joined a young Englishman carrying a weighty volume of Francis Younghusband's *The Heart of a Continent*. This was not casual reading but in fact his guide book, for Tom Broadbent explained that Younghusband was an ancestor on his mother's side and he was planning to travel in his footsteps. Nobody could claim a more revered forebear in Central Asian exploration. Treating the volume with biblical reverence, Tom unfolded a route map of the fabled trek from Manchuria across northern China and over the Himalaya: the fuzzy ochres of the atlas plates led us over the Galphin Gobi, the desert of Zungaria and the Silk Road oases of Turkestan—Hami, Turfan and Kashgar—then south skirting the dreaded Tarim basin to Yarkand and finally crossing the Himalaya into Kashmir via the previously unexplored Mustagh Pass. The map had originally been retailed by Stanford's Geographical Establishment, London—still in business today in Covent Garden and where I had been not two weeks before to purchase a new set of maps. Tom would be setting out from the site of the former British Legation near Tiananmen Square at 6:00 a.m. on April 4th—exactly one hundred years to the hour after Younghusband left on his intelligence-gathering mission to assess the threat of a Russian invasion to the Chinese Empire. This was of concern to the British who, in administering the Indian subcontinent, much preferred a Chinese to a Russian neighbor. A century later Tom's worries were not concerned with the "Great Game" of Victorian power politics but the contemporary challenge of overcoming access restrictions. All but a handful of towns were nominally "open." Viewed from the West it appeared that the bamboo curtain was down. But one only needed to step off China's main street to realize that was a gross misconception.

Tom's enthusiasm was inspiring. Undeterred by inexperience at the age of twenty-two (He confessed having never walked more than six miles before!), he had inherited the when, where and why of a journey. The British pioneering spirit lived on: Tom had bought a stout pair of boots, a comfortable rucksack and one or two survival gadgets, and with a full week to spare was on the threshold of successfully keeping his century-old appointment. Already acquainting himself with Chinese ways, he was receiving acupuncture to combat difficulty in sleeping. I felt it augured well to ask the descendant of Younghusband to make the first entry in the diary where I planned to keep comments and greetings from the people I met on my journey.

* * *

Back in Jiayuguan again, I had no choice but to lodge in the town's *binguan*. I awoke to the early morning street broadcasts and gazed out upon a cast concrete monument of a peasant and worker, striding forth, united arms outstretched, pointing along China's socialist road, which also happened to be the road out of town that I should soon be following myself. During my absence, I had been refining my equipment in the light of experience, and the biggest change was to use a new model of shoe. The manufacturer claimed that a shock-absorbing "gel" pad made the shoes 30 percent more protective in terms of cushioning. That was all scientific jargon; I translated it into meaning that every third mile was of no consequential stress to the legs. I was asking these shoes to carry me 1,000 miles, for there was no chance of replacing them with anything similar en route. Until recently, Chinese shoes just came in small, medium or large. And my size was thirteen. . . .

I had also greatly improved my stock of maps. Now my route was charted by English and Chinese maps, the latter in particular being an enormous improvement on the 1:6 million wall map used previously. With these and my improving Mandarin, I would be able to confront peasants with wayfinding queries. I had taken care to learn geographical terms which the Chinese often use in combination with cardinal compass points to create place names. If all else failed, I would fall back on

Operational Navigation Charts (ONC) composed from satellite photographs. Their provenance might cause suspicion if found by security personnel, though a more immediate and practical problem was that place names were transcribed using the old Wade-Giles system rather than the Pinyin alternative. (Jiayuguan was Pinyin, Kiayukuan was Wade-Giles—both are the same place.)

Perhaps the hardest fact to comprehend was the sheer distance of the run. My mind was incapable and unwilling to contemplate such a distance, and therefore as a psychological aide it was strategically wise to view the run as a series of steps. It would be of no help, when tired and weary, to pull out a map with the distant Yellow River beckoning some weeks away. As though to represent my method of one chunk at a time, I cut my maps into manageable stages with conceivable targets on their right-hand edges. The first piece of what resembled a jigsaw Dragon, the tail, was a 155-mile stretch to Zhangye. Apart from the mental benefits of this strategy, such a small map could be comfortably and safely inserted in the pocket of my shorts. With this positive action, I left the *binguan* for the post office.

I had planned to obtain postmarks from settlements en route which, along with my own comments, photographs and any diary entries by my hosts, would be a verification of my passage through the country. I should need to be wary in areas where a quick telephone call could muster the local Public Security Bureau, but this I would play by ear. My experience in the Jiayuguan post office was a learning one. It seemed no matter how small the gap between myself and the counter, a peasant would attempt to occupy that space. Half a dozen hands, holding crumpled paper pennies, were proffered in the face of the clerk and whoever shouted "*tong zhi!*" (Comrade!) the most was served first. Eventually, after my own fair share of barging in, the clerk obliged by franking a postage stamp affixed in the diary. It thudded down like the firing of a pistol for a race.

* * *

Jiuquan, fifteen miles out from Jiayuguan, was an insignificant dot on the map of the Hexi corridor, but it was also a substantial county town with a long history, having been garrisoned and resettled under the Han

Emperor, Wu Di. The Emperor was pleased with the way his general Huo Qubing had colonized this first territory within the walled kingdom and made it safe for commerce, and to express his gratitude he sent him a present of ten jars of wine. But since ten jars were not enough to distribute to all the troops, Huo Qubing refused to drink any of it himself and poured all the Emperor's gift into the town spring. Either he was China's first socialist, or he was making a dangerous comment on the scale of imperial gestures.

I had hoped that my experience of the previous year might have lessened the sense of alienation I felt when surrounded by staring small-town peasants muttering "*wai guo ren.*" But when I was engulfed by middle-school students released for lunch, it was as menacing as ever. The uniform of the Cultural Revolution may have given way to the first expressions of individuality in Beijing, but in Jiuquan, where only government-owned stores existed, the students were still a tidal wave of green and blue, brightened only by the knotted red Young Pioneer scarf at their throats, symbolizing a piece of their national flag.

The sexes behaved quite differently towards me. Girls continued on their way, often hand in hand or with little fingers linked in friendship. Boys also held hands but were more cavalier, yelling to their comrades should they miss seeing me. They caused unashamed havoc on the street, doubling back on their bicycles for a second look at the *lao wai*, but although English was their second language, they were too timid to attempt to communicate beyond a giggling squeal of "Hello" and "Okay" once we had passed.

A quiet room and the sight of a bed eased my sullen mood as I brewed a mug of *moli hua cha* and pried the shoes from my heels. Just fifteen and a half miles and I was wrecked. Fitness, taken for granted before, had been lost during my period of illness and injury. Reason was deserting me, and once again China, the walled kingdom, seemed an untouchable and mysterious fortress in which I was serving a sentence, being punished for the audacity of starting such a journey. Quitting, even to the point of inventing a face-saving scenario in which I was arrested and deported, seemed the only chance of parole. At present, sleep was the only escape.

Awakened by hunger in the early evening, I ate *jiaozi* in a small *fandian*. Neglecting to have brought my own chopsticks (essential to minimize the risk of catching hepatitis), I wiped the grime off those provided and tucked into my feast of thirty dumplings. Two soldiers at an adjacent table, smoking and swigging beer, glared at me until their own *jiaozi* arrived, after which they paid me no further attention. At six o'clock food was on everyone's mind. Steam rose from woks, families squatted on their haunches, knees level with shoulders, scooping and slurping noodles into their mouths. A wheel squeaked on the bumpy cobbles as a grandmother pushed a bassinet slowly along, using it as much to aid her own locomotion as a cot for the toddler. As I nodded and smiled to them, the old lady informed the child that I was a foreigner.

Twelve noon and midnight Greenwich Mean Time were prearranged tuning-in times for mental telepathy sessions with my family. For three precious minutes I could tune in to advice I knew to be logical and positive and it is what saved me on the brink of submission. The uncertainties of my first days in China, repeated here again in Jiuquan, were rehearsals for more testing times ahead. On the eve of departure they represented a final psyching up of my will and determination to achieve my goal. These days had brought me close to breaking point, but, somehow, I had survived.

* * *

Winter had left the oasis bare, dry and dusty. Views which were punctuated by the dark green of clothed poplars the previous autumn were featureless. Peasants were reaping the harvest of a season's work then; now they were just beginning the work of plowing the land with donkeys, camels or water buffalo. At the edges of the fields many grave sites were noticeable, for the Qing Ming festival, in which the Chinese respect their departed by decorating the conical burial mounds with white pennants, had recently passed.

The cold allowed me to jog in relative comfort without sweating except where the rucksack rested on my back. It did, however, demand additional calories. In Shang-ba I was followed by a group of thirty or more people, inherited in the post office, to the *fandian* where they watched me eat *mian tiao tang*. It was piping hot, tasty and looked good with bright green chopped spring onion sprinkled on top. The audience was amused not only that I had my own chopsticks but by the size of them—child's length to save weight.

The night's lodging was taken care of by a man I met when I stopped to eat a jar of fruit at a village store. Slinging my rucksack on his back, he marched me off to his farm and the chance of a nap before supper.

As I opened my eyes, the Chinese characters of a newspapered ceiling came into focus. At the head of the *kang* a black and white portrait of Mao hung on the wall at such an angle that he appeared to be gazing down directly upon the bed's occupants. Outside, the preparation of dinner was well advanced with plenty of steam, crackles and sizzles coming from the cookhouse. While a young boy stirred a vat of bubbling gruel, his father, Pan Rui Ji, made *jiaozi* by sandwiching meat and vegetables in pastry. More commonly boiled or steamed, these were fried. What a feast! The gruel, *xiaomi xifan* (millet seed porridge), could be eaten with sugar and thus doubled up as a welcome sweet dessert. The "*zha*" *jiaozi* were delicious and between us we ate fifty or more.

Our full bellies were to form the foundation for a heavy spirit-drinking session after two of Pan Rui Ji's comrades arrived with a large and ornate bottle of *mao tai*. A low table, on which Pan Rui Ji's wife put two candles and four tiny porcelain egg cups, was placed in the center of the *kang*. It had surprised my hosts that, as a man, I was a nonsmoker and therefore they seemed pleased their guest was willing to participate in this other show of friendship. The seal was broken by Pan Rui Ji and he filled all four cups.

"*Tong zhi men! Ying guo peng you huan ying! Ganbei!*" (Comrades, welcome English friend. Bottoms up!)

Down it went in one gulp, all competitors untroubled and swiftly displaying their empty cups. A trail of fire blazed between tongue and stomach.

"*Peng you men! Ying guo! Ganbei!*" (Friends, England! Bottoms up!)

The second time it was not quite so devastating, my organs having received a warning of the strength of this fearsome liquid. We all showed each other empty cups. The laughs became louder, the smiles broader and the eyes more expressive. In the shadows behind stood the wives and children giggling and chatting. Seizing the flask, much to the men's delight, I poured the next round and proposed the toast: to China.

"*Peng you men! Zhong guo! Ganbei!*"

They were enthralled and complimented me on my Chinese. A longer interlude ensued (thank goodness), giving the men a chance to "roll their own" in yesterday's news. The candles served as lighters, illuminating the exhaled smoke rings and glinting off the white of their eyes and teeth. We talked about national leaders, a conversation instigated by Mao looking down on the four of us. "*Mao hao ma?*" (Is Mao good?) "Good, good," they replied chuckling. Reaching for the *mao tai* (named after the place in which it is brewed—nothing to do with Mao), I poured another round, rebuffing their halfhearted refusals. This appears to be a traditional aspect of the drinking ritual, the seizing of one's cup beyond the pourer's reach, together with a loud and enthusiastic repetition of "*gou, gou, gou!*" (enough, etc). After a few seconds, the drinker succumbs to the persuasion and his cup is filled!

"*Peng you men! Deng Xiaoping! Ganbei!*"

Imitations of drunkenness followed, yet we all knew there was little chance of leaving any spirit in the bottle. Pan Rui Ji poured the next round, chasing the cups off and under the table, ignoring the refusals that were becoming altogether more convincing pieces of acting.

"*Peng you men! Wan li Chang Cheng! Ganbei!*"

With the spirit taking its toll, the two friends failed to down their *mao tai* in one, and had to be carefully watched by Pan Rui Ji to make sure they emptied their cups in their mouths and not on the *kang*. The end of the flask was divided equally, though everyone seemed unselfishly willing to go without. The final toast was to friendship: "*Peng you men! You yi! Ganbei!*"

Uttering sighs of relief, Pan Rui Ji asked his wife to make tea. In just twenty-four hours my morale had soared from the brink of defeat to a heightened appreciation of the privilege I held in entering the heart of China and experiencing camaraderie of this nature.

A shaft of sunlight illuminated my rucksack on the dusty floor. My tongue and throat were parched, and as I stirred, Pan Rui Ji's wife brought in a flask of hot water. The men were slow to rise, eyes reluctant to open and limbs to bend in the dawn chill.

Diary, April 11th: Corn Seeds Farm

Off at 8:40 a.m. after a breakfast of *hong tang shui* (raw cane sugar in hot water) and bread. Potential blister sites on first metatarsals. Crossed massive stretch of desert— flat stony plain, nothing in sight except derelict watchtowers. Cold eddies rush past. Visibility closed in—

couldn't see Qilian Shan. Over twenty-five miles today.
Crossing this waste, I am in awe at the courage and
tenacity of tradesmen, travellers, pilgrims and missionaries who have trekked along this very track. . . .

Whilst travelling through the Hexi corridor, one can be relatively
confident that there will be some kind of settlement every twenty-five to
thirty miles. The pioneers of this route, which much later became known
as the Silk Road, travelled by camel train. Each daily stage involved about
ten hours of trekking, and the beasts of the caravan could be relied upon
to amble at a steady three miles per hour—which resulted in staging
posts at approximately thirty-mile intervals. The snowy Qilian Shan to
the south provided many springs fed by the glacial meltwaters, and
around these watering holes caravanserai became established. These
inns of the oases thrived on the business of the passing merchants who
needed refreshment and shelter. Accurately described as the forerunners
of the transport cafe, they offered a comprehensive service: animal fodder
and water, hostelry and sustenance for merchants. Carters hired their
animals and guide services, since few caravans ever made the entire
intercontinental journey. Effectively, it was a network of routes along which
merchandise was passed from one trader to another. Apart from the hostile
terrain and extreme climate, there was an ever-present danger of attack by
bandits. Plunder of an eastward caravan might yield gold, silver and glass;
the looting of westbound travellers, fine embroidered silks and jade.

Within the confines of the Middle Kingdom, the rulers of the Han
Dynasty took it upon themselves to protect the Silk Road by extending
the Great Wall to Jiayuguan and later to Yumen (the Jade Gate). Beyond
Yumen the route was guarded from forts and watchtowers, a chain of
which penetrated to Dunhuang and into Lop Nur. Once outside Chinese
territory the goods were traded to Persians and Turks who crossed the
Pamirs to Mediterranean ports for distribution to Rome and beyond. The
term Silk Road was originally coined by the German explorer von
Richthofen in the nineteenth century, but it had been an established trade
route between Europe and Asia from the days of the two great empires,
China and Rome.

Inevitably, too, the route became an artery for the dispersion of
knowledge, culture and religion. In 139 BC Zhang Qian was dispatched

by Emperor Wu Di to make contact with an ally in Central Asia in order to put down a tribe who were disturbing the border and the Silk Road. Unfortunately, the recalcitrant tribe got to Zhang Qian before he reached his support team and it was thirteen years before he managed to return to the Emperor. By then everyone had lost interest in his original mission, but Zhang Qian was able to tell his master about the Himalaya, the Pamirs and Afghanistan and the existence of a great empire further to the west—Rome. The part of Zhang Qian's report that interested Wu Di the most was not his account of precious metals or glass, but his description of a breed of horse that was strong and swift. The quest for a horse like this would play an important part in China's history and that of the Great Wall.

Qingshui means "clear water" and describes the health-inducing properties of the streams running off the Qilian Shan. The Silk Road passes straight through the village. Now the only traffic is an occasional truck or local bus emblazoned with "Lanzhou," the provincial capital of Gansu. In autumn the old men had watched over melons amid a litter of rind gobbled up by piglets. It seemed they had not budged—only their fruit had changed, although the dismal display of bruised and shrivelled apples did little to entice the bus passengers. A small Moslem inn, its sign written in Islamic and Chinese script, promised more attractive fare. It felt warmingly encouraging to recognize the two characters of the word *fandian*, yet I could make nothing of the Arabic scrawl below. Inside there were pictures of Mecca and an Islamic calendar, reminding one that this northwestern periphery of China has always been a racial mosaic, the result of an interaction that began on the Silk Road two millennia ago.

The proprietor, cooking under religious and seasonal restraints, served up a plate of noodles and egg. Producing my diary, I gestured for him to write with Arabic script, though he was unable to do so. No doubt the mastering of literacy in Chinese is task enough.

My hosts for the evening were the eighth team of Zhong commune on the edge of Qingshui village.

Diary, April 11th

A woman and her children, about twelve and fourteen, give me tea as the boy reads my letter of introduction written by Han Suyin. Hard bread dunked in tea, a choice of *hong cha* or *moli hua cha* (black or jasmine).

Wash socks and burst a small blister and nap until 6:30 p.m. My limited Chinese falsely impresses on them my overall standard—they waffle on—if I don't respond they shout it louder.

Perhaps the possibility of someone, even a *wai guo ren*, not speaking Chinese never occurred to them. Deafness seemed the obvious barrier. With a breakdown of communication, it appeared the evening was heading for a stare-out until the boy produced a dog-eared school textbook. Superficially, at least, just an English language reader—yet behind its innocent cover was an incredible programme of political indoctrination produced to brainwash schoolchildren's minds. The first lesson was an adoration of the Communist Party:

> *The Communist Party is a great, glorious and correct Party. It is the core of leadership of the whole Chinese people. Chairman Mao is the Great Leader of the Party. Long live the Communist Party of China! Long live Chairman Mao!*

On to lesson two, "What is the date today?" which held more practical promise for China's budding interpreters.

> *Today is May 5th. It's Marx's birthday. What day is Lenin's birthday? It's April 22nd.*

During the Great Proletariat Cultural Revolution even the teaching of a foreign language was seen as an opportunity for propaganda. Young minds were not exempt from a disturbing and intense vocabulary; on the contrary, it was the harnessing of the rebellious spirit of youth that was the burning core of the Cultural Revolution. The words jumped out of the book at me: political, correctness, capitalist, incorrectness, ideological, punishment, red banner, glorious, bury, imperialism and that nastiest of all, criticize. Every word hit me like stones thrown by a rioting mass—a witch hunt in the school yard; children, so naturally cruel en masse, putting their lesson of hatred, aggression and criticism into practice. Surrounding, throwing and chanting, "We are Chairman Mao's Red Guards!" Louder and more menacingly, "We are Chairman Mao's Red Guards!!" Screeching and spitting, "We are Chairman Mao's Red Guards!!!

Red Guards!!! Red Guards, Guards, Guards!!! . . ." They stopped. I looked up. Around me thirty or more peasants, children near and adults behind, watching and waiting on my every action. They were kind, harmless and friendly people building a new China from the dereliction.

Official China was cautious, slow, paper pushing, and red sealing—as inflexible as it ever was. One further lesson in the book—*Lenin and his Passbook*—captured the mentality that was my number one enemy. Lenin arrived at his office gates to be stopped by the security guard and asked to show his pass. Lenin searched but could not find it. Another worker entering the office reproached the guard, "Comrade, everyone knows Lenin. You should let him pass." The guard refused. "The regulations state that no one is allowed to enter the office without showing their pass." Lenin supported him. "The guard is a good comrade. It is correct he should not let me enter. The regulations must be observed." This mentality trounced all preconceived hopes I might have possessed of officials bending the rules to let me "pass." I was only William Lindesay after all.

Diary, April 12th: Yuanshanzi

Bread and tea for breakfast. Visibility poor, couldn't recognize the farm of the Qingshui people from last year. Some people plowing a field shout at me—at first I continue—then look around—I can't believe it! It's the people of the oasis!! This chance meeting in the desert put me in high spirits for the whole day. As I jog along the track, across the wadis, and past a beacon tower or two, I grow eager to engage in a physical battle with the Wall rather than this mental one at present. It seems as though the Wall is hiding, viewing my form and strengths from its beacon towers—but not ready itself to challenge me. At threeish I reach the small oasis of Yuanshanzi calling in on old friends! They remember me. I'm drinking black tea as the kettle boils away on the stove, and the old man Li Zisen reads an account of my proposed journey from *Silk Road News* (the newspaper of Chinatown in Liverpool). It's 4:20 p.m., I've done about twenty-one miles today. Front of right ankle a little sore. Slept for one and a half hours until 6:30 p.m.

These meetings with old friends really boosted my morale. It was reassuring to be sheltered under this sturdy roof, to drink water the boy had drawn from the well, to eat eggs from the chickens which pecked grain in the yard, and see noodles made from wheat flour ground under the millstone. We huddled around the stove with burning faces and cold backs for the room was drafty as the wind blew strongly outside, making the lamp flicker and our shadows dance on the walls.

Li Zisen produced his personal stone chop and tin of red sealing ink from a locked trunk. He proudly made his mark at the end of a short message, the result of much coaxing on my behalf:

> I am Li Zisen of Yuanshanzi village, Gaotai County of Gansu Province. You came here to drink water. Because when I was a boy I wasn't taught how to read or write, I have very little to say. Although the Great Wall is regarded as a formidable project, in my own eyes it is just a dusty wall through sand hills.

> *4/12/87, Li Zisen*

Breakfast was a real treat—*mantou*, freshly baked. Most farms had offered bread at some stage, but usually rock hard. Seeing *mantou* prepared just increased the hunger pangs. Steam billowed from a huge cane basket as the water bubbled gently over glowing red coals in the morning chill of the cookhouse. The result was a huge basket of stodgy warm steamed buns to feast on with a jar of jasmine tea to warm frozen fingers. It was the best breakfast yet.

Shortly after leaving the village of Yuanshanzi, I passed through *yuan shan zi*, which are small rounded hills. Having taken a liking to this logical naming of places, I applied my Chinese to the map of China on an etymological tour. I rafted through the gorges of four rivers—Sichuan; ballooned above Yunnan—South Clouds; ferried across the Huang He from He Bei—north river, to He Nan—south river; and took a train from Nanjing—the south capital, to the north capital—Beijing.

Li Zisen's impression of the Wall in his locality was not surprising, for at best it was immemorable: a crumbled mass, a linearity upon which windblown sand settled. Few substantial lengths of Wall remained in the region and these were greatly diminished from their original defensive stature.

Villages meant food. Food meant stopping, but there was always a risk. Nanhua was typical. I was hungry yet fully understood the hazard of eating at a *fandian* where an audience would gather. As a precaution, I donned my navy Ultrafleece trousers to hide my recognizable red shorts. Stopping to photograph a length of Wall being incorporated in the structure of dwellings attracted attention. Now I had continual company into the village, like a flock of seagulls hovering aft and bow of a ship entering port. It was not a style of entrance that helped me, being headed by half a dozen cyclists, wobbling all over the road, with an inner escort questioning my nationality, name, destination and the whereabouts of my companions. Curiosity was killing them, yet they could not know that in highlighting my presence they were endangering my security and could bring these mysterious travels to a halt. I ate quickly and left quickly. The scar of indigestion was only temporary.

Up to now I had experienced no problems in finding a bed for the night, but that evening at a small commune I drew a universal blank. My letter from Han Suyin went unread, my Mandarin only gained the response "*Ting bu dong*" (Don't understand). Dogs snarled, women giggled and mere toddlers, identifying my foreign devilness, whooped around yelling at my intrusion until two old men escorted me into a courtyard. There we met a dignified elder, who beat the farm dog away to make quiet for my introduction. This was my chance. He read the letter and thumbed the notebook. All four of us went inside to drink tea. Almost certainly he was the commune leader, and a hierarchy existed that accounted for the uncharacteristic refusals of hospitality. Consorting with a *wai guo ren* was clearly the sort of decision which could only be taken by the commune leader. It made me all the more appreciative of hot food and a warm bed that night once I had been positively vetted.

Diary, April 13th: west of Linze

Quite an audience gathers, peaking at twenty-six! It's a strange feeling, totally exhausted, wanting food yet being the exhibit of the village. That's the price of hospitality. I want relaxation; they want interest. Given my own room at ten o'clock. The two little boys watch me prepare to sleep, enjoying fiddling with my torch. Under the watchful gaze of Mao on the wall (who else?).

I'm surprised that Mao is so highly revered in heartland
China—every place I've stayed in seems to have some
Maoist relic—if not a picture—still holding wallspace
some eleven years after his death.

The provincial map of Gansu and the ONC agreed on one thing: that
a major section of Wall would be found east of Zhangye. Until now they
had forecast different stories. The ONC, compiled as it was from satellite
photographs, appeared quite reliable for physical features, though tracks,
roads, the position and size of settlements were often inaccurate. I relied
increasingly upon the Chinese map, which seemed accurate for villages
and roads, the only reliable reference points. If my heart beckoned "east
of Zhangye and don't spare the legs," my head at least proposed a more
patient and cautious approach. I waited for the Wall so the Wall could
wait for me. Now, following a paved road, the pressure of wayfinding
was off—but the heat was very much on. Altitude and sun singed my
forehead, nose and ears and the tarmac burnt my feet. In other respects
luck was with me as I breezed through Linze town, calling in at the post
office for a postmark and getting a much-needed dose of vitamin C with
a jar of pineapple. Making use of the adjusted hour, I continued walking
long after the energy to run had deserted me. Some workmen watching
a television outside a building beckoned me over. With everything going
well and feeling sociable I responded.

They ushered me in to meet their bosses, Cheng Shouli and Jia Yi. Cheng
was a huge man, happy and smiling, with a round and rosy face with a spiky
beard. He shook me by the hand repeatedly, letting out sporadic gestures
of approval interspersed with orders to his men and sentences from my
diary. Was I hungry? Thirsty? Tired? I was waited on, mouth and foot. A
kettle of glutinous rice, egg and pork was placed before me with a bottle of
beer. Cheng pried its top off with his teeth to the cheers of his comrades.
Before the last mouthful of food was chewed, a second helping was on its
way. In came the ubiquitous enamel basin, stencilled with red peonies
outside and in. Hot water, a cloth and soap—my first good wash for a week!
Finally some traditional Chinese medicine for the feet—soy sauce in hot
water, a remedy highly thought of by the heroes of the Long March.

Some of the men returned to the television outside, the black-and-
white picture flickering through the window and door. Cheng and Jia

with some comrades stayed, talking over tea within the limits of my vocabulary. How old was I? Perhaps twenty-seven. A wife, children? They were all married with families in Gansu. Cigarettes, how much in Britain? My shoes, so light, here—feel them! So big! What size? Forty-eight! English? No, Japanese. A yeah. . . . His sleeping bag . . . it's so small, is it warm enough? Yes, duck feathers, Chinese! How many miles along the Wall? The Chinese were as undecided as anyone. All opinions were aired. *Wan li Chang Cheng*— that's 10,000 li which is 3,100 miles. Jiayuguan to Shanhaiguan is about 1,865, I told them. Out came the maps, Chinese and English. We pieced together the Dragon jigsaw on the bed. Reeling off the route was easy to me: Wuwei, Huang He, Ningxia, Yanchi, Jingbian, Yulin, Fugu, Datong, then Bohai. Places were just one aspect of the journey, but personalities such as these men were more memorable. They took a genuine interest in my adventure. The prelude was ending and new ground and new contests with the Wall lay ahead. I had succeeded in exorcising the panic that had existed at the start. China, as I always knew she would, was supporting me with the infrastructure my run needed.

What these men did for a living remained a mystery until Cheng Shouli's diary entry could be translated:

> Mr. Will, you have a strong desire to see the most ancient of Chinese sites, the Great Wall. My partner and I express our sincere welcome to you.
>
> Today you arrived at Shajingzi; it is a timber center that resulted from the ideology of Mao Zedong's May 7th speech, ordering intellectuals into the countryside for reeducation by manual labour. My partner and I are some of the cadres of the forestry bureau of Zhangye county. Our city is a pass from the Great Wall to the Silk Road and we have many ancient sites including a Buddhist Temple of Western Xia kingdom. Once again welcome you to Zhangye.
>
> *Cheng Shouli, Jia Yi, April 14th, 1987*

It was in May 1966 that Mao decided it was time the white-collar cadres got their hands dirty and learned from the workers and peasants whom he believed were the core machinery of the nation. Hence, the May

7th directive was issued. Cadres would go to the countryside to learn how to sow and harvest wheat, tend animals, construct irrigation projects and terrace hillsides. During the next decade peasants were the most desirable rank; paper pushers, researchers, bookworms were regarded as good-for-nothings. It was a devastating directive, forcing breadwinners to leave their city families for the remote countryside, yet it was responsible for huge areas of land being pressed into production and ambitious engineering projects being completed. This timber yard was an example, for an enormous amount of labor must have been used to afforest the desert fringe. But labor has never been a scarce resource in this giant of nations where, more than anywhere else, one is acutely aware of the labor-intensiveness of many achievements. Indeed, going to the countryside to labor was nothing new, for Qin Shi Huang pressed hundreds of thousands into workgangs to build the first Great Wall.

At rest my pulse rate would normally be under fifty bpm. Now it beat out at seventy-five, the alarm bells of overtiredness. The first piece of map, now sweated and worn to illegibility at its fold, had almost been traversed. Zhangye was a safe place. Just a few months earlier it had been added to a growing list of approximately 400 towns and cities that foreigners are permitted to visit freely. Conveniently located as a stepping-stone at the midway point in the Hexi corridor, it was a place to rest and recuperate following my first week on the run. After 167 miles with a fifteen-pound backpack my aches and pains deserved a twenty-four-hour recharge.

Zhangye provided all that I hoped for—a room to myself, hot water, my first shave for a week and a chance to vary my diet with fish from the Blackwater River and lamb kebobs from the Uygur street vendors. Clean and well-fed I was on a high, confident enough to jettison some superfluous equipment. I parcelled up my Gore-tex sleeping bag, jacket, balaclava and gloves in white cotton and posted them back to Beijing. Now the backpack was over three pounds lighter. I was honing myself for my next round with the Wall.

With Jiuquan and Wuwei, Zhangye was a long-established garrison town on the Great Wall which grew in importance when the Han Dynasty expanded its empire westwards. Zhangye has the largest recumbent Buddha in China—it was the first evidence of my journey that indicated the Silk Road was an artery for the dissemination of the Buddhist faith that originated in the kingdoms of the Himalaya.

The doors were disproportionately tiny compared to the size of the temple. A rationed light entering through them enhanced the aura of eeriness about the body of the dying Sakyamuni, a colossus some sixty-five paces in length, as tall as a house and with slender tapering eyes the height of an adult man. The head and feet of the Buddha were flanked with lines of deities which, illuminated in the half-light, presented a most horrifying array of human emotions and expressions. Faces were hollow-cheeked, popeyed and scarred, downmouthed with misery and frozen with terror. One body was obesely grotesque and potbellied, the next sorrowfully rackribbed. They stood, as they have done for 900 years, scowling, glaring and horrifying in the darkness. They were not Chinese in appearance with their round eyes, long faces and big noses. The followers of the Buddhist faith had introduced a totally alien culture and art form into the Middle Kingdom, which had left this reminder amazingly undamaged during the Cultural Revolution when the Red Guards had been encouraged to destroy all traces of a prerevolutionary past.

Out of bed by six, I had beaten the sunrise, full of anticipation of finding a major section of Wall by nightfall. Squads of middle-school students ran around the streets, their plimsolls smacking hard on the tarmac, heads thrown back panting and puffing, arms waving about uncontrollably. An old woman, just a couple of generations away from them in age but an epoch away in composure, sliced the unbreathed air with gracefully deliberate sword strokes, as if repelling an unseen enemy. Like the students, I was a runner not a fencer, yet each and every one of my strides was as purposeful as that mandarin's sword strokes.

▬▬ 6 ▬▬

The Rice Bowl of Friendship

In the eating of coarse rice, the drinking
of water and the using of one's elbow
for a pillow, joy is to be found.
— *Confucius,*
The Analects

Though it was two months before "*Da Shu*"—the great heat of midsummer—the noonday sun, high in the sky, possessed a fearsome intensity. The gently undulating desertscape, empty and desolate, lacked any objects to make shadows, creating an absence of perspective. Ahead lay continuation. Distance. Limiting this panorama of bleached and shimmering ochres was a faint outline of the Longshou Shan to the north. Alert at the outset, but with eyes now grown weary with constant straining, I surveyed this desert for the Wall. Perhaps the maps were inaccurate, or my estimate of progress was too optimistic. With each stride, I became more defensive, for in the realm of the desert only the sun and wind prosper. Even the Wall, the Emperor embodied in "the Dragon," is a temporary intruder. The elements are the genuine rulers.

Sun and wind have contested above the Wall for two millennia. The sun's rays baked the rammed wet earth to the hardness of rock during its construction. Ever since, the wind has set about to destroy the Wall, this symbol of alliance between sun and Emperor. Howling sandstorms, which convert day into premature dusk, have degraded the Wall into a shadow of its former self. During the preceding 125 miles only the skeletal framework of beacon towers remained. Between them, the flesh of the Wall has largely disappeared, reunited with the surrounding sands. In the role of detective, searching for the wind's victim, I peered towards the break of slope edging the corridor, for it was there, according to the ONC map, where the Wall would emerge. Expectation became imagination as rock colors mirrored the subtle shades of changing sky. However, the linearity of the Great Wall once seen is not soon forgotten, and much as I yearned to be reunited with the Wall, I knew it was not there.

As I became fatigued, my urgency and enthusiasm gradually diminished. It was only then, having sunk into an unobservant mood, that I saw something as unmistakable as the Wall come into view. Descending from the piedmont of the Longshou Shan was a Wall so variable in condition that it appeared crenellated. In Britain my wayfinding policy is governed by the opinion that the map is always right, but out here I had less trust in a map constructed by a cartographer's interpretation of satellite photographs. Such maps were more than likely to be wrong until they proved themselves right. But if they were accurate, then the Wall would be a constant companion now for some days towards the next safe town of Wuwei.

From afar the uneven outline appeared like the backbone of a dinosaur; it was an intermediate condition of Wall hitherto not encountered. Its base was widened by the banking of sand and it crumbled easily, for large clods of rammed earth lay on the sands. Animals could easily mount its banked sides, and shepherds driving their sheep and goats to and fro between plain and foothills had further damaged the structure. Once in the corridor the Wall changed direction. Now assuming the general northwest to southeast trend, the Wall was no longer oblique to the prevailing wind and improved markedly in condition within a matter of miles. In time it became more continuous, bigger and thicker, retaining the shape and height created by its builders rather than one forced on it by the elements. Now it was over twice my own height and beginning to exhibit the blocked shape of the wooden frames into which damp earth was compacted; I could even detect fibrous organic material, probably bamboo, within the structure. It seemed quite incredible that bamboo, still in widespread use, not only in China but the whole Far East, was used by the civil engineers of the Han Dynasty to separate layers of rammed earth as the height of the wall was built up. Bamboo also speeded up the drying-out process and helped retain the shape of the block once the wooden frames were removed to expose the Wall to the baking rays of the sun.

On the smooth and flat surface in the lee of the Wall, I was able to keep a good pace, and for the first time since leaving Jiayuguan wayfinding was simply a case of following the Wall. Soon I was back in the company of two familiar routes: the Silk Road and the railway line linking the remote northwest autonomous region of Xinjiang to the rest of China. Lying close to what looked like a railway maintenance depot was a small shop selling cigarettes, *mao tai* spirit, beers, unidentifiable dried foods, and serving food in a room next door. I waited beneath a scenic poster of a snowy Mount Mustagh Ata in Xinjiang while the cook enthusiastically planned the entry he would write in my diary and tried to cook at the same time. The eggs were burnt, but the effusiveness of his welcome was more than compensation:

> We live beside the Great Wall, Situn shop, Dongru village, Shandan County, Gansu Province. The Great Wall of Ten Thousand li starts from Shanhaiguan in the east and reaches Jiayuguan in the west. Today this English friend arrived from far away—it shows a great willpower and gives us an unforgettable impression. We express welcome, congratulations and sincere hope that you succeed in your journey.

> *Liu Xi Shi, Twelfth Team West Tun, April 17th*

At dusk it was time to leave the Wall, cross the railway line and find shelter. The peasant family I approached mistook my request for an inquiry about the distance to Shandan and kept assuring me it was forty-five li. Now was the opportunity to make a further deposit of confidence in the journey's coffers. Ungrudgingly, I bade them farewell and stumbled back towards the Wall to select a good site to bivouac. There were some hollows, almost caves in the Wall, used by shepherds and peddlers. Then, hearing voices, I froze. Two people were running and shouting. It was the two sons of the family I had just left, begging me to return.

The boys were almost twins, looking like dwarfs in their baggy suits and adult's caps which hung over their shaved heads with such a generous overlap. They proudly escorted me into their home, to the delight of their parents. I immediately set about allaying any suspicion they had towards me by producing my notebook, letter of introduction and photograph of three generations of the Lindesay family. This last was far more captivating than any words could be. The children of my family were given the most attention, especially the blond-haired ones, for the Chinese perceive the typical foreigner as a golden-haired, blue-eyed being. Which was my wife, they quizzed; how many children? How disappointed they were when they realized I had none. "I'm only thirty, too young," I joked. It was a story line I learned to change in the future. Bachelors of thirty were not common in China.

The crowing of roosters gave warning of sunrise as I stretched my stiff muscles in the courtyard. As the sun's huge red disc edged above the horizon into the purple chill of dawn, the boys led me back to the Wall before the village was awake. We reached an irrigation channel, a swift and icy torrent, which broke the dawn silence as intrusively as its very presence in the desert. Beyond stood the more familiar intruder in these parts, the Wall, spotlit along its crest by the deep red glow of the sunlight, intensified by its own natural color. Like an ocean changing hues with the sky, the Wall would project many characters. At the moment it was being particularly helpful in revealing itself, yet I remained wary of falling into a false sense of security. Indeed, every day was filled with uncertainty, even more so when the Wall headed directly through a closed town like Shandan, which was fast approaching, along with all the usual worries it posed.

Perhaps at this stage it is appropriate to introduce the law enforcement organ of China, the Public Security Bureau (PSB) or Gong An Ju, as I had learned to call it. The native population has more reason to fear it than the foreign visitor, who might ordinarily have contact with the PSB only at the port of entry into China, or perhaps in seeking a visa extension. In the eyes of the Chinese the Gong An Ju has a serious identity problem, since tens of thousands of crimes went uninvestigated during the Cultural Revolution. Muggings, murders and ransackings were allowed if targeted correctly, for the Gong An Ju is inseparable from the Party and government. Punishment still often depends on the whim of the local Gong An Ju; the names of convicted criminals are posted up in their home neighborhoods to shame their families. For violent robbery, embezzlement and wrongdoings against the state the penalty is death. Before executions the criminal's family must buy the bullet (costing one yuan), and the bodies are passed on to hospitals and universities for research purposes. We in the West call it a deterrent; the Chinese "killing a chicken to scare the monkeys." It is highly effective, for the crime rate in China is negligible compared with Western nations.

The Chinese have an inborn fear of the "dog-legs," as the Gong An Ju men are unaffectionately known. Out on the streets, they appear to be everywhere, wolves prowling round a flock of sheep. A Gong An Ju officer is rarely seen without a cigarette; it is the first thing anyone they apprehend will offer, smiling desperately so as not to lose face. Their profile is obvious in paramilitary green tunic uniforms and peaked caps rimmed with gold braid, which also appears on their epaulettes and sleeves. They are un-armed, except for the special duty units deployed to guard buildings of particular sensitivity, like the embassy districts of Beijing. There are the plainclothes units too—watchers. One student told me they were every-where, every neighborhood had one, every hotel. "They should be out solving crimes, not spying on ordinary people," he complained. In one way they are shrouded in mystery, in another, the training of recruits, they are open for all to see. On most days, in the area of Beijing's Kunlun and Great Wall Hotels, one can see large crowds of Beijingers cycling home from work stop at the roadside to watch a Gong An Ju circus: unarmed combat, weapons practice in the upright and prone positions and, what the audience likes most, motorbike and pillion skills like glorified wheelies. But it is a skillful and slick display with a purpose to deter.

Observing the role and profile of the Gong An Ju was fascinating and essential, for I was fully aware they were an opponent in my own Great Game of the day. No, I certainly would not be asking one of the boys in green the way out of Shandan. Thankfully, it was not the time or the place to get to know each other.

* * *

Once the attempts to cultivate the land had yielded to the desert, the condition of the Wall improved. Within the environs of Shandan town it was fragmented, pitted by caves, penned by animal shelters and criss-crossed by tracks. With only the wind as its enemy, it stood fifteen feet high and ten feet in width, a monumental Wall, impossible for a man to scale. The relief of the desert gave the Wall no need to divert from an arrow-straight course. Nothing drew one's vision away from the Wall, for there was no backcloth, only deep blue sky whitening at its edges into bleached sandy ochres blotched with white salt pans. Within this vista there were only three forms—sky, desert and the Wall. And the Wall was center stage. Here at least the Emperor had achieved eternity, for "the Dragon" was a structure that matched the elements.

The serenity of the desert is stunning, a silence of piercing perfection; a sunlight so constant as to be the beam of a spotlight. Myself, alone on this stage. On target. Focused on the Wall. How long this has been the dream. The only dream. Right from the very moment of waking, through each stride of physical preparation. This has been my world. These are my footprints. The patience, isolation of thought and devotion is being rewarded with a landscape distanced from contemporary travellers. This is my privilege.

Both the ONC and Chinese maps were accurate in showing the Silk Road, now a sheet of soft and shining tarmac, cutting through the Wall. Close by loomed a huge beacon tower, making passing traffic look like toys in comparison. From the seclusion of the Wall's shadow, I watched a donkey cart, a green jeep and a truck go by in a period of thirty minutes. It was time to plan the late afternoon and evening. Fengcheng village appeared too far to reach by sunset. Besides the distance, I had already sensed a gradual climb developing as the Wall began to undulate towards the Yanzhi Shan. From the ONC, which depicted relief by shading and contours, it appeared this range of hills was a southerly tongue of the Longshou Shan extending into the heart of the Hexi corridor. So, taking advantage of my high morale, it looked like the ideal opportunity to sleep under the stars, and with that plan in mind, I diverted away from the Wall to obtain food. The best to be found was *mantou*—one of my favorites—just coming out of the baskets at a village bakery. Incredible luck. Back on the Wall, I was feeling relaxed and content, even with the prospect of the bread-and-water supper and breakfast ahead of me. Training half this distance at home in Britain, I would have demanded a cow between two bread vans to satisfy my hunger. Yet out here bread was all that was in the larder. Bread was a feast. So bread I would eat.

As the Wall gained height, the desert acquired a scant vegetation cover. These were grazing hills for sheep and goats. The Wall became a little fragmented in these more exposed sections, though it still remained an enormous structure edging east towards the Yanzhi Shan. A cool evening breeze came off the hills into my face whilst the sun from behind cast a lengthy shadow across the gravel trail. It was time to rest. I crossed to the northern side of the Wall to escape the breeze and choose my place.

There were many small dugouts in the Wall, with rings of stones and ashen twigs scattered around where shepherds could keep vigil on their stock. But there was too much activity nearby for me to settle for the night. Dogs were barking. The noise grew louder. Two dogs. Coming towards me. Quickly putting my rucksack back on I grabbed four or five stones. They ran, barking and growling, kicking up the desert dust as they screeched to a halt about twenty yards away. Stealthily creeping on their forelegs, they stretched their necks, snarling to show overfull mouths of canine teeth. My heart pounded out the adrenalin, the chemistry of performance, necessary to fight for survival. I feigned throwing. They knew the decoy. I pelted the leader of the two, replacing each release with another rock. In they came, working together in grisly partnership. I kicked and threw, shouted and cursed. My dream was ending. They would strip my flesh to the bone. Never had I kicked so quick and hard, my right leg, left too, like the pistons of an engine. They backed off. The shepherd approached yelling and throwing stones too, but in came the dogs again. It was close to disaster. Jugular veins severed. No blood transfusions—not even matching blood—hundreds of miles from help late at night—death by dogs in the desert. I stared them in the eyes, snarled back at them, continued throwing. Slowly I walked away, continually throwing. The distance between us grew.

Out of danger my heart soared. I pulled my Ultrafleece trousers over limbs that had been inches away from being consumed. The thought of rabies did not concern me as much as the likelihood of being living dog food. Sleeping out was not going to be as straightforward as one hoped. I was not going to be a dog's dinner at any price.

Still very shaky, but with a good-to-be-alive feeling, I labored on, following the Wall through the foothills. All physical strength had long been exhausted. Nervous energy had been used in repelling the dogs. Weak and famished, I came to Fengcheng village and approached a cluster of smallholdings not one-third of a mile from the Wall. Dogs seemed to be everywhere. One grisly beast, tethered by a rope, relayed my arrival to another. As it charged, I lost no time in preparing for battle. But peasants fended it off with sticks and I managed to cross a threshold safely. My hosts in Fengcheng, or "the village of the dogs" as it would always be known to me, were the Yin family. The weather, still bitterly cold in the evenings, meant that they preferred to confine themselves to a small room, with a stove, less than twenty feet square. The room was roasting. My hairy limbs and large feet came in for a good deal of attention from the children. The little girl, Yin Lanlan, perhaps eight, looked very like her mother, Liu Huiming. (Children inherit their father's name and wives keep their own name after marriage.) She wore an orange-red jacket embroidered with peacocks, symbolic of the Empress in China. Her brother, Yin Jianxi, was a couple of years younger and looked like, well—China: a baggy dusty suit as a top layer, smiling rosy-cheeked face, shaven head, black plimsolls, with ground-in dirt on his hands and ankles, all topped with an army-green cap. These children loved "my own" children. To gain respectability I had by now deemed it wise to inherit a wife and child for the journey's duration. "*Ta shi tai tai, erzi*" (She is wife, son) I announced, pointing to my sister-in-law, Hilary, and nephew, Bob, in the family snapshot. A family man in China is regarded as having good virtue and character. The development of the Chinese character for good testifies this, for it is formed by combining *nü* (woman) with *zi* (child) to give *hao* (good). In Chinese eyes a man must have found goodness in the possession of a wife and the fathering of a child.

The laying out of neatly folded multicolored quilts was the sign of bedtime. Yin Lizhong and I went outside to relieve ourselves, he pinning their dog to the ground with his foot pressed firmly on the whimpering animal's neck. In this small intermontane basin the night air was icy. We were perhaps 2,000 feet above the general altitude of the Hexi corridor. Back inside we stripped off, me to reveal my Lifa vest and shorts, they to reveal yet another full layer of clothing. We lay out, five of us in a row. There was no fire under the *kang*, but the cinders of the stove still glowed, and being like sardines in a tin meant that we benefited from each other's warmth. After thirty miles my muscles ached, my joints were stiff and my face burned. I was justifiably shattered. What a day of extremities it had been. Stunning Wall, demon dogs and the inheritance of a wife and child in the evening.

Bad weather of sorts arrived during the night. The wind rattled the door and shutters, billowing the newspapered ceiling below the eaves. Rain lashed down. Semiconscious, I imagined crossing the Yanzhi Shan in the storm. Once the diffusive light filled the room my worst fears were confirmed. Outside there were blizzard conditions. If it had not been for those dogs, I would now have been buried in snow, frozen and wet for lack of my Gore-tex sleeping bag mailed prematurely to Beijing. What fortune from adversity!

Yin Lizhong needed to fetch coal from the yard. Accompanying him there, I could see there was little prospect of any rapid change in the weather. With the dry powder snow swirling around, visibility was less than one hundred yards. It was even too bitter for the dog, now blanketed by snow and as indistinguishable as the coal heap, to show aggression.

The family gave me no reason to be concerned in having to delay my departure. Hour after hour the storm continued and no visitors came to the farm. Liu Huiming prepared noodles while the rest of us stayed on the *kang* covered in our quilts. The children were captivated by my rucksack clips and the sharp click which the molded buckles made. Inevitably we worked our way inside, to the torch with no switch, the compass and the footcare products. To entertain them I carried out a comprehensive foot examination, while the little boy found a scratch on his finger worthy of a dab of antiseptic cream and an Elastoplast. The parents, let alone the children, had few possessions for entertainment. Yin Lizhong read a book, while his wife busied herself with cooking and cleaning. The children amused themselves with a game using bottle tops.

After *xiu xi*, the customary period of rest following lunch, I agreed to staying put for the day. The wind had abated yet the sky possessed what I interpreted to be the grey-white fullness of snowflakes. Demonstrating romanized writing in my diary encouraged the children to produce their own writing materials. In exercise books they diligently copied out characters into boxes about an inch square that were further subdivided into quarters so that the composition of each complex pictogram could be constructed accurately. It was an appropriate time for Yin Lizhong to write his thoughts in my own book.

> Dear Mr Will,
> You came to my home and slept for one night yesterday, April 18, 1987. On the second day the weather changed and we had a whole day of snow, which created difficulties for our British friend Will, who couldn't continue on

his journey. He and my family slept together without asking for anything. In this short time we have built up sincere feelings of respect between our two countries. In my home, people of the two countries sat on our bed talking and laughing, eating our steamed bread and drinking green tea. My whole family felt happy and enjoyed the pleasure. What an unforgettable time! We admire the Briton's willpower and his kind easygoing attitude. He came from far away, having no fear of the rains, the hot weather or the poor food of the peasants. It makes an unforgettable impression on us. We warmly welcome Will to China and are happy to have made a friend today. At least we would like to wish you success on your journey; may you receive good fortune all the way.

> *Your Chinese friends, Yin Lizhong, Liu Huiming, Yin Lanlan, Yin Jianxi of Fengcheng village, Laojun, Shandan County of Gansu*

It was that kind of kindred spirit encompassed by this tribute which gave me the confidence to step out from day to day, safe in the knowledge that somewhere along the way I would be offered the rice bowl of friendship.

Diary, April 20th

Dawn brings a crystal-clear day. Fengcheng village is surrounded by snow peaks. After a noodle breakfast, I leave the Yin family. Back on the Wall I meet three shepherds. The Wall becomes less continuous as it enters the Yanzhi Shan. I tread in virgin snow, crunch, crunch—look up to feel on a real high. Raising both arms with clenched fists I shout, "China, the middle of China!" The Wall follows the pass at about 8,500 feet (according to the ONC), deteriorating with height because of the beating it receives up here from the weather. The hills are full of shepherds, snuggling in their huge skins out of the wind. Over the pass, downhill, with the wind behind, I'm skipping along—the miles fly. By midafternoon the descent to the corridor is over. A

bottle of fruit in syrup at the first village I come across.
At 7 p.m. the wind is still buffeting behind. Approximately thirty-five miles done, the Wall has petered out.
I'm taken in by an old man; his family is large and he
shouts at his daughters who don't respond to my smiles
or nods. Some of his sons, still in their teens, appear to
have fathered children that are very aggressive. After
noodles and bread, I'm given a room (shed) to myself.
The old man holds an oil lamp over me to show a crowd
of visitors. Stretched out, I feel just like a corpse with
sympathizers paying their last respects.

With nothing more than the hair on my head protruding from the quilt,
I didn't engage the villagers' interest for a very long time. It was good to have
privacy, particularly among such a strange family. The eldest daughter, a
giant of a woman over six feet tall, never showed any sign of personality—
she merely obeyed her father's orders. She was his personal servant. The
sons had the bodies of boys but the heads and expressions of much older
people. One toddler had squinted eyes and was half-witted and quite
rough. He was manhandled by the others and withstood falls and collisions
caused by his own lack of coordination, which would make any normal
child cry the house down. I wondered what method of birth control existed
in this village. A likelihood was that marriages were arranged at very early
ages and perhaps partners were consanguineous.

When the shed door banged open I was already awake. I expected to see
the old man; instead, pink, hairy, snorting nostrils surprised me as much as
I surprised the calf that clumsily tried to turn around, bashing its head.
Pushing the beast outside, I dressed, patching a couple of small blisters and
dabbing the pressure points on my toes with Vaseline. Anxious to leave this
odd place, I bade the old man farewell and resumed my way to Yongchang
at sunrise.

Cold, tired and hungry, I looked forward to the prospect of a large
breakfast. Meals and a good bed for the night were the highlights of the
journey in this region where no Wall remained. Within sight of the bell
tower of Yongchang, I ate a noodle breakfast, supplemented with *bingzi*
(pancakes) and a jar of fruit—all washed down with fruit tea. This was a
specialty tea, served in porcelain cups with a saucer and lid. Crystal sugar,
dried apricot, date and some other unidentifiable ingredient were added to

green tea. With a full thermos of boiling water on my table, I enjoyed a good half-dozen delicious cups. From my table in the *fandian*, I could observe main-street life of the market town: an unhurried and timeless scene, repeated all over China, presided over by the bell tower at the center of the town. The bell, of importance in feudal China, was rung in daylight hours as the yardstick of the working day imposed upon the peasants by their landlords. A drum, also housed in a tower, was beaten in early morning and evening. But minutes, hours, even days were not important. The peasant communities' only markers were the seasons, sunrise and sunset. Although I carried a watch myself, it was of little use, for time was relative and became increasingly so the longer I was away. The peasants slept with the onset of darkness, awoke at dawn—and I with them. When the sun was high and hot it was noon. As for meals I employed the camel principle, eating when convenient, although I was hungry and thirsty most of the time. The exact observance of time was only of importance when other people were involved—during "British Telepathy" times at eight in the morning and evening (noon and midnight GMT).

Diary, April 21st: beyond Yongchang

With a belly full of food, I always find the world a better place. China is no exception. The wind blows up from behind. Since it is my aim to follow the main line of Wall between its two terminal points along a predominantly west to east direction without any major deviations to the north or south, I'm not expecting to see any Wall until beyond Wuwei. The road is unpaved; many of the truckers passing stop for a banter, often to offer food or a cup of boiled water. They carry thermos flasks with them. I've zigzagged along the whole length of the Hexi corridor. I am now back at its southern edge in the lee of the Qilian Shan. The wind whips up the dust and sand in the noncultivated areas of the desert. My big breakfast set me up for the day's push towards Wuwei. Late evening I seek refuge with a young farmer. His grandmother is deaf, but she responds warmly to my smiles. I'm given delicious jasmine tea, sugar and *bingzi* on arrival. Then the main meal of noodles with eggs before a small, but not intrusive, audience.

The dignified old lady was cared for by her grandson. Such respect for elders is typical of the Chinese social system. There was a warmth of seasoned caring in her every gentle action, and she took obvious pride in her appearance. There are still distinctions of classes in China today, even within the peasant community. Perhaps this lady was a member of a rich peasant family of landowners before the revolution. She wore all black, a padded coat with high collar and woven toggles, and narrowing breeches that highlighted dainty ankles and, of course, tiny once-bound feet in black plimsolls (though not the ordinary slipons). Her thick grey hair was perfectly groomed and fastened in place. Straightbacked, noble and contemplative, she sat on her throne with hands tucked inside the opposite sleeves of her jacket. There may have been unit and commune leaders within this hamlet of Changlong, but this fine old lady was the mandarin.

Wuwei, the most easterly of the Han Dynasty prefectures of the Hexi corridor, was within reach of the morning's effort. After two weeks running under the constant observation of the Qilian Shan, I was beginning to make an impression on the map. Those snowy peaks that had become a familiar southern witness to my daily progress through the corridor were tapering in height towards the southeast. Downgraded and renamed as the Lenglong Ling, they would continue to escort the Silk Road towards Lanzhou, the provincial capital of Gansu. The Wall behind was all built during the Han Dynasty. Ahead, beyond Wuwei, there was the promise of the older—the original—Great Wall of Qin Shi Huang. In the meantime there was the opportunity for recuperation—and preparation for what looked to be one of the most remote stages of the route, along the southern edge of the Tengger Desert to the Huang He. The mighty Yellow River, which at the outset had seemed too distant a target to contemplate, was now within my grasp. Perhaps just a week away in time, I was nonetheless under no illusion whatsoever that in order to reach that great river there would be doubtless many rivers to cross.

7

Many Rivers to Cross

Problems shall arise, though I hope to
rise to them.
                              —*Sir Francis Younghusband*

The regulars of the tea house found me a streetside seat. They could
not have seen many foreigners before, because Wuwei had only been
classified as an open city at the beginning of the year. The proprietor
brought over a porcelain cup of tea leaves, and she was followed swiftly
by a man with the boiling water. There was a choice of three teas: jasmine,
black—favored by the Moslems—and spicy fruit. The men, mostly
elders, came to the tea house to pass the time with playing cards,
mahjong, or just talking about the price of tobacco.

Like so many places in China, Wuwei was a large town that few
people outside the country, or even province, would know very much
about. Out in the street the conforming masses streamed past, bicycles
alike, posture alike and clothes alike, the anonymous image of Communist China that strikes most foreigners. How privileged I was to be seeing
through this uniform facade to the individuals, to families with names,
faces and personalities, cookhouses, *kangs* and courtyards. I had found
friends in a nation of over one billion people.

That was a number never too far away from anyone's mind. The
giant billboard poster overlooking the square was hand-painted on the

order of Beijing's demographers, fearful of a manifestation of the Malthusian prophecy. Twenty years ago the message from Mao had been quite different, as the people were encouraged to have the largest of families. Now the model family above the square cherishes just one child, significantly a daughter. The policy was not a change of direction but a reversal—from go to stop.

The recent reforms have provided new artistic outlets for the men who had previously painted only birth control, road safety and political slogans. Advertising has arrived in China, and the ad men are seizing upon the Great Wall as a brand mark. Unconsciously, I had listed them since my very first days in China: tires, fans, generators and televisions. Appropriately the Great Wall TV in Wuwei showed the Wall. I had made a point of drinking Great Wall wine and lemonade, was amused at using Great Wall toilet paper (yes, they do have it in China nowadays) and pondered whether Great Wall corned beef was as good as Fray Bentos.

The tea house was the kind of place to stay all morning. Most of the old men clearly did so. There must have been lavatories nearby for the flow of boiling water was neverending. A little space at the top of the cup was the cue for a the man patrolling with the big kettle to tilt his black-bottomed pot high above the table and skillfully hit the target of tea leaves with an arc of boiling water without so much as a splash, let alone a drip from the spout. It surely must take hundreds of gallons of practice to attain such a mastery, as well as a working knowledge of hydraulics to minimize turbulent and torrid flow.

The quality of teas and their ability to withstand a multitude of infusions does nothing to increase the takings for the proprietor of the tea house. It is as much a social provision as a commercial concern. The hot water keeps coming for a price of two mao (four cents). With jasmine tea the first brew is the most fragrant. Subsequent infusions have the stronger flavor of green tea as the leaves swell up to occupy almost half the cup like a subterranean colony of seaweed. One sits thinking, sipping, observing.

The centerpiece of the square is the galloping horse of Wuwei, a charger so fast that it treads upon a swift. This cast replica forms the backdrop to the snaps of a score of photographic peddlers. A fall from grace has created many vacant sites in the nation's city squares, factory units and school compounds. Once produced in production line numbers, the statues of Chairman Mao that for three decades overlooked

China's public places are now being dismantled. In Wuwei it seemed right and proper that the horse, an animal that played such an important role in the expansion and defense of the walled kingdom in the time of Han Wu Di, should occupy pride of place. This horse, the *Tian ma* (heavenly horse) was not indigenous to China. Instead, the Emperor could only provide his cavalry with the Prejevalsky horse, hardly a thoroughbred and no match for the Xiongnu and other Hun tribes, who were accomplished horsemen upon their much swifter and stronger mounts. With such a strategic advantage, the "outsiders," who pursued a largely nomadic life, could make quick raids into the walled kingdom of Han Wu Di and normally escape back to the wilderness, a land which held terror for the Emperor's men. When the "Great Traveller" Zhang Qian returned from Central Asia after some thirteen years, he told Wu Di about the *Tian ma* in a land called Ferghana (now in Soviet Central Asia). The strategic importance of these horses was immediately apparent to the Emperor, so he despatched several expeditions to acquire some *Tian ma* for himself. The third expedition succeeded in bringing a supply of chargers back to Chang'an for breeding. Now the Han Dynasty could compete on equal terms with the horse specialists to the north of the Great Wall.

A flood with jasmine tea, I had to leave the tea house; otherwise, I might have stayed the whole day. For a couple of hours I had relaxed, escaped from the task and felt refreshed by the break. A few last pleasures remained, such as subjecting the heavy growth of Western beard to the barber's blade, and drinking local beer—from the *Tian ma* brewery, of course. Then I set about organizing my next step into the unknown.

According to the maps my primary method of routefinding —in the absence of any surviving Wall—would be in following a railway line to Zhongwei on the Yellow River. This had the advantage of directness, as the permanent way stretched across the desert. But without tracks or roads there were unlikely to be many settlements, and these were going to be much further apart than the camel train yardstick of the caravanserais. My hope was that track maintenance gangs would need depots at more frequent intervals.

At the crossroads I entered the signalman's hut to make friends, "ask for permission" to follow the track, and take shelter from the cold drizzle. There was little chance of taking the wrong path—this was the "central line"; westbound was Xinjiang; eastbound was Ningxia, Nei Mongol and eventually Beijing. In China all roads and railways lead to Beijing.

Now to follow the permanent way, banked high, curving into the distance. Beside the track was a narrow flat path caked in oil and grease from passing engines. In over a couple of hours I should reach the Wall again, about fifteen miles farther on. My constant pace was only interrupted by the approach of trains, which shook the earth as they thundered by and further saturated the air with moisture from their plumes of pure white steam that contrasted with the grey drizzle sky. At a station depot the double line branched into a multitude of tracks, grimy and greasy points and coal-littered sidings. Old men scavenged for fragments of coal. Retired engines that had played their part in opening up China's frontiers during the "Great Leap Forward," now derailed, awaited a sentence to scrap. Their still active successors, the dinosaurs of the engineering world, would soon face extinction, too. As the use of diesels spread to every province, the last remaining steam engine factory in Datong, Shanxi, would grind to a halt—unless the train enthusiasts of the world convinced China Railways that one day they would regret the move. However, there could be no place for sentimentality in the building of a modern socialist state. Massive and black, greasy and hot, smooth and heavy, these red-spoked workhorses which "flew" cast-iron flags on their sides were entering their final terminus. But they had conquered deserts, valleys, passes and mountains; as well as withstood ice, snow, heat, sandstorm, rain and humidity.

The three most significant and progressive Wall-building periods promised to be represented on this stage of the journey towards Zhongwei. The original Great Wall built by the first Emperor of unified China, Qin Shi Huang, was likely to be found close to the Huang He. Qin Dynasty Wall-builders had used existing walls of the Warring States kingdoms of Qin, Zhao and Yan as a framework for the first continuous northern defense, which stretched from Lintao (near Lanzhou) all the way to the Yalu Jiang, the river boundary between Liaoning Province and North Korea. I could only hope that all the farming in the Yellow River valley had not destroyed the first Great Wall. The successors to the Qins were the Hans—dedicated Empire-builders who extended the Wall through the entire corridor of Gansu Province to beyond Dunhuang. Between the Hans and the Mings was a period of some 1,150 years during which the

Walls were maintained. Small spurs were often built; however, it was not until the Ming Emperor Zhu Di (1403–1424) that a complete reconstruction, by reinforcing old Wall and building new, was embarked upon. The Ming Dynasty was keen to build the strongest, most formidable Wall in China's history, for it had seized power from the preceding Mongol Dynasty of Yuan, which for a century had been the foreign ruler of the Middle Kingdom. Once the founder of the Mings, Emperor Taizu, had banished the Mongol Khan from Dadu (Beijing), it was left to Zhu Di and Zhu Qizhen to make sure the Mongols would never seize power again. No amount of wall-building was too much of an undertaking for this principal aim, and Zhu Qizhen was largely the innovator of an Interior Great Wall, some of which was present in this region of southern Gansu.

Three hours outside Wuwei it was the Ming Wall that I first came across. Simplistically, in this area the Ming Walls describe a loop—a double defense being thought necessary to ensure the security of the fertile Yellow River basin. Now I was on the northern Wall of that loop, the exterior wall that formed a frontier with the Tengger Desert. However, it was surprising that a construction some twelve centuries younger was no more impressive than its ancient Han ancestor. The Wall retained no geometric shape or apparent height; windblown sand had banked up against it to a level of almost ten feet above ground. Above this "tide mark" imposed by the sea of shifting sand protruded a mere one and a half feet of crumbling and shapeless rammed earth. Clearly, the appearance and repair of the Great Wall in these desert regions depended upon the type of desert. On a gobi-type terrain, stony and encrusted, there was less available weaponry for the wind to use as erosive material. In the "shamo"—sand sea desert—the loose sand mounted a two-pronged attack on the Wall, as a weathering force and as a banking.

My hunch that there would be depots along the railway line was correct, but two where I called to beg for food had bare larders. It was two o'clock. Once one meal time has passed it is a long time to the next. There are no snacks in between. Eating follows a lengthy process of starting a fire, baking, steaming or boiling. Everything is eaten there and then. There are no leftovers.

Alongside the Wall and railway track, which now ran parallel to each other, there were plantations of trees. It was here, at the edge of the Tengger Desert, that cultivable land was being eaten up by the same shifting sands that swamped the Wall. The condition of Wall improved noticeably as the trees shielded the land from the wind and reduced erosion at the desert fringe. From the elevation of the railway line the plantation appeared to be up to two and a half miles in width. As the young poplars come into bud, they introduce a green tint to dull brown sands. Yet there is no valley, no river, nor even a stream here. These trees were planted by man and sustained by monthly water rations—part of the "Great Green Wall" across the whole of northern China to halt the desertification of land. This curtain of forest gave me a sense of security, hiding the desert wastes beyond.

By late afternoon I found a smallholding in the shadow of the Wall. All that they offered was tea. A peasant, obviously a visitor, offered to find me a bed and meal. Off we went across countless miles of impoverished farmland, he riding his bicycle and no doubt baffled by my refusal to accept a lift on the back of his "Flying Pigeon." Anger built up inside me at having to detour so much, and then after an hour we arrived—at what passed as a village street, a street of baked and rutted mud, littered with blowing sagebrush, scavenged by dogs, with one boarded-up and padlocked general store. I thought my food would come from his family; instead, he dropped me inside a *fandian*. All they had was flour, soy, chili, garlic and beer—and some rooms in the back. I thought twice—no, ten times—about staying there, but my legs did not think at all. They had stopped for the day.

The food was hardly a feast, despite being well seasoned with the available condiments. By the time I returned to my room word had already spread of my presence, and the other lodgers and children filtered in to watch me as though they had a right to visit. No knocking at the door. I had paid one yuan for this! After a two-minute audience I impatiently ushered them outside, securing the door by tilting a chair under its handle. Lighting two candles to brighten up the spartan cell, I soaked my feet in boiling water and drank some beer, only emerging from my fortress under the cover of night to urinate, repelling a lurking dog in the process.

The day started clear and bright, and as I passed through the Great Green Wall, the poplars and pines gave a perfumed scent to the cool air. Even bird life was fostered within this forest: sparrows and possibly the Chinese cousins of our redwings and blue jays. The Great Wall became better preserved, standing high and straight-edged along its top. For once there was some company—a shepherd who kept his flock out of the forbidden zone of the forest by throwing clods of earth at any animal tempted by the greenery. Up the embankment a railway maintenance team were working on the line, using longhandled rakes to comb back the gravel on to the ties. They were a mixed force of men and women in baggy suits and caps adorned with the railway logo. One of the girls was a stunning natural beauty, her black hair shining in the morning sun. With rosy apple cheeks and big, wide-open timid eyes, she would have been the envy of any city girl the world over, yet she was shovelling gravel to keep the trains running across the Tengger Desert. The gang leader wrote:

> We are the workers from Tumen railway maintenance district. Tumen station lies on the Gan-Wu line between Gansu and Ningxia. Just 200 yards away is the Great Wall. South of the line, about two and a half miles away, is the town of Tumen.
>
> *Wang Xing Yang, April 25th, 1987*

An engine hooted in the distance and we all scrambled down the bank, watching it haul its long line of green passenger carriages en route to Yinchuan, Ningxia's capital, according to the destination boards posted on every car.

Running upon such a rough surface, I glanced up only occasionally. To see green tunic clothes was not at all rare, but to recognize the gold-braided sleeves and epaulettes of the Gong An Ju was nothing less than shocking. Perhaps they were just returning to their homes in the country-side? As we drew near each other, they stopped and blocked my path, saluting in unison and holding up open palms to request me to halt. Smiling, I greeted them with "*Ni hao*" as one of them produced a red-covered identity card from his breast pocket. He held it open at eye level and pronounced very slowly, "*Gong An Ju. . . . Wo men shi Gong An Ju*" (Public Security Bureau. . . . We are the PSB). Optimistically and naively I tried to have a friendly parley with them; however, they were not to be fooled, amused or diverted by my extroverted miming. Off we marched, me leading—our destination "two and a half miles east."

Walking as quickly as possible, I made it hard for the two arresting officers. They were short men, and I could hear them slipping on the gravel as they tried to keep close to me. Even their breathing became heavy. Eventually they grabbed me by the arm to tell me to "*xiu xi*" (have a rest), giving themselves the opportunity to mop their sweaty brows and regain their wind. The Gong An Ju were just officials doing their job—yet they stood between me and Shanhaiguan. Walking them into the ground was the only way to vent my anger. As we approached a railway depot, I realized my arrest had probably been the result of a telephone tipoff from the *fandian* village. I had only myself to blame. But I told myself this was merely a delay not a disaster, and I prepared to memorize the route that we would take back to Wuwei, which was where I was told I was to be taken.

Nearly three hours later the jeep arrived with a Gong An Ju driver and his suited comrade.

"Hello, I'm from the Foreign Affairs section of Wuwei government," he said confidently.

"Really. Your English is very good. What's . . . "

He interrupted sharply, "Give me your documents, please." I rummaged in my bag. "Show me everything, passes, permits." I handed over just my passport and letter of introduction.

"UK, yes? London? Visa's fine," he flicked repeatedly through the pages. There was a brief pause. "This part of Wuwei county is not open to the foreign guest." That was the cue for my puzzled look. "You cannot visit here unless with special documents," he said in a strained tone. "My leader in Wuwei city would like to meet you."

"Like to . . . or wants to?"

"Wants to, must!" he said with a Hobsonian chuckle. "Let's go."

After so long on foot, climbing aboard the green Beijing jeep felt sacrilegious. The track was incredibly rough; surely a wheel would come off or the axle break—something?! My head banged on the padded ceiling as I grabbed the handles on both back doors rigidly. Ribs dug into my guts, more noticeable because of my weight loss of recent weeks. Once on the open road we sped along its center, our blasting horn scattering the cycling peasants to the sides of the road.

Four plainclothed and three uniformed Gong An Ju officers awaited our arrival. In their presence the interpreter assumed a more official and interrogative manner.

"Give your passport to our leader! You have entered an unopen place without taking out a valid travel permit."

"Can I receive a permit to continue my journey?"

"The Alien's Travel Permit can only be issued by the Public Security Bureau in Lanzhou, our province's capital. You can go there by train."

He went over to the leader's desk and talked for several minutes. I scanned the room. Cupboards and drawers were all padlocked. To think that there were undoubtedly Alien's Travel Permits in this very room. Above me on the wall was an incredibly detailed map of the county. It must have shown every fragment of Wall! If only . . .

"Sit down now, please! My leader has decided. Listen to him."

Holding up a bilingual document, he began to speak. We stared each other in the eye. "My leader says you have committed an offense by not taking out the travel permit in Lanzhou. He has a book which tells the Public Security Bureau how to regard your crime. We can punish you! This is our law! Our leader is a good man—he thinks you have a good attitude and does not want to punish you. But you should be criticized! As an alien you must, must pay attention to open and unopen places. You can go to Lanzhou tonight or tomorrow. We suggest you stay in the Wuwei Hotel— it is best suited to the foreigner there. That is all. You can go."

As soon as I entered the crowded street outside the Gong An Ju headquarters, a new phase of my journey had begun.

Diary, April 26th

Up at 6:00 a.m. and on to the road heading south, having memorized the route that the jeep took yesterday. A minute's waiting—and a lift from two men in a big truck going to Xining (Qinghai). At my drop-off point, about twenty-five miles down the road, I walk up the track towards Tumen for half an hour—then hitch a ride in a truck full of bricks. In the back among the bricks my hands freeze to the bone and eyes fill with dust. I hold on tight. The men are driving somewhere north of the Great Wall. At 9:15 a.m. I bid them my heartfelt thanks exactly at the point of arrest! "Full steam ahead" along the railway line for about three miles, then breakfast (three *baozi* and several bowls of sweetened *xifan*—rice porridge) at a signalman's hut by a bridge across a gorge. I follow the Wall off to the southeast now, across country towards Dajing. It is hilly and windy, though there is plenty of company in these hills—shepherd boys and totally black Chinese miners. Primitive stuff: open-cast method—on the surface digging with picks and shovels. At Dajing I'm paranoid at being apprehended, although hunger forces me to take a risk and sneak a meal. A huge crowd escorts me through the village, whittling down to a single persistent man who leads me to believe there's a bed for me in his home. On entering Peijiaying, this village gossip broadcasts "Englishman on the Great Wall" to everyone in sight. The big letdown is that he takes me to a *fandian*. Not again. "*Bu yao, bu xi huan fandian*," I tell him sternly and march off to puzzled looks in search of somewhere more suitable on the edge of the village.

Although a capacity audience of peasants crammed into the room they had turned out in vain. The performance was cancelled. The star exhausted. His props—the photograph, torch, expanding sleeping bag and a plastic whistle would stay offstage safe in the rucksack. He felt aggravated at their refusal to return to their homes. Guilty, too, for he realized his obligation to provide entertainment in return for food and shelter. Nevertheless, he stretched out on the *kang* to sleep before their very eyes. But the peasants stayed. They tried to provoke a reaction with a hubbub. They prodded his body, stroked his hairy limbs, fiddled with his rucksack and shoes, determined to earn a performance, persisting, enraging him. A rap on the ankle and then the shinbone. It was more than he would tolerate. He reacted.

Rolling over from the prone position, levering myself sharply up, I opened my eyes to the unmistakable gold braid and green uniform—the stern face of the Gong An Ju.

The officer inspected my passport surrounded by the frenzied peasants. He had to shout at them to get back and calm down. What a premiere they had witnessed. These simple people, full of excitement in what they were seeing, had little comprehension that the denouement of this scene could be no further performances in the whole of China. The show would end its run. As I resigned myself to the inevitable, the officer returned my passport and gestured for me to stay put. Off he went, repeating his instructions to the prominent menfolk.

This was my chance to escape. I only needed a short time. With unlaced shoes, I barged through the jam-packed room, out into the yard to assess the whereabouts of the Gong An Ju. Heckled, apprehended and followed by the men, I passed through a fence into the pigsty—to the giggles of embarrassed womenfolk. No Gong An Ju was in sight. Perhaps half an hour of light remained. Returning inside to don my Ultrafleece suit and lace up my shoes, I pulled my rucksack on, looked happy in shaking hands with my host, and to shrieks of disbelief parted the waves to the door. With straining faces and serious tones they begged me to stay. The light faded rapidly as a few boys tried to jog beside me on the track into the countryside. Soon my unwanted escorts grew tired. Alone and free, I looked around to see a few faint lights of Peijiaying in the distance. All fatigue had vanished.

There was no moon that night. With no light other than the constellations above, I could guide myself from the sound of my footsteps upon the gravelly path. It grew colder and colder. Often I stumbled or tripped, yet resisted the urge to use my torch for fear of diminishing my improving nightsight.

I contemplated the course of my preliminary encounter in my own "Great Game." This one remained to be concluded. I put myself in the shoes of the opposition. A search party would be out at sunrise. Feeling that my head start held sufficient edge to exit from Gansu Province, I veered off the track to bed down. Encasing myself completely in the mummylike sleeping bag, I gazed up at the sky. It was a restricted view, like that of a frog in a well. The Chinese had a similar perception of the world, with the Great Wall acting as the wall of the well. The Middle Kingdom stood alone, isolated, yet the masses wanted to jump out of the well and have links with the lands around its edges. Frogs leap exceedingly well. A star then skidded across the heavens. That was surely a good omen. "Catch a falling star—put it in your pocket, save it for a rainy day," goes the song. Perhaps God's speed was now with me.

The contest began again at dawn. It was only after breaking bivouac that I realized how cold it was. Immediately, as I stuffed the sleeping bag into the small sack, my fingers chilled to the bone, my teeth chattered and my whole body shivered. Using the insulating mat as a shield from the icy wind, with foil side bodymost, I hobbled off along the track; sore, stiff and starving. A flagging spirit, yearning for the simple comforts of life, was soon lifted, for there, about a half mile to the south, I spotted the Wall at the foot of the Wu Jiao Ling. The hidden way beyond the Wall was the safer route for me.

Sunlight reflected off the hardened mud path winding across the fields. Seeing three small figures come along the track gave me the hope of finding breakfast. They were schoolchildren, well wrapped up in padded jackets, caps and headscarves. Arriving at the Wall, I called on the first farm whose smoking chimney showed signs of cooking in progress. The occupants were a jolly fat woman, brushing the dust from the yard, and an old Moslem with a black skullcap. Steamed bread and black tea were offered, the piping hot gulps thawing my throat and leaving a trail of fire to my empty stomach. The Moslem watched me in total silence, occasionally pushing the enamel washing basin filled with *mantou* towards me. He contentedly rubbed tobacco, stuffing it into his long black lacquered pipe decorated with silver fittings. The smoking of a pipe of tobacco is a period of rest—a *yi dai yan*; though once he had lit up and started puffing, I realized he was having something more than a break. He was getting an "extra hour of daylight"—the name given to opium by the Chinese.

Diary, April 27th

The Wall is grassed over to a considerable extent, and even looks like it may have been built from such clods. Beyond, the foothills of the Wu Jiao Ling are forested with conifers. I follow the Wall along a straight course for a good twelve miles; it then fragments, eventually disappearing. The only way through these hills is to rejoin the track. There is little traffic—a couple of big trucks, one of which had a Ningxia plate. The land slopes towards the basin of the Huang He and I can detect the greener and darker hues of a village—Bai dun zi. These mammoth mileages begin to take toll. My left foot is particularly troublesome—no bathing, change of dressings or socks since Wuwei. It's also the hottest day to date—up to 80°F. Thankfully, irrigated land around Bai dun zi gives me the chance to bathe. At 5:00 p.m., reasonably confident that I've outrun the "dog-legs" into Ningxia, I call in on a small work unit.

"*Zhe shi Gansu ma?*" (To establish where it is not.)
"*Bu shi, zhe shi . . .*" I interrupt, "Ningxia?"
"*Bu shi! Na li Nei Mongol!*"

Inner Mongolia? Out came the map from my shorts. Obviously they were correct, and, yes, the village of Yingpanshui was just across the provincial boundary. On the premise that the security bureaus of each 'parish' were primarily concerned with keeping their own districts foreigner-free, it now seemed unlikely that they would unduly trouble themselves further in continuing their pursuit. Safe within an autonomous region, and the desolate Inner Mongolian one at that, I looked at my map to see the closest town of note was over 185 miles away. I felt secure. For once, I was quite content to be surrounded by so much sand.

These men were mining folk—with good washing facilities. It was the opportunity for a long-overdue pedicure—soaking, piercing, rubbing, dabbing, hexing and patching. Putting my feet up by wedging them high above my body on the wall, I tried to rejuvenate my lifeless limbs. These had been my longest days. Aside from the distance covered— something I could thank a dedicated physical preparation for—the time since Wuwei had been a serious drain on my nervous energy and wits. But a good heart and strong legs would have been as nothing without my entire devotion to the journey born from years of yearning, strengthened by previous failures, fuelled by a unique compound of adrenalin that kept my high hopes still burning bright.

Diary, April 28th

It showed just how cold it was, for in a mere twenty minutes my flasks of boiling water were chilled by the wind. Meanwhile we ate breakfast—rice, *mantou* and *jiu cai* (like a green onion shoot). I link up with railway that will hopefully show me the way to Zhongwei. Remoter and hotter. More encounters with four-legged friends— serves me right for trying a head shot of a camel foal. Mother charges me. I go steady on the water, relying on the railway peoples. Two trains pass—Lanzhou to Hohhot and Beijing to Lanzhou. The drivers give me a thumbs-up and the passengers, gasping for air by dangling from the windows, call frantically. Reach Gantang at 7:00 p.m.—totally lame.

Gantang was the station, a collection of sidings and adjacent ram-shackle buildings, most of which were concerned with the quarrying in the mountains nearby. The afternoon was punctuated by regular explo-sions and echoes from the blasting of the rock, stockpiled here awaiting freight. With shoes feeling full of blood (I had felt my own explosions—of blisters underfoot), I could only limp by walking on the outside edges of my pathetic feet. At the sight of such a lame, thin and sunburned being, the quarrymen pushed a seat under me and brought out a pitcher of ice-cold water. Off came the shoes; my socks stuck to their insoles with dried blood and pus, baked hard by the hot sands underfoot. In turn, my socks were welded on to my feet, the dressings board hard, pulverized and sticky. The quarrymen gathered around, pained expressions on their own faces, as I dipped the deathly feet into water and drained bloody fluid from the skin bubbles. The blisters on the inside heels and the balls of each foot stung to hell and throbbed. The thought of the remaining miles to Zhongwei was frightening, for it was excruciating enough just to hobble a few feet or so into the quarry leader's shack.

Diary, April 28th: Gantang

Dear English Friend,
     This is a plaster stone quarry. You came here from far away to journey along the whole of the Great Wall. You are a Great Man! We feel that your willpower and revolutionary spirit are worthwhile for us to study.
     We wish you luck, dear English friend.

Gantang Plaster Stone Mine
Zhongwei County, Ningxia

The inspiration of the Chinese people's revolutionary spirit was the Long March, a retreat by the Communists from the jaws of the National-ists. An army of over 80,000 left Yudu in Jiangxi Province, southwest China, to arrive one year later at the village of Wuqi in Shaanxi Province. Only 4,000 survived the campaign, yet out of such supreme hardship the unique hybrid of Chinese politics was molded from Communism and the very personal philosophy of Mao Zedong. It was that ideology, spread to some 200 million peasants along the route of the Long March, that culminated less than fifteen years later in Mao proclaiming the foundation of the People's Republic of China, a "New China," from the balcony of the Gate of Heavenly Peace overlooking Tiananmen Square in Beijing. I could identify at least with the hardships of these Long Marchers, who gained the outright popular support of peasants along the way. If the Chinese identified me with their founding heroes, that was a great honor—though an undeserved one.

Officially, China has no religion; however, the parable of the good Samaritan seemed to be played out every night, and the underlying doctrine of Communism is a very Christian one. China has come closer than any other nation to creating an equal society—albeit at a level which the World Bank would classify as "Third" World. Nevertheless, the facts are plain to see: no poverty, equality of pay. Officially the work of the peasant, worker and cadre is regarded as being equal. Individuals rank least in importance in their society—families, communes, units, provinces and China come before "self." That was the reason for an unquestioning offer of hospitality in return for nothing but friendship. They were not selfish. The quarry leader was a typical example. He prepared a stew of potatoes, dried beef and dried mushrooms when it would have been easier to serve me noodles from the commune kitchen. It was a real treat.

With a contented stomach, I rested my feet as much as possible. The pain grew so intense that I was forced to take two painkillers. I slept belly-flopped on the *kang* with my legs bent up at the knees supported by a couple of pillows.

The day which promised to produce hitherto unimaginable levels of pain dawned bright and sunny. The facts were simple. Ahead lay Zhongwei where I could rest for as long as the blisters would require to heal. Here I was, lame at Gantang, some forty-five miles away. But there was little here. No matter how much it hurt, I had to move on.

Starting off was the most painful. Once that threshold had been endured jogging seemed more tolerable than walking. In the former foot action, heel-strikes and toe-offs were much shorter. As the sun lifted into a cloudless sky, hot air billowed up from the baking and blinding sand dunes at the railway's side. I felt hot and dizzy, imagining, hallucinating how my feet used to be: springy and healthy. Now they were bloody, swollen, sweaty, festering, lifeless and spent. Could I die of blisters? Is there someone out there sticking pins in a photograph of me? In stamping frantically on the rocky surface, I get agonizing injections of pain, glorious pain. Am I going insane? The more intense the pain the less it hurts—maybe there is a finite amount of pain in each foot? I cannot be beaten by a little pain, stingy twinges! I could run without toes, with broken bones, with no shoes. Forget it. Get the job done.

Nineteen miles from Zhongwei is the maintenance depot and station of Changliushui. There is a standpipe there. It is no hallucination. Out of that tap flows water, ice-cold water from the reservoir in the rocks deep below. Had this been six miles farther on, I would have collapsed. But the tap was there at Changliushui, and I crouched under it, cooling my searing skin and throbbing head. It was truly the water of my life.

The Samaritan of the day was the stationmaster. Huddled under a blanket, cold and shivering one minute, hot the next, I was clearly not out of danger—in more ways than one. He could pick up the phone or try to bundle me on a passing tram to Zhongwei out of concern for my health. With this thought, I got off the bed, topped up my jar of tea, walked backwards and forwards and pronounced boldly, "*Mei guanxi*" (No problem). "*Ming tian wo hao le.*" (Tomorrow I'm fine.)

The sight of a huge wall map of China above the bed had a positive influence on my attitude. Here was a country occupying a third of Asia and I had journeyed throughout the whole of Gansu. With that "pink corridor" behind me, the big blue river bend of the Huang He lay ahead. Each step brought me closer to prolonged rest! The station possessed its own China Railway seal which was proudly stamped in my diary. My bed was made from two wooden benches pulled together in the waiting room. It was impossible to sleep, despite the Nurofen tablets—added to which there were "train quakes" each time an engine passed through the station.

On a murky and cool morning, drugged by four painkillers, I set out, determined to reach Zhongwei before they wore off. The track looped like a meandering river around steep-sided gullies. Some of the floors of these miniature valleys held splashes of green. Soon the valleys widened, and the peasants had doubled the area for cultivation by terracing. An emerald green of brightness that meant food, people, and a limit to the desert. These were the first rice paddies I had seen on my route, small plots of production that contributed to the sustenance of this vast nation.

Now the mighty Huang He, the Yellow River, flowed through a gorge well below the level of the desert. It was a muddy color, much the same as the dunes themselves. Like models, barges criss-crossed the channel, chased by their own chevroned ripples which became breaking waves on the river shore. Neat plots, rectangles of green and yellow, edged the bank like a patchwork blanket.

High above the water, the Great Green Wall shielded the valley from the advancing sand dunes. Beyond these trees the waves of the giant dunes, with their golden sunlit crests and shadowed troughs, were even more like an ocean. Squares of straw that floated on the surface of the sand waves, like the giant mesh of fishermen's nets, attempted to hinder the movement of sand into the tree belt.

China's second-longest river, whose headwaters rise on the Qinghai Plateau to the west, must traverse many a landscape on its way to the sea. Unlike the Great Wall, which is undeterred in its course by any terrain, the Huang He must weave an altogether more tortuous route. Like this great river's, my journey is from the desert to the sea. If I were to throw a log of wood into the channel below, would it, I wonder, beat me to the Yellow Sea? Or would it become stranded high and dry somewhere along its course?

ıl 8 lı.

A Land of Fish and Rice

Give me a lever and I will feed the earth.
—*Old Middle Eastern farmer's saying*

I feared the consequences of overriding my body's pain-sensing mechanism by taking a double dose of Nurofen. The blisters, two on each foot in perfect symmetry, were bigger and worse than ever. I wondered whether I had truly overstepped the mark. Not only might I lose the journey, I might lose my feet. They were ghastly, raw and infected.

By the time I reached the Zhongwei Ningxia *fandian* I had ransacked my first aid kit, wallpapering my feet with moleskin, Elastoplast and lint. I had also swallowed my entire supply of painkillers. It was now necessary to reach for stronger stuff. I carried two antibiotics, Tetrabid and Penbritten. One was suited to infections producing pus, the other viral complaints, but I had completely forgotten which was which. There was no time for shilly-shallying. Both were broad-spectrum medications. I chose the large yellow and brown pills. The patient started the course and told himself that they would work wonders.

An hour later the hotel attendant, realizing my near-complete inability to walk, had fetched two large flasks of hot water from the boiler. Attempting to cleanse the wounds in a tepid bath was a killing necessity, excruciatingly reflected by my face in the bathroom mirror. It was wrinkled, pot-eyed and hollow-cheeked; the last week had taken its toll. Dabbing the four wounds very gently to dry them, I swore that the "gang of four" was not going to defeat me. Yet trying to walk to the bed was unbearable—impossible. I had to crawl back on hands and knees.

During the night, the pain worsened. I found it impossible to sleep, morbidly checking my pulse rate by watching the wound throb on my inside heel. I saved my big physical effort to reach the dining room for breakfast, where the hotel staff suggested a hospital visit, for which they provided a bicycle and a guiding waitress.

It was May 1, International Labor Day and a holiday in China. Appropriately, British Bank Holiday weather was the order of the day with rain making the red banners and silk pennants go limp. But at the hospital I received prompt attention. The doctors and nurses gasped and chattered when I revealed the "gang of four." Lancing the wounds, they daubed them with iodine. Like ink on blotting paper, the purple pigment spread over, between and up my toes. "*Wei shenme?*" (How?) they asked, screwing up their faces with looks of agony. "*Jiayuguan bu hen jin—ba bai gongli!*" (Jiayuguan isn't very near—500 miles!) I replied. The doctor grinned admiringly, gave a slow, understanding nod of his head, and a thumbs-up. "*Hao. Hen hao*" (Good. Very good), he repeated approvingly.

For a modest charge of two yuan I was prescribed some "goodies" to take back to the hotel. The waitress collected these on my behalf from the dispensary. They amounted to a long cotton bandage, two newspaper cones full of tablets—sealed with a twist, and three boxes of plasters. If ever a fitting event of heroic endurance was required to endorse a brand of plasters, there could be none more appropriate than the Long March.

With my inability to walk—in fact, barely stand—I could begin to comprehend the driving force behind a real cause. The Long March of the Red Army under pursuit by the Kuomintang is unmatched in human history: 3,853 miles of hostile terrain, day and night, crossing twenty-four rivers and eighteen mountain ranges in a period of exactly one year. Each man carried in the order of sixty-five pounds of equipment and was shod with straw sandals. These were ardent Communists, fired by the dream of a New China under Mao, who marched at their head. Over thirty years later, after that dream had been realized, teenage Red Guards taking part in the Cultural Revolution yearned to temper themselves in recreating the hardships suffered by their fathers on the Long March. They embarked on "New

Long Marches," making crossprovince pilgrimages to places where the Marchers passed or along sections of the hallowed ground trodden by the Red Army itself. Fueled with youthful fervor, quoting from the *Little Red Book* of Mao's teachings, they too wore straw sandals. Most Red Guards were teenagers, yet many took their young brothers and sisters along with them—children full of Maoist pride—and marched several hundred miles. Probably not since those days of the mid-sixties had such mutilated feet as mine been presented for inspection in China. In just looking at their pitiful state, I realized my own intense belief in my own cause. In normal circumstances, I would have been unable to continue long ago, yet, unbelievably, here I was in Zhongwei, some 500 miles along the Great Wall without having conceded an inch of the way. That made me feel good—very good. Curling my toes to feel the pain, I played down the agony and yelled, "Only 900 miles to go!" Then, slapping on four of the wonderfully aromatic tiger-bone and musk Long March plasters I hobbled outside into the street to buy some treats. This was worthy of celebration.

Despite it being a national holiday, the streets of Zhongwei were crowded, with the shops and stalls open. The variety of food on offer was a change from the desert markets: there were green vegetables, an abundance of eggs, bean curd, and of course fish—mostly alive in troughs. The general store was well stocked: half a dozen black "Flying Pigeon" roadster bicycles protected in cardboard; the hardware section of woks, pots, kettles, ladles and scoops; a clothing section with straw hats, green caps, Mao suits, towels and bedrolls. Passing the dried food counter—too much of which was unidentifiable—I purchased from the pyramidal displays of jars, tins and packets, shopping for vitamins and protein to aid the tissue repair of my feet. I returned to the hotel clutching jars of pineapple and apricots, tins of smoked fish, chocolate and ten hardboiled eggs from a stall at the curbside.

That night I managed my best night's sleep for over a week. On awakening, I was encouraged by the sight of my healing wounds. Feeling positive, I considered a likely day on which I might hope to set off again. To rush my recovery would, however, be foolish and critical, for once I had left Wuzhong, on the east bank of the Yellow River, there existed a great chasm of closed country throughout East Ningxia, Shaanxi and Shanxi until the city of Datong. That meant no opportunity to rest and therefore no chance to make mistakes. Now was the time to plan ahead—visas, money, and a target for the end of this spring stage of the run.

At breakfast I spoke my first English for a month with two architecture students from Beijing's Qinghua Daxue—the "Oxbridge" of the country's educational institutions. Their English was excellent, and over our prolonged sociable breakfast of unlimited eggs, *mantou* and *xifan* (an enamel basin full between the three of us), we spoke on a number of subjects. Two waitresses joined us at the large round table.

"She watched you arriving in Zhongwei," said Zhang Wei Yi. "You looked like a wild animal—so dirty, a foreign devil!"

"Chinese people are often afraid of the foreigner," added Zhuang Wei Min.

"How many foreign visitors come here?" They relayed my questions to the girls.

"This year, you're the first!"

"Last year?"

"More than twenty." Then I faced a barrage of questions that fell into a series commencing with "In your motherland . . . what do people like to read . . . think of the Iron Lady, Mrs Thatcher . . . the USA . . . the Soviet Union . . . how big are your apartments?"

Zhuang then looked serious and said, "Are there any questions which are impolite to ask you?"

"Not at all. Feel free to ask anything," I replied, expecting to be quizzed about salaries or girlfriends.

"Please tell us something about AIDs," he said gravely.

"We hear that many foreign people, especially Americans, have this disease." They looked genuinely afraid. All I could do to allay their fears was to preach a nutshell moral philosophy, one which liberals would describe as being Victorian. They nodded understandingly and Zhuang added, "There are also men like this in China—in Beijing Opera—quite common. Thank you for answering us."

"Many Chinese want to go to America, don't they?" I asked.

"It's true. Students especially who get the news magazine—*Newsweek*—do you know it?"

"Of course. But I think you shouldn't be dissatisfied with your own country. China is a great nation."

Zhang interrupted, "We know *Newsweek* is propaganda."

I continued. "Yes, the West is richer but we are becoming selfish, only money counts. We are losing our respect for others."

"Maybe the reforms will do that in China," said Zhang.

"But you have the chance to learn from our mistakes."

"We are honored to hear your ideas. You criticize your own people as we do ours. We hope to visit your motherland one day."

"Chinese people will always be welcome—they have helped me so much."

"Can we do anything for you now?" asked Zhuang.

In fact there was something. "I want to extend the visa in my passport—at the Gong An Ju—will you write a note for me?"

The Public Security Bureau was next door to the hotel. Out of the padlocked cupboard came the seals, tins of red ink and book of regulations, but there was little hesitation in granting me a visa extension of some two and a half months—more than sufficient time to see me through stage one. That was a major headache over, for lying awake some nights before, it had occurred to me that the PSB of Gansu could have alerted their counterpart in Zhongwei to my escape.

The second bureaucratic hurdle of the day to be tackled was the Bank of China. Though I had a considerable cash reserve remaining from a large black-market transaction of Foreign Exchange Certificates into renminbi, I considered it wise to leave Zhongwei with enough cash for unforeseen costs. One of the criteria for a town or city being categorized as "open" is the availability of "reasonable standard accommodation" and foreign exchange facilities, a fact which I challenged the Bank of China clerk with at his blank look when presented with a Thomas Cook "Great Wall" traveller's cheque. The cheques even had *Zhong guo Yinhang* (Bank of China) in Chinese characters overprinted on them. After some time, he admitted the cheque could not be cashed because the bank did not know the exchange rate. The RMB yuan is linked to the US dollar and never varies, but still he refused to exchange it. Demanding to see the manager, I then insisted they telephone the provincial capital, Yinchuan, to get the day's official quotation. Following the booking of this long-distance call the rate was duly obtained—the same as it had always been. Then came a test for arithmetic—the deduction of commission and the discrepancy between the calculator and abacus. The transaction took almost two hours to complete.

After two days in Zhongwei, I cautiously thought about leaving — the blisters were healing miraculously, at a speed I had never thought possible. The wounds were looking clean, dry and scabbed; clearly, the choice of antibiotic had been wise. Over the next couple of days I ate well, piling in the proteins to heal the flesh, and feeding off the memories of 500 miles of Wall to prepare myself psychologically for the next stage. The point at which to adjourn for the summer lay at an unknown place in the great expanse of closed territory ahead. How much further I could proceed depended upon the temperature, though now I was beginning to believe that somewhere in Shaanxi Province was quite conceivable.

To consolidate my achievement I set about mailing back all exposed film to my contact at the Midland Bank in Beijing. A lengthy process at the post office ensued, since paper envelopes for packages are not accepted. Instead, cloth bags have to be made from calico—purchased from a textile shop. Some time later, I returned to the post office to start sewing—only to realize that soft padding of contents is another requirement. I went out to the general store to buy a small towel. Meanwhile, back at the post office, all needles were now occupied by peasants stitching up their own parcels. Ten minutes later, I patiently sewed up my own bag to the standard of security and neatness acceptable to the postal clerk.

* * *

I had been told that the original Great Wall of the Qin State (Warring States period) could be found on the banks of the Yellow River, but my enquiries in Zhongwei as to its whereabouts all met with ambiguity. Responses like, "It's too far and very dirty," or "a taxi will take you there," or "the temple of Gao is more interesting," were the recognized code for not being allowed to go there alone. I naturally remained steadfastly determined to inspect one of the oldest components of the Great Wall.

Heading southwest out of Zhongwei at sunrise I left the paved road to zigzag through fields along a maze of tree-lined tracks spanning canals and channels. Every mile I questioned the nearest peasant. The answer was either "near," "far," or "not here," meaning he didn't know. But replies of "near" and "far" did at least suggest I was on the right track.

The next step was to ask a multiple choice question: "*Duo shao gongli—wu, ba, shi*?" (How many miles—five, eight, ten?) This really made them commit themselves. Once they had quoted a distance, I asked them again and if they stayed with that figure it was likely quite accurate. Instinct was always the final judge and soon I emerged at the river.

The Yellow River is second only in length to the Yangzi at 3,935 miles, but has a much smaller volume. Its basin is largely arid or semiarid and only in its source region, shared with the Yangzi on the Qinghai Plateau, is there high precipitation. I now needed to cross the river. The ferry was operated by a hand-turned chain and pulley mechanism. On I clambered with sheep, goats, chickens and bicycles for the 100-yard crossing. There on the south bank, tucked away behind a village close to a coal depot, I found remains of what I believed to be a Warring States contribution to the first Great Wall of Qin Shi Huang. Little more than several hundred yards of the Wall remained, almost perpendicular to the river channel itself. Yet it was an enormous structure—more of an elongated mound than a wall, from the top of which one could see across the whole fertile strip to the desert beyond. Admittedly, I possess no great archaeological expertise, and I brought back no artifacts or vegetation to carbon-date the site with; however, this previously unseen scale of structure with its widespread base and immense height held a real aura of age. Moreover, its location in protecting the alluvial river plain was very much attuned with the aim of the Chinese Kingdom Wall-builders in separating their agricultural lands, here in the very cradle of Chinese civilization, from the wilderness of the nomads beyond the Wall.

Across on the north bank there was no trace of the Wall continuing, only flat fields perfectly plowed, with seedlings sprouting in the furrows. I was content at having found one surviving remnant of the old Wall. To the east the Wall could only become younger. I was satisfied, too, at the condition of my feet. The tiger-bone and musk plasters were securely in place, and doing a fine job.

Gone was the dusty fawn desert. Here the plow cut slices of rich dark earth. An inheritance left by thousands of years of river flooding. A soil with fabric and moisture, brimming with the energy to produce food.

Running through this garden of produce, I felt my days were no longer lonely. The color of the earth and greenery was restful to the eyes that had gazed upon so much desert. Everywhere was life: in the village markets; on the tracks as peasants moved their barrows of vegetables, chickens and squealing piglets; and in the fields where they guided the plow, planted, and separated the seedlings. It was a landscape abundant with water: wide canals flowing, narrow brooks gushing, keep-ponds reflecting and channels trickling, all moving the nutrient-rich waters of the Yellow River to the fields. Life existed both in and upon the water too—ducks for banquets and quilted jackets, and the silent moment shattered by a fish plopping in a pond. This was Ningxia, a land of fish and rice.

Concern at having made no progress for several days kept me going late into the evening. Remarkably, after some thirty-seven miles, my feet were perfect—they had exuded so much pain of late that surely they had no more to give. Perhaps the delay they enforced was a mixed blessing, for I now felt in good physical condition to tackle the large distance ahead, but first there was the short-term target of recrossing the Yellow River tomorrow to reach the open town of Wuzhong. To achieve this it was necessary to use all the hours of daylight. At sunset I bivouacked in a sheep pen, quite dry and not unpleasant to the nose.

Sleeping as solidly as I could ever remember for a night under the stars, I broke camp and was jogging before the chill of the dawn could discomfort me. Just on opening time, I was the first customer for a breakfast of *you tiao* (grease sticks—like doughnuts) and *dou jiang* (soy bean milk) at a *fandian* in Qukou. The "doughnuts" looked better than they tasted but the soy bean milk was delicious with a little sugar added. With that full belly, I was nicely poised for a big mileage. Outside, however, I met a schoolteacher who spoke just a few words of English. He was so enthusiastic about my journey that it was difficult to refuse the offer of tea at his school. This honor involved no detour and we arrived before the children of the village. Some of the teachers slept there, and when I recited my route to them they insisted I accept one of their children's atlases to take with me, a twenty-four page booklet with simple but interesting maps. I was particularly interested in a world projection that placed China in the central position. In order to accommodate "*Zhong guo*"—the Middle Kingdom—in its rightful place the hemispheres are shifted. The Americas have become the Eastern Hemisphere and the Euro-African-Asian continents, the Western Hemisphere. The Pacific Ocean is central and China is the Middle Kingdom. As the teachers escorted me to the school gates, the children were starting the day by exercising to music in the dusty playground. Upon the schoolyard walls were large-character slogans one of which I recognized—"Study hard, keep fit and make daily progress," a maxim of Mao. Above, the red-and-gold-starred national flag fluttered in the breeze. I left the school with my treasured souvenir. A few ounces of weight, certainly, though a memento for which I was prepared to shelve my pledge of collecting nothing but names. Doubtless there were countless thousands of them in classrooms and satchels across the whole People's Republic, but with my lifelong fascination for maps, this atlas was very special to me.

Perhaps the teacher who wrote in my diary was a geography teacher.

> Huang He is the second-largest river in China and flows over nine provinces on its journey to the sea (Qinghai, Sichuan, Gansu, Ningxia, Nei Mongol, Shaanxi, Shanxi, Henan and Shandong). But the river is not wide here and it contains much sand and silt from the soil erosion of the Huangtu Plateau. The Qingtongxia control project is nearby.
>
> *Wang Xingwen,*
> *State Qukou Farm Middle School,*
> *May 6th, 1987*

This geographical entry of Mr. Wang summarized the problems of the Yellow River: small volume, eroding and laden with silt, temperamental and needing control. The Yellow River basin has suffered famines due to drought one year and devastation from flooding the next, deservedly earning the title of "China's sorrow." Since Liberation there have been projects to regulate its flow, storing floodwaters for times of need by damming. Here at Qingtongxia there is a reservoir, dam and bridge.

The latter concerned me the most, for I needed to cross that bridge—likely a bastion of security—in order to reach Wuzhong. In my approach, I felt like a log of wood cascading to its fate amongst churning white waters that could toss it like a matchstick on to the rocky sides of the gorge. Yet there was no alternative; the current was too strong, for I had the momentum of 660 miles behind me.

At first the river filled the air with its watery hum and hiss. Then a braided channel came into view, stepped across by separate island-hopping bridges. Truck drivers queued, clutching their papers and taking the opportunity to sit on their bonnets for a smoke in the sun. Ahead lay sentry boxes, huts, checkpoints with barriers and numerous officials. It was no time to lack confidence—I broke into a jog, assumed a middle-of-the-road position and casually breezed by, acknowledging the bureaucrats with a smile, wave and "*Ni men hao.*" Incredible! Over the Yellow River without a question being asked—I could barely believe it. Now out of the turbulent waters, I entered the peaceful flow of the countryside beyond with a renaissance of energy in my legs that I vowed would take me to Wuzhong by nightfall. As the sound of the waters faded, I pictured myself crossing the mighty river once again after my summer recess, for the Yellow River's course describes a huge loop to the north and the Great Wall crosses its torrent twice along its path. For once, I felt entitled to look ahead and be positive.

The tall poplars and weeping willows, whose branches often draped down to eye level, provided shade on my afternoon push to Wuzhong. This region claimed to possess the oldest established irrigation system of the Yellow River basin. The engineers of Qin Shi Huang had constructed canals once the fertile alluvial strip had been protected by the Great Wall. There were armies to feed in these newly colonized lands. Large acreages were pressed into production and the Qin Qu (canal) was dug in a network on the east bank of the Huang He. Just as the Wall-builders had used bamboo, so the same wonder material was here hollowed out to be used as piping for bringing water up from the canal to the rice paddies and keep-ponds.

Diary, May 6th: Wuzhong

A group of boys excitedly escort me to a lüguan where I rent a room for five kuai (the spoken form of RMB yuan). I eat in the back room of a Muslim *fandian*. The proprietor takes a real pride in his establishment: serviettes! chopsticks in paper! It's a family operation—his sons are chopping, tossing and mixing in the cookhouse, thudding choppers and knives on wood, clanking ladles and spoons on woks around searing flames of foundry-like proportions. His daughters serve the guests, efficiently topping up their fruit tea, wiping the tables and providing the diners with piping hot

towels to refresh themselves with. The *mian tiao* is the
best I've tasted, washed down with two beers. This
place possesses a peaceful ambience that I've never
before experienced in China—a perfect place in which
to linger and toast myself for crossing the Yellow River.

In one respect Wuzhong reminded me of Hong Kong. There one sees
Westerners and Chinese, and English and Chinese signs. Here in the
"Ningxia Huizu Zizhiqu," Ningxia Autonomous Region of Hui Nationality, a Moslem community has established itself within a predominantly
Han nation. Arabic script was written alongside Chinese; many people
wore the skullcap; they could purchase their holy texts, talk with imams
sitting cross-legged on woven rugs, and pray freely without interference,
facing towards Mecca at the appropriate times of day. Newly built
mosques were tiled in glaze, and civic buildings of Islamic style attempted to recreate the mosaic splendor of the Middle East. It would
seem that China is allowing some of her many minority nationalities to
retain their cultural heritage and form of worship in a largely agnostic
country.

Wuzhong was the last town from which to report my progress back
to Britain before my summer break, and the post office was the first at
which I had seen professional letter writers awaiting custom, all sage-like
with long white beards, pipes and nicotine-stained fingers. The skill of
calligraphy is an art form of the Chinese practiced by scholars and
mandarins through the ages. The wonderfully atmospheric pictograms
are produced using the "four treasures of the studio"—the ink stone, the
slab, the brush and the paper. The letter writers now use five additional
treasures—fountain pens (made in Shanghai), pads of paper, envelopes
(airmail or white, sketched with a "scenic spot"), eight-fen stamps for
internal postage and glue for sealing the letter. One such man of letters
produced a quite handsome script, and *pro formas* of his love letters were
available to prospective clients, surely as romantic as a bunch of flowers
to a Western girl.

The populous valley of the Yellow River was merely an interlude on
what was almost entirely a route of desert, semidesert and mountains
that had festered with hostilities along the Wall. It was with optimism
that I left Wuzhong, knowing that by the day's end I would have

reentered the desert and be reunited with the Wall. That was a place left to nature and there was only a Wall left to withstand the elements.

North of Wuzhong I prepared to cross canal country to Lingwu, lands watered by the Qin Qu and Tianshui (heaven water) canals. Wuzhong had been the sixth town on my route that foreigners were permitted to visit although most of them were clearly not main destinations, for during that time I had not seen any non-Chinese—until a vehicle drew up beside me. Out jumped two Americans, Steve and Eugene, seismic exploration engineers, accompanied by a driver and "Charlie" Wang, their interpreter. Out came our maps to illustrate this roadside scouting. Steve was able to give me a quickfire description of the desert and loess country ahead, distances between villages, sandstorm warnings ("they come and pin ya down for days") and the condition of the Wall. "You're sure to pass the camp—stop by, take a rest and shower—plenty of iced beer—just a couple of miles south of the Wall outside Dingbian." With no other islands of safety available, that kind of offer was going to be difficult to pass by. Eugene took our picture at the back of the Toyota pickup with me holding open his map of China. At his request I marked my route and autographed the map. Steve promised, "I'll be telling the guys to expect a special guest." And off they drove.

That was my first opportunity to assess the reaction of foreigners to my journey. Steve Wetstein was an oilman who knew the Chinese well, having surveyed the Taklamaklan in Xinjiang. "They contract us to do a job—then the PSB hassle us over permits to go out and find the goddamn stuff." Eugene was new to China, a manager visiting the site. "It's been hell just to get clearance for a day. But what a day," he added. "Meeting the Brit running the Wall!" It was not until they asked me to estimate the distance to Jiayuguan that I made a significant calculation. I had covered over 600 miles. It was the first time I had realized the fact.

My legs had been trained on miles, yet the maps I carried had a scale of kilometers. Most Chinese, however, used their own peculiar unit of distance—the li, a flexible measure which considers the nature of the terrain (as any sensible measurement for travel on foot should). The li is approximately one-third of a mile, though an uphill li is much less, and a downhill one much more. At the end of each day's running I 'guesstimated' my distance of travel by analyzing the map, considering detours and zigzags, the hours on my feet and pace. Then, using the instinct of fifteen years' training, I computed a figure which erred on the conservative side by 10 percent. The underestimation of training totals had been a long-established method to allow me to swear conscientiously I had gone the distance. For a distance athlete there could be no more unacceptable belief than to think one had trained 100 miles in a week when actually one had done less.

So, east of Lingwu I celebrated my record with just one gulp of water, for the day was cool as the sun's rays were filtered by the dusty atmosphere. Then it was on to Shaanxi, no resting on numerical laurels. For now, as I left the Yellow River valley, desolate country lay ahead once more.

9

Under the Veil of a Sandstorm

If we fail to reach the Great Wall, we are
not men. We who have already marched
twenty thousand li.

—*Mao Zedong,*
spurring the Red Army north on the
Long March

The amber sky to the northeast forewarned of the problems in
crossing East Ningxia and Shaanxi. Here was a huge wedge of desert,
surrounded by loess tablelands that released dust so light that winds
could suspend it high in the atmosphere to produce an orange-brown
filter for the sun, a dust that rained down to irritate the eyes, block the
nose, and create an earthy paste in the mouth and a cement between the
teeth. This was the third major desert on my route, the Mu Us Shamo,
tucked under the western arc of the big bend of the Huang He. Yet
agriculture is attempted to the very limit of this sterile frontier, between
these barren dusty hills where no springs surface nor irrigation channels
flow. Peasant smallholdings congregate around wind pumps marking
the site of ground wells, the water from which allows the cultivation of
a few hardy crops. But without the protection of a Great Green Wall, the
plight of these subsistence farmers is unlikely to improve. Indeed, by
grazing sheep on the sparse vegetation they only invite the dustbowl
conditions to worsen.

By evening, the Great Wall out in the desert to the north seemed
beyond reach, for the sky looked increasingly sinister with the threat of

a sandstorm. With sunset, the desert and sky were indistinguishable. My priority was shelter. North of Gu Yao Zi I approached a group of workers gathered around their radio as the "Internationale" preceded the sounding of seven o'clock Beijing time. My arrival in their courtyard was surprising enough. They switched the radio off and immediately made a place in their home for me. It seemed the more remote and hostile the environment, the more quickly people accepted me.

Diary, May 8th: north of Gu Yao Zi

Despite the dismal surroundings, the men are a jovial bunch and we take a formal photograph in the yard with my camera perched on a bicycle as a tripod. Dinner is cooking. A constant amount of brushing goes on here: the yard, rooms, beds—after an hour a film of dust has blanketed everything from the natural fallout of the sky. The walls, ceiling and any adornments are soiled— linear scrolls of calligraphy and portraits of Marx, Engels, Lenin and Stalin. Happiness at the end of a long day is a plate of *mian tiao*, tea all evening, a foot bath and a chance to wash myself and socks.

As darkness fell, we kept ourselves shut inside and well provided with liquid to prevent our throats from drying and voices from croaking. Showing my hosts any maps always provoked differing opinions and advice with regard to my route. "*Mu Us Sha mo san ge Chang Cheng*" (The Mu Us Desert has three Great Walls) was a fact they agreed on; though which was the older and newer were matters of heated discussion. Nevertheless, a Great Wall existed some sixteen li north; its age was of little concern to me.

The day began with much the same routine as it had ended: washing, cooking and the inevitable sequence of brushing the dust off of everything—shaking one's clothes out in the yard, beating bedrolls, dusting walls, shelves, beds and floors, and finally splattering water upon all ground surfaces, inside and out.

I moved off, compass in hand, under clear skies, to cross plowed fields whose friable dusty carpet held not a drop of moisture. Treading upon these strange surfaces, my feet broke the encrustation with a crunch to release puffs of dust with each footprint. For once, the slopes exposed to the wind made easier going as I began to realize that the distance of sixteen li I had been given contained a sizeable factor to allow for the difficulty of a march that took one hour to complete.

The Great Wall followed a series of low ridges along its west to east path, and from afar possessed a distinct shape between moundlike watchtowers. Upon closer inspection, however, it exhibited an advanced state of dereliction. There was no Great Green Wall, so the Great Wall itself marked the limit of cultivation; northwards lay a totally empty tract of desert that was the Autonomous Region of Inner Mongolia, since the line of the Wall here marks the provincial boundary.

My progress accelerated, for, as was usual, a track of sorts existed alongside the Wall, and after some three hours, I caught occasional glimpses of a second Wall to the southwest which appeared quite substantial. It was two early twentieth-century geographers, Clarke and Sowerby, who established the location of these different walls while exploring the Mu Us Shamo. The region was known to them as the "Ordos," a word derived from "hordes," being originally descriptive of the Mongol archers who inhabited this vast region of desert. Switching my course to follow the second Great Wall, I was soon to notice the parallel intermittent remains of a third Great Wall from the Sui Dynasty (AD 581–618), a rampart representing the reunification of the Chinese Empire after some four centuries of internal strife.

The Han Dynasty had given way to a series of several coexisting "kingdoms" ruled by self-styled emperors, a division brought about by the numerous incursions of nomadic barbarians who invaded at a time of peasant revolt and military discontent. The new kingdoms themselves adopted the more stable agricultural economy of the people they had overrun. When China was reunited as one empire under the Sui Dynasty, Emperor Yang Zhian resumed the building of the Great Wall to deter invasion from the Turks, who had now become the enemy north of the Wall. The Sui Emperor built a 220-mile section to the south of the Ordos in the year AD 585, using a workforce of 30,000 men. Previous rulers of the Walled Kingdom had attempted to improve relations with the barbarians in various ways. Yang Zhian went to the extreme of sending royal brides to the leaders of the Turks, a sacrifice indeed for the Chinese princesses condemned to life and death beyond the Wall.

After frequent famines, grain production was stabilized and sur-
pluses produced for storage. A system of citizenship was introduced that
is still in use today, and a census was conducted. One of Yang Zhian's
sons, Yang Di (a rogue by all accounts), assembled a huge labor force to
construct an artificial waterway linking the two great river systems, the
Yangzi and the Yellow Rivers. The Grand Canal was a transport innova-
tion, later extended to encompass Beijing in the north and Hangzhou in
the south, which allowed the movement of foodstuffs from the more
plentiful south to the less prosperous north. Together with the two
natural river networks it linked up, the Grand Canal joined the Silk Road
as one of the great trading routes of the Chinese Empire.

The Sui and Ming Great Walls, running side by side barely fifty feet
apart were, in fact, separated by some 950 years. After the Sui came
China's golden age, during which the Tang Emperors abandoned the
Wall as a line of defense and took the attack to the barbarians beyond it
to the north. Perhaps the track I was following had witnessed the march
of Tang warriors en route to that front for battle with the Turks, Arabs or
Uygurs. But it was more commonly used as a trade route, transporting
the goods of merchants and the crafts of artisans whose skills flourished
within the commercial environment. Foreign languages, other than the
Tang mother tongue, might well be overheard from passing merchants.
They would be travelling in relative safety, free from racial hostility,
towards the Tang capital of Chang'an, the greatest and most cosmopoli-
tan city in the world. The census of AD 742 recorded the foreign
population (out of a total of 2 million), to be at some 5,000 persons drawn
from all Asia and its peripheries. These were Hindus, Jews, Arabs,
Mongols, Koreans and Japanese. Not only had the Great Wall become
redundant physically with territorial expansion, but the very philosophy
of Wall-building to isolate China from foreign lands had been shelved.
Contact with the world outside reached a peak, with the Silk Road
playing a vital role. Arts, music and literature scaled new heights. In the
enduring state of peace and security, Tang poets could look back at the
construction of the Great Wall and be thankful that, for the time being at
least, China was under no threat from barbarians. The poet Li Bai (AD
701–762) recorded the end of bloodshed with approval in his poem,
"Fighting South of the Rampart."

The Emperor's armies have grown old and gray
Fighting thousands of li from home
The Huns have no trade but battle and bloodshed
And have no fields or plows
Only wasteland where bleached bones lie in the yellow sand
Where Qin built the Great Wall to keep the Xiongnu at bay
The Han in turn light beacons of war
Those beacons are forever burning
Fighting and marching never stops
Men die on the battleground to the sound of clashing swords
While the horses of the vanquished neigh piteously to Heaven
Crows and hawks scavenge for human guts
Carry them off by beak and hang them on the branches of trees
Generals, archers and porters are slain upon the bushes and
    grasses
They schemed and fought for nothing for
The sword is a cursed thing
That a wise man brandishes only when he must

The dream of eternal peace held by the Tang Dynasty crumbled in the early tenth century as the Empire, shaken by an internal military revolt, fell prey to a succession of foreign rulers who governed partitioned sections of Empire. The following Song Dynasty retreated to south China under attack from the northeast, and now the Great Wall lay outside the diminished Empire's control. The Jin Dynasty adopted a defensive Wall-building policy again, in recognition of the invasion threat from the north. But no Wall was strong enough to deter the ransacking of China by the Mongol ruler, Kublai Khan. It was the splendid and powerful Ming Dynasty that finally ousted the much-loathed Mongols from China, and it was its elevated mud Wall that now ran fifty feet from the Sui version.

Running between these two Great Walls, it was impossible to ignore the thousand years of history they represented, and not to think of the men who had perished here far from their native homes. The poet Wang Chang Ling sums up the futility of warfare.

The ancient battles along the Great Wall
Were spoken of with lofty praise
But antiquity has now been changed to yellow dust
White bones jumbled amongst the grass

For myself, I valued my 600 miles and treasured so many kindly gestures of friendship from individual Chinese. These were rich moments, wonderfully intangible blessings that no manmade forces could take from me.

The weather was getting worse again. The sheer volume of dust particles suspended high in the sky diffused the sunlight and made it seem later than it was. The real menace of dust clouds, however, is the spread of disease. Detouring from the Wall, I readjusted my face mask and approached the village of Gao Sha Wo.

A chanting tempo led me to some middle-school students engaged in an exercise routine to music. "*Yi!—Er!—San—Si!*" yelled an instructor, and the students responded with lively chops, jumps, stretches and kicks.

Refreshed at the village store with two jars of apple in syrup, I approached a remote farm where I was startled by the sight of two animal corpses—not sheep, but dogs. Then followed a predictable threshold encounter as a loose guard dog charged and I threw clods of crumbly earth that at least temporarily blinded the beast. In response to my request for shelter a peasant escorted me to the leader of the *danwei*, or unit. Production teams operating in a specific geographical area are in turn controlled by a brigade, several of which form a commune (*gong she*). The team leader billeted me on a very remote smallholding. Whether this was to keep his team from inspecting me, or me from inspecting them, I could not work out.

Despite the advanced weeks of spring, the family and I slept upon a heated *kang*, along with assorted cats, hens and a curly-tailed black piglet which had been promoted from farmyard to farmhouse during the weaning stage.

Diary, May 10th: Wallside at Ba sha shu

Suffering the heat of the *kang* and the body heat of the three sons sleeping alongside. The mother awakens us at 6:30 a.m. The sons are out plowing within minutes while breakfast steams in the cookhouse. The black piglet feeds there too. I feel sickly, with a headache and a bursting bowel. The mother acts as a guard to keep their wild dog at bay—as I squat by a mud wall, she's forty yards away, holding a big stick and stones to repel the beast that feasts its eyes on the flesh of my backside. Set off within the hour, though incapable of running—really hot, thirsty and nauseous. Leave the Wall to meet a road which leads to a depot of some kind. I gesture sickness, get some boiling water and a sympathetic draping of bedrolls. I am left quite peacefully staring up at the smoke-stained ceiling as the men work.

Diary, May 11th: Niu Mao Jing

The old man Feng, the team leader, speaks so loudly that it appears he's arguing with everybody, getting in a hundred words for every ten of the others. They bring me a jar of oranges for breakfast, and the self-styled morning checkup finds the patient more comfortable with temperature lowering. The worst moment was a late evening encounter in which forty villagers invaded, jabbering, glaring, shouting, sitting on and pushing against the bed. My temperature soared, with frustration and beads of sweat running down my face. In the late afternoon, at the end of a prolonged "*xiu xi*" with my face to the wall, there is a tap on my shoulder. "Hello," says the voice (not poor student standard). It's an official delegation—a smart English teacher from the County Middle School and the leader of Foreign Affairs. . . .

Despite the hopelessness of my predicament, I levered myself up sharply, brushed aside the bedroll and, looking extremely happy, introduced myself.

"I've come 2,000 li—all on foot from Jiayuguan in Gansu."

"Are you well? Comrade Feng told us a foreign friend was sick."

"I've recovered well. Tomorrow I'll be able to continue along the Great Wall."

"Perhaps you should come with us, we have a car outside, to the hospital in Yanchi?"

His phraseology, although interrogative, held a suspiciously directive ring.

"No! No! Then my foot journey would be broken. Do you understand? Every li must be on foot."

The suited schoolteacher then interpreted expressively to his austere comrade.

"I'll leave here tomorrow on foot," I continued.

"Would you meet our county leader then—as you pass through Yanchi?" I confirmed my willingness to do so, while plotting a possible escape route along the second Great Wall, which passed well to the north of the town.

Li Dong turned to the Foreign Affairs leader saying, "It's an honor, we feel, to welcome a determined man—we want to help you."

"The best help to me is advice. . . . Maps? What is the country ahead like—perhaps as far as Yulin?"

"I know it well," said Li Dong. "After Jingbian the mountains start and the people become so poor. Tomorrow we can discuss all you want," he added. "Twelve o'clock, it's good for you?"

"Fine, twelve noon—where?"

"Just walk into Yanchi—word of your arrival will come to me quickly. A foreigner in Yanchi! Goodbye. Keep warm and eat more."

"*Zai jian!*"

"Oh, your Chinese is good! *Zai jian!*"

Unbelievably I could celebrate being left alone to proceed. But for how long? It seemed likely that if I did not meet them tomorrow they would search for me. Equally obvious, too, that a leader of Foreign Affairs would be aware of the rules and regulations concerning foreign visitors—yet he had agreed to leave me here, free to continue on my way tomorrow. Perhaps my firmness and confident manner had merely delayed the inevitable—brought about by Feng's concern for my well-being. Yet I could hold no grudge whatsoever against this kind old man. He wrote:

> We are working for China Railways based in Niu Mao Jing village—about twenty miles from Yanchi county town. Mr. Will—you rested here to recover from an illness. But we are sorry that we were unable to care for you well. Wish you good luck all the way.
>
> *Feng, May 10th, 1987*

In Yanchi I waited at the first main intersection, marked by a small roundabout, and admired the rare sight of cornflowers and marigolds. A crowd of peasants was quick to gather around, overflowing into the road and causing passing truck drivers to blast their horns. Mr. Li appeared from nowhere and confidently brushed through the encircling townsfolk.

"Good morning! You are well recovered now?"

"Well and strong. This morning was an easy forty li."

"Many important leaders want to meet you."

"Really. . . . Are you sure you can spare the time away from your students?"

"No problem. Until two o'clock we have—"

I interrupted, "*Xiu xi!*"

"*Xiu xi; dui!*" he chuckled. "Oh, your Chinese is very good!"

As we walked briskly up the crowded street, totally oblivious to the cyclists, many of Mr. Li's students called out to him. Mr. Li responded briefly, telling them I was the "foreigner of the Great Wall." We reached a crossroads and stopped.

"Everything you need is here. That's the post office. Here is your hotel, and over there is Yanchi County Government building." The sentry guards at the gate looked menacing. We crossed over and breezed inside, up some stairs and along a network of corridors. Mr. Li reminded me that I would meet the leader of the county and the Party Secretary. There were two men and one woman in the neat office. After prolonged handshakes with all present, the leader delivered his welcoming speech, as another woman entered to serve tea in blue porcelain-lidded mugs. He spoke for a minute or so, after which Li Dong stood up to translate.

"We admire your strength and determination in crossing our desert homeland to inspect the Great Wall. Anything we can do to help you, please ask. We most sincerely welcome you here."

Then the county leader wrote in my diary:

> We the various nationalities people of the county wel-
> come our friend Will to come to Yanchi County for his
> inspection of the Great Wall on foot.
>   Yanchi County is situated in East Ningxia and was
> liberated by the Party forces and established as a revo-
> lutionary base area in the year 1936. It is located between

a desert tableland, "the Ordos" and loess plateau, and it is a region of both agriculture and animal rearing. The climate is typically continental in character and includes the following weather: drought, wind with sand, sunshine in abundance, and a shortage of frost-free days.

The county produces three treasures: salt, fur and young sheep, and sweet licorice root, all of which are well-known products throughout China and the rest of the world.

The Great Wall crosses our county from the west to east. It is the remains of the Sui and Ming Dynasty Great Walls, which are very well preserved in Ningxia.

You came here along your route from Jiayuguan on foot. Your spirit is respected and admired. We sincerely hope your journey will be a success. Please return here again.

County Magistrate, Wang Shi Ying
County Office Secretary, Zhu Lei
Representing The People's Government
of Yanchi County, Ningxia

Meanwhile, we were joined by Li Dong's comrade, Ta Chun Yu, a fellow English teacher from the Yanchi No. 1 Middle School who announced that a banquet awaited us at the hotel. "They have been ordered to provide the best food," added Mr. Li. We were served by smiling waitresses, with ornate chopsticks on best "Jing de Zhen" rice-design porcelain. "We don't often eat much meat like this," said the young teacher. Mr. Li and his comrade then had to return to their school. "What a story I have to tell my students." But he was delighted to learn I had now decided to stay the night, and he immediately invited me to inspect the town with him at the finish of the school day.

Stopping briefly in the hotel entrance to look at the town plan, he pointed out the remains of the Great Wall in the vicinity. "There are two Ming Dynasty Walls, and one Sui Great Wall." The first Wall, just ten li north of the town in the Mu Us Shamo, was the oldest, built in 1474. Then, in 1531, when it was found to be too far away from the town's garrison, the massive grey small-bricked structure towering over us, it was "moved" south along the same path as the Sui Wall. Tufts of grass grew out of its pitted surface. Even more than the Great Wall out in the desert, these city walls evoked the passage of time, as their dereliction contrasted with the surrounding stark, socialist-style buildings. Our echoes beneath the walls disturbed a pair of crows scavenging upon its top. Taking wing, they croaked raucously, echoing the calls of Ming guards watching for the hordes of Mongols to appear from the Ordos four centuries ago.

In a small park, grandly named the Revolutionary Park in honor of the heroes of the Red Army, Mr. Li asked the curator to open up the museum, where we examined photographs, maps, weapons and uniforms. "Just sixty miles south is Wuqi town—where the *Chang Zheng* finished," he explained. "North Shaanxi is the birthplace of the Liberation—now let's go to my home to talk about your Long March."

Li Dong's home was small but well provided with a refrigerator, radio, pictures, and more books and newspapers than I had seen on my entire journey. Such a collection was hardly surprising for an academic family, for Mr. Li's wife was also a teacher. They had met as students of English at Shanghai University. The Fudan University of that city is renowned throughout China, and Li Dong's mastery of English was testament to its excellence. "Very lucky to study in Shanghai," he reminisced. "Ningxia is a small region—very poor. I came to Dingbian— which is just across the border in Shaanxi—during the Cultural Revolution. In those days, we were young and wanted to take part in the Revolution, especially in Shaanxi Province."

From these experiences he was able to inform me of the route ahead. "After Jingbian the Great Wall is well preserved outside the river valleys—there flow the young waters of our Yellow River, but," he warned, "the tableland between is difficult to cross—the heat of day can be very bad. When we marched to Beijing in the 1960s, Shanxi was the worst area; we crossed the mountains around Taiyuan in high summer, sleeping by day and marching at night over the mountain paths with flaming torches." Although I did not realize it at the time, Li Dong was describing one of the New Long Marches of Red Guards—and it seemed he had played a part in one of the most famous marches of all, from Shaanxi to Beijing.

Mr. Li's two children played in the *hutong* outside, while his wife, whose command of English was adequate, offered us tea or coffee to drink. "We bought it on our last visit to Shanghai two years ago!"

"I'll try the coffee then."

He tried to tune the radio in to "Voice of America" but the interference was too bad.

"You must miss your family?"

"Of course—but I feel that the help and friendship of your people stands for my own family's support out here in China."

"Yes, the peasants are kindly. Did you know that in Nei Mongol a stranger may enter any farm to rest or eat? But," he added, "in the town things are different—another country almost. My students, for example; the best want to go to Beijing, Shanghai or Guangzhou—and stay there— earn more money, but what about the family? And they act badly, noisily, only for themselves—no code of life."

"The China I've seen seems very caring towards others though— with respect."

"The older people, yes. We've been taught to serve the people first." Our coffee arrived and tasted exceptionally good. It was the first I had drunk for some six weeks. "Drink as much as you can!" he said, laughing. "Only foreigners seem to like it—you're the first visitor to our town for two—no, three years!" That was a problem for a student of English, he emphasized. "I read the *China Daily*, usually two weeks old, as often as possible," pointing to a wad of newspapers on the floor.

"Perhaps in some months' time you can read about me there," I joked.

Before setting off back to the hotel, Li Dong confessed he had important information for me. He explained that the Yanchi Health Committee had received a worrying telegraph that morning. He was serious. "You should take great care with your cleanliness when living with the peasants." Notification had been received that rats and mice had been found dead by the thousands along the border region with Nei Mongol. Action had been rapid to prevent traffic across the border, for the PLA (People's Liberation Army) had been deployed in the region. "It's a disease—but I don't know what to call it in English." That was the first time he had struggled for a word. "My dictionary"—he flicked anxiously through the pages—"this is the word—look, it's this." He held the huge book open with his index finger pointing to the words— "bubonic plague." A shiver went down my spine. I was so shocked that I was at a loss for words. I immediately recalled the sight of the festering dog corpses and my own recent illness.

"What will happen?" I asked. "Will they broadcast the news?"

"Never, no! That would just cause panic amongst the peasants. I've told you because, as an outsider, you may be in danger." I was particularly concerned at news of bubonic plague in China being broadcast and causing worry to my family, who would not know my exact location. "Tomorrow some experts in health will travel to the border area to make an investigation—you will be gone by then."

We walked back to the hotel, passing by Mr. Li's place of work, the No. 1 Middle School. Surprisingly, many students were just leaving the premises.

"This is a night study class—the examinations are soon—the rewards will be places in Beijing, Shanghai; a different life, so competition is very high."

I wondered how a bout of the plague would reduce the intensity of such a contest. However, it was no time for joking as Li Dong bade me farewell. "I know you are determined—you will complete this great journey. Nothing can stop you!" Giving him my heartfelt thanks for all his hospitality, I ran inside the hotel with a new attack of diarrhea. . . .

It was virtually impossible for me to sleep. I kept seeing Li Dong's index finger underlining "bubonic plague" in his dictionary. Morbidly, I considered my personal hygiene and how it had become lax over the weeks—by now I thought nothing of using the grimy chopsticks provided in *fandians* instead of my own. And how often had I drunk from jars, caked with inground dirt around their rims. A different vigilance was also necessary in view of Mr. Li's information regarding the presence of the PLA in the region. If military and official personnel were on the move along roads and through villages, it was more critical than ever to keep out of their way. The relaxed policy in Yanchi was one thing, but out of the county things might well be different.

The parallel Great Walls of the Sui and Ming Dynasties passed through the northern edge of the town. Once out in the countryside the condition of both improved considerably. In the flat and dull light of dawn the Ming Wall possessed an earthy purple appearance in contrast to the red and yellow sands of the Ordos. The Sui Wall was merely an elongated mass of those very sands and separated from the Ming Wall by a trench—a feature that was incorporated within the Ming defensive structure in order to accentuate the height of the Great Wall to invaders. From afar the defense appeared discouraging enough, yet at close quarters, when the Hun needed all his courage, the Great Wall effectively "grew" a further six feet.

The trench soon became a well-travelled track providing shelter, security and navigational aid in crossing what was otherwise sparsely populated desert. The travellers were largely salt merchants. Mounds of salt blotch the landscape as white patches, and the salt lake that gives its name to the town of Yanchi was located beside the Great Wall towards Dingbian. A local legend tells of how the people inherited the mineral, as told me by Li Dong in my diary:

> Several thousand years ago the Salt Lake was a freshwa-
> ter lake. One day a white horse came to the desert here
> from heaven and it taught the people how to cultivate
> the land and cure their illnesses with medicines made
> from the licorice root. The horse respected the people
> and the land here, but the powerful Emperor Yu Huang
> was enraged when it became known that his people
> were taught by a heavenly horse. The Emperor ordered
> the horse to return to heaven—but it refused and ran
> into the lake. The next year the local people found more
> and more salt in the lake—they believed the horse had
> given them the mineral they so desperately needed.
>
> *Li Dong, Yanchi No. 1 Middle School*

Running the "salt road" between the Walls, I crossed the provincial boundary of Ningxia into Shaanxi, the hotbed of revolutionary thought and headquarters of Mao Zedong in the 1930s. Upon that border, close to the village of Yan Chang Bu, the surface of the Great Wall, golden now with the reflected desert light, is pitted like a honeycomb with cool and shadowy enclaves. Each of these one hundred or more caves is large enough to shelter a couple of men. The Great Wall of the Ming Dynasty, built as a border defense against the banished Mongols, became a last defense once again some 400 years after it was built. On the incised loess plateau to the south, the remnant brigades of the various surviving fronts of the Red Army had established their base at the end of the Long March. The exodus had finished—the fighting had not. Nationalist forces under the direction of Chiang Kai-shek encircled the Gansu-Ningxia-Shaanxi liberated area. Along the northern front of that region, corresponding with the line of the Great Wall, a frontier war raged once again. The caves in the Wall were dug for shelter by the 359 Brigade in 1936, led by Wang Zhen who, much later, in 1988, was to hold vice-chairmanship of the People's Republic. They fought the Nationalists in the Liberation War, and then under a common threat, formed a united front with Chiang Kai-shek to repel the new foreign aggressor, Japan, whose forces had crept across Inner Mongolia to become the modern barbarians to the north of the Great Wall.

When the Long Marchers arrived in Wuqi, the region was sparsely populated, a land of barren dusty hills and sterile semidesert. Even today the region seems inhospitable enough. In 1935, there were no houses, no wells, and no food production. Yet the Reds not only survived here, they actually prospered through a spirit of self-sufficiency admired through-out China. This self-help philosophy, exhibited through collective labor by Wang Zhen's 359 Brigade in the Nan Ni Wan valley, became a maxim of the Communists. They reclaimed barren land to produce wheat and corn and dug dwellings into the loess hillsides. It was a Communist pioneering spirit immortalized in the words of the revolutionary song sung by the workers as they terraced the hillsides:

> *The flowers in the basket are fragrant*
> *Please listen to the song that I'll sing*
> > *for here we are at Nan Ni Wan*
> *Such a good place now with good views*
> *Scenes full of crops and animals*
>
> *Before, there were no people here*
> *Only barren hills—how much it has changed*
> *It's like south of the Yangzi River*
> > *brought here to the north of Shaanxi*
>
> *At this "South Yangzi" here in Shaanxi*
> > *the flowers bloom all over the hills*
> *We thank the comrades of 359 Brigade*
> > *who fought the enemy and farmed the land*
> *We must offer the flowers to those heroes*
> *They should be our models*

The collective work ideology that the song embodies epitomizes the entire post-Liberation development program, a plan founded on workers and peasants joining hands in labor for the common good of their unit, village, county and motherland. Even in the reforming China of the eighties this spirit is still evident. Often I had seen villagers, their bicycles parked at the field's edge, working together at harvesting, watering, or digging ditches. It is a community spirit that also motivates schoolchildren to clean classrooms, brush out their yards, paint brick walls, plant, water and weed saplings.

The hollows dug by the 359 Brigade provided welcome shade. Sitting within one, sipping water from my canteen, I faced the compounding problem of dehydration from the heat, and from the diarrhea that had now plagued me for almost twenty-four hours. These caves would have made an historic bivouac site, but in view of my condition I decided it would be wiser to refuse the tempting invitation to sleep with the ghosts of 359 Brigade and seek out the American surveyors I had met near Wuzhong, who must by now have assumed I'd passed them by. Entering Dingbian, I perked up my morale by reviewing progress—now I had entered the fourth province on the route—Shaanxi! Then I was caught short, which reduced morale and much else.

Diary, May 13th: Dingbian

The eyes of Dingbian stay fixed upon me—as though the whole town is aware of my toileting in the alley behind the bazaar. I pass at least half a dozen Gong An Ju officers, who just glare too. The silver trailers of the seismic camp are indeed very difficult to miss. The scene resembles the invasion of the planet by advanced beings. Like flying saucers landed on the earth in the Middle Ages—silver windowless shacks, rows of Toyota jeeps, gargantuan seismic vibrating trucks sitting among the mud huts of Chinese peasants, whose simple transport is the donkey cart, whose work vehicle is the plow pulled by an ass or camel. I meet Steve Wetstein, who gives me a private air-conditioned cabin vacated by a guy on leave. I'm shown the shower and the Mess—complete with videos, a refrigerator full of goodies and stacks of books and magazines. As I tell the men of the bubonic plague rumor, Steve recalls seeing two Beijing jeep ambulances in the border region during the morning, yet he admits to being complacent about such scares: "Been working the armpits of the world too long," he says. A hot shower to rid myself of the Ordos dust is the most welcome luxury, although steak and boiled potatoes came close. The diarrhea continues, but with no dysenteric suggestions. The men seem to have adopted the Chinese habit of turning into bed early.

The time needed to digest my crack-of-dawn fryup was spent examining detailed maps in Steve's cabin. Laying my eyes on OS-quality maps (no doubt specifically surveyed for oil exploration use) gave me a final boost of confidence for tackling the route as far as Jingbian. My big problem, said Steve, would be the dust storms. He gave me a pair of perspex goggles.

There was a knock at the door; it was Charlie Wang, the interpreter, who no doubt had come to say farewell. But he looked concerned and serious.

"The Gong An Ju are here. They want to see his documents." Our hearts sank.

"Hell, Charlie! What's the game? You know this guy doesn't have the papers!"

"They want to see him," Charlie muttered meekly and left.

Steve and I looked at each other. "Don't worry, Steve—it's not your fault. I'll be off now, okay?" I opened the door, and there stood two Gong An Ju officers beside Charlie Wang.

As we drove back to Dingbian, flung side to side in the rear of the Beijing jeep (the suspension of which I was now familiar with), I repeatedly cursed my stupidity at having gone to the camp at all. How blind I had been, anxious to benefit from creature comforts while ill, when quite clearly the warnings had been there all the time. When I had met the two Americans near Wuzhong, they had related their hassles with the PSB over permits—and they were contracted workers in the country. Of course, I should have guessed an informer would be active at the seismic base to watch the activities of six foreigners amongst ninety Chinese.

It was still early and our arrival at the Gong An Ju headquarters, where the officers and their families slept, appeared to have caught the hierarchy unaware. After a frustrating wait, four officers eventually arrived to conduct the interrogation. Smoking, yawning, hawking into spittoons, uniforms hastily pulled on, shoes unlaced, it was galling to have to face such slovenly representatives of the nation's law-administering force.

However, they were predictably equipped with the booklet entitled *The Law on the Entry and Exit of Aliens to the People's Republic of China*, and lost no time in quoting me Article 29.

> *Whoever travels to places not open to aliens without valid travel permit, or forges, alters, misuses or negotiates entry or exit certificate in contravention of the provisions of the present law may be subjected to such penalties as warning, fine or detention for not more than ten days by the public security organ at or above county level.*

My fine words, as relayed by Charlie Wang, about the spirit of my journey and the wholehearted support of the Chinese people were not making much impression. They were more concerned with my geographical movements, yesterday, last week, from the beginning at Jiayuguan—even my previous visits to China. How could I finance all this travel? Did my government pay for me? (answer yes and I would be a spy). After much note-taking and report writing, Charlie Wang told me that they would have to consult the provincial capital, Xi'an. Meanwhile, I could return to the comforts of the seismic camp to await their conclusions next morning—without my passport. Keeping up my optimistic front, I requested an officer to write a contribution in my diary. Surprisingly, one of them obliged. I expected a scolding and was nonplussed when it turned out to be a tribute:

> Dear English Friend,
>
> How are you? You came here for the first time, financing your own travels. The weather is difficult for such a journey—but with your iron will and confidence you are bound to complete the entire route. I hope you reach that destination successfully. Welcome you here once again. Goodbye!
>
> *Ji Wen Qiang, Dingbian Gong An Ju, 5/14/87*

In the evening as the men drifted back to camp from field surveys, all, with the exception of Steve Wetstein, seemed too tired, disillusioned or depressed to be concerned with an adventurer's problems. Their manner to the Chinese was patronizing. They were out here in the desert for the money and just counted the days to their next leave in Bangkok or Bali.

To be psychologically well prepared for the ruling of the Gong An Ju would be advantageous, so in the comfort and solitude of my shack I contemplated the likely outcome of the directive from Xi'an. The worst punishment would be the implementation of Article 30:

> *The Ministry of Public Security may order serious offenders as listed in Article 29 of the present law to leave the country within a time limit, or to expel them.*

Faced with that catastrophe, my only hope would be in getting the foreign media to support my cause. A combination of lesser punishments was possible: fines, detention, confiscation of film and written records, and transport back to the last approved city from which I had come. I could only hope for something from the latter penal category. Whatever their decision, given an inch-wide gap, I would do my utmost to wriggle through.

* * *

Steve Wetstein drove Charlie Wang and me down to the Gong An Ju headquarters after breakfast. It was a miserable day, fit for a funeral. The sky was dull brown with dust. We followed a big truck along the pot-holed road to town. The men riding outside stared down at us in the Toyota Prairie Rider. One of them plugged a nostril, then snorted to fire snot that narrowly missed our vehicle. It was the kind of morning when one noticed all the nasty and disgusting habits of the Chinese.

On the headquarters exercise ground there were about thirty men and women moving halfheartedly to vigorous strains of music. The semiuniformed officers reluctantly flung a leg here and there, and stretched an arm this way or that way. I had seen more life and expression from octogenarians exercising in Beijing.

The anxiously awaited moment arrived. Initially, my expectations were falsely lifted by Charlie Wang's staggered translation.

"The Shaanxi government of Xi'an wish for you to continue on your journey"—he paused, my hopes soared—"but only if the People's Liberation Army would agree, too." My heart sank. "It's bad news for you that they did not agree. You will be punished in three ways," he continued. "One—you cannot continue; two—you will have to return to an open place, Yinchuan city, if you want to stay in China; and three, you must pay a fine of one hundred yuan. When you pay the money, we will put you on a bus to Yinchuan in Ningxia. You can travel to Beijing easily from there. Now give the officer the money and he will return your passport."

I delved into my bag and pulled out a wad of renminbi, counting out the necessary sum on the table.

"Okay. This is your receipt of paying. Sign here. Your passport—check it, please." It was in order.

Around the corner from the headquarters, Charlie Wang inspected the row of ramshackle minibuses. "This one, Yinchuan six kuai," he beckoned. I was the first passenger and clambered inside to occupy a seat in the rear corner. Charlie Wang and an accompanying young officer stood waiting for the bus to depart. The storm intensified. Visibility was down to tens of yards, and I could hear the sand grains singing abrasively against the metal body of the bus. A few peasants pressed their faces against the window to gaze in at me. One by one, other passengers arrived, haggling with the conductor for a cheaper price on their voluminous baggage. This was my funeral. Outside stood the murderers, Wang and a representative of the Gong An Ju, and the mourners—envoys of peasants who had welcomed me. Just as my whole odyssey was about to be condensed into a minute's recollections before burial, I was interrupted by a rapping on the window. Sliding it open, a blast of grit blinded me. "Shut it, aye-ah," cried the surrounding passengers. Wang and his escort had knocked to tell me they could no longer see. "We're going back—I'm sorry but good luck!" and off they ran, disappearing within a few strides.

"*Hao le! Hao le! Zouba Zouba—a!*" (All right, all right—we're going!) yelled the conductor. The engine fired. Standing up I heaved my rucksack from beneath a peasant's seat and yelled, "Stop, okay, stop!" Treading upon bags, baskets, bedrolls and boots I lurched to the door, slid it open and jumped out into the sand-charged air. The swirling dust and grit was horrific. As the few people remaining outside charged blindly for cover, I dug inside my rucksack, relying entirely on feel (as my eyes were tightly closed) to pull out my goggles. They had given me the inch that I needed—and underestimated my determination—by a God-given few seconds.

◖◖ 10 ◗◗

Three Border Towns

Often in the rainbow wandering in af-
ter the rain I seek the shadow of the
Great Wall, proud and comforting.
—*Yang Lian, "The Burden"*

Under a blotched amber sky outlines became mirages, shrouded by
the sandy cloak of swirling dust. Billowing parched air, laden with dust,
scattered debris—sagebrush and tin cans—underfoot. An improvised
orchestral melange—rattling shutters, slamming doors and flapping
canopies—played against the continuo of sand hissing on roofs and shop
fronts. Bazaar stalls were left bare, their proprietors fled; the whole place
was depopulated of townsfolk, robbed of sight and choked of breath by
the passage of this suffocating cloud.

A life support system was necessary to venture outside. Like a true
alien now, weirdly equipped with goggles and mask, able to survive the
intoxification that the native population could not, I cautiously plodded
out of town. How I relished this storm. Of the hundreds of thousands of
footsteps along the Wall—across desert, plateau, mountain and valley—
that single step off the bus was, together with the first step, the most
significant, my symbolic gesture of perseverance when presented with
the slightest of opportunities, one determined step ahead of my opponents. It was a vote of confidence in the distance covered and an act of
faith on that which remained.

My plan was to lie low in the seismic camp until the storm abated. The encampment of aluminum shacks looked even more like visiting spacecraft in the eerie light. I made my presence discreetly known and was given a room.

Diary, May 15th: Dingbian

At midday a glimpse outside tells me the sky is filled with dust despite the brighter orange-brown glow. Later on it began to rain mud drops, which dampen the dust down for a clearer evening. The crew returns early, and after I tell Steve Wetstein the plan, he gives me an OS-standard map—showing every farmhouse beyond Jingbian. . . .

When my wristwatch alarm bleeped at 2:45 a.m., I leaped up and fumbled to silence it. Dressing by torchlight for this "graveyard shift," I had no difficulty in focusing thoughts on the task in hand. This was my last night in Shaanxi.

The sky was crystal clear, its stars twinkled more brightly than I had ever known, and the moon was full: high, big and brilliant, the perfect heavenly torch for a march by night. Stumbling across an open field, I reached a tree-lined track that led east to the Great Wall. Its silhouette against the moonlit sky was not difficult to follow. Dogs barked unseen. It was about four o'clock in the morning. I was in heartland China with the moonlit Great Wall at my side. My spirits soared. I was determined to capitalize fully on the opposition underestimating my capabilities. I recalled how underestimation had played a critical part in deciding the direction of the Chinese Revolution. During the Long March, the Nationalists had underestimated the marching pace and ability of the Reds. The Reds reached a crossing point on the strategic Golden Sands River (the upper reaches of the Yangzi River), plugged the holes of a scuttled boat and ferried across to catch the Nationalist guards with their pants down—stoned on opium and playing mahjong.

As I progressed slowly due east, the sky began to lighten before a pink halo edged above the hilly horizon, a color which was soon flushed throughout the whole eastern sky by the emergence of the giant red disc of the sun. Within ten minutes, the sun was golden and the sky azure, a light so clear it was difficult to believe that just a day before this peaceful and serene landscape was swept by a vortex of sand. On a hillside above the hamlet of San Lou Tan I stopped to have my packed breakfast—jam butties and *Jian li bao,* an electrolyte health drink produced by the Guangdong Sports Science Institute and the official drink of the Chinese Olympic Team. The ingredients were a blend of mineral water, pure orange, honey and ginseng—a tasty mixture that I had found particularly effective for ridding dust from the mouth during my stay at the seismic camp. As I looked back toward the west, my nighttime passage was now revealed in bright sunshine, and from this vantage point I could use the 1:50,000 scale map to examine the landscape. This arable belt was clearly defined and perhaps four to five miles across. To the north was a yellow sand sea; to the south was the gullied fringe of the elevated loess tableland. Breaks in the Great Wall larger than 300 feet were indicated on the map, and individual farms were identified with family names. There was the Qi Jia (Together Home), the Chang Jia (Often Home) and the Li Jia (the Li family Home). Many of the hamlets were marked as being communes by the suffix *gong she.* The land around them was subdivided into grids of one square kilometer labelled with team names and numbers: "the Dong Guan Yi Dui" (the East Pass Team No. 1). And for the very first time I could give my location as a six-figure map reference.

Many of the towns in this region include the character *bian,* which means border, referring to their location behind the Great Wall, historical frontier of the Empire. Additional security was provided by the construction of town walls (as at Yanchi and Dingbian), while hopes for a life without conflict are reflected in the prefixes to *bian—Ding, An,* and *Jing* mean stable, peaceful and calm respectively. At Xi Bei Wan I left the Wall to enter Anbian, "stable border," nestled in the bend where the Great Wall changes direction from east to south. Part of the village's main street was still cobbled blocks that had perhaps a couple of centuries ago been trodden upon by Qing peasants. This feudal scene was further enhanced by the smoky atmosphere from streetside food vendors, the clatter of horse and donkey hooves and the main-street prominence of the farrier. But there were red stars and Hags on the buildings and the people crowding me were clothed in tunics. This was Republican China, where I was a rare independent foreign visitor and the people were too wonderful to bypass. The sight of my camera with its large lens barrel had the children hiding behind one another, peering out with their peeping eyes, half-expecting a photograph to appear immediately. I stood there for a few minutes playing photographic games with the crowd. But the thought that there was bound to be a Gong An Ju officer enjoying the show was a reminder to move on. Like the Pied Piper of Anbian, I jogged away, with thirty or more children running beside me, hopping and skipping with delight. The Great Wall now embarked upon a southeast loop towards Bai Yu Shan across a desolate gully-infested tableland. Having been warned off it by Li Dong, I would now follow a section of sealed road towards the third border town, Jingbian, and perhaps relocate the Wall above the valleys of Yellow River tributaries.

By midday the sun dealt out the hottest conditions yet encountered. My feet were burning and legs yearning to stop, for they had already done a day's work. After a jar of apricots, I walked and was glad of any onlookers that I attracted. In particular there were three middle-school girls—it was Saturday, and a half day for schools. One of them distinguished herself as the only representative of the nation's secondary education to attempt to use her knowledge of English seriously—although her questioning did help me cover a few more miles without worrying about the heat. Approaching Hao Tan commune, we caught the sound of a distant fracas. Gradually, the nature of the sound became distinguishable: the frenzied unison of drum and cymbals, the ring of bells and shrill voices. That made the event unmistakable—it was my lucky day—the Beijing Opera had come to town.

Here was a kaleidoscope of color beyond belief within a dusty desert place, as refreshingly different as discovering Van Gogh's "Sunflowers" amongst the murky Manchester factories and figures of Lowry. A sword is brandished above a trailing satin sleeve, the fiery orange of dancing flames. Yellow silk of Sun and Earth is the Emperor's color, embroidered with a red-tongued golden dragon. Moods swiftly change as these vivid silken robes shimmer in the hot caressing breeze, or are suddenly enlivened by the dramatic overtures of a white-bearded man toward a timid young maiden. The musicians, accommodated at the side of the cast-concrete stage, produce a mixture of melody and sound effects to fit the action, emotion and body language. The conflict of a sword fight is created by rapid and voluminous thrashing of drum and cymbal; remorse and contemplation by the sad drone of the two-stringed *er hu*;

gaiety by the birdlike chatter of the *dizi* bamboo flute; and tranquillity by the subtle plucking of the moon guitar. Exits are made to a flurried finale of everything that the orchestra can muster.

Backstage is the open-air dressing, makeup and green room rolled into one. The trunks of this travelling troupe lie open, overflowing with the finest embroidered silks. Masks, beards, bald heads and headdresses lie strewn in apparent confusion. Oblivious to the crowd of peasants, a young girl makes up as the Empress. She picks up color from a tiny paint-box, guiding herself with the use of a palm-sized mirror. She pales her oriental complexion to eggshell smoothness. Her slender tapering eyes are accentuated. She pouts her lips to paint on their apex a slim scarlet rosebud, and rouges her cheeks to the subtle tint of a ripening apple. Only then does this girl allow her face to be dimpled by a smile of majestic beauty. Crowned with a headdress of red silk and silver she enters the stage, followed by ladies of the court to a deafening fanfare.

The manager of the troup, Zhang Shu Lin, wanted me to stay until the end of the performance, but I had already spotted the Gong An Ju seated amongst the commune dignitaries. The last thing I wanted would be to interrupt his enjoyment of the opera—for that reason I had to leave. However, I assured Zhang Shu Lin, by gesturing with impeccable "Give Us A Clue"-style miming, that I would be posting my camera's contents to him at The Traditional Opera School, Xin Zhuang Village, Chun Rong Township, Ning County, Gansu Province.

Diary, May 16th: east of Hao Tan "Gong She"

Strains of the opera took a good fifteen minutes to fade away, being carried downwind (along with a great deal of sand) in my direction. That indicated how slowly I was now shuffling. My legs are so incredibly stiff. At four o'clock I entered a work yard stacked high with logs and planks and was instantly well received by a couple of men who gave me water, a wash basin and one of the little "terraced" rooms.

Feng Jin Hai, the eldest of the four residents here, was prompted into demonstrating his calligraphic skills by the interest I had shown in a textbook of character styles. The procedure for this art form was conducted, like so many Chinese customs, according to the teaching of the great philosopher Confucius. His guidelines for keeping the "four treasures of the studio" necessary for good writing in fine order were impressively adhered to, for the condition of the materials reflected the state of mind. Feng proudly produced his equipment from the safety of a padlocked cupboard. The ornately carved ink slab was wrapped neatly in paper, the ink stone rested snugly in a box, and the hairs of his brushes were protected by newspaper cylinders tied with thread. His young comrade assumed the role of student by preparing the ink. The ink stone is ground on the wetted slab in a circular motion, mixing the ink with the spot of water in the well of the slab to achieve a good consistency. While his student toiled, Feng removed his cap and jacket and prepared the paper. Symmetrical folding acts as a guide for the spacing of each character. Feng was satisfied when the ink had become thick and consistent, and the sound of the grinding had become smooth. We all gathered around as he dabbed his brush gently but firmly in the well of the slab. Holding the loaded brush in his fingers perpendicular to the paper, he made deliberate and precise strokes of direction and pressure. Some were tapered, others wide or hooked, straight and curved. There were eight characters in all. He placed his brush on the table and in the absence of a chop seal, signed the work with his name and address. It read "English friend travelling the Great Wall," Feng Jin Hai, Hao Tan Forest Farm, Dingbian County, Shaanxi. His stunning scholastic art, produced in such simple surroundings from basic materials, was a testament to the discipline imposed by the written character. They were so much more than the transcribed words. Translation could not express it. Each character possessed feeling, personality, depth and history. Now, whenever I see Chinese calligraphy, I shall always visualize the brush strokes of the Master Feng captivating the devoted attention of his student and admirers.

It was rare to eat anything so late, but the young and cheerful wife of one of the men had a large basket of eggs and started to poach some. We all ate a large quantity—I ceased at a very contented figure of nine, finishing off with a bowl of the salty soup in which they had been boiled.

Diary, May 17th: Hao Tan to Jingbian

The late supper induced a much-needed deep sleep. A later start today saw me continue along the road between the sand and the loess, but the continued hot spell and constant dehydration to match prevented me from reaching Jingbian by nightfall. I'm just outside the town at a team lodging—five people in their twenties. Two girls spend all their time making up, fixing long hair and painting nails that appear to be a great tease and frustration to the three boys there. They seem like helpless unguided children. There's nothing in the larder apart from eggs—so I have a very big omelette which ends up covering half the area of a large wok. I have eaten over twenty eggs in as many hours.

The prospect of a hot water breakfast meant there was no point in hanging about. I was up and away so early that the gates of the unit were still padlocked. The seven miles into the sunrise of Jingbian were largely downhill into a valley holding a Yellow River tributary. It took an hour to reach "Calm Border" with legs noticeably starved of carbohydrates. That deficiency was corrected by wolfing down *you tiao*, rice, and *mantou*, topped by a jar of apricots, though the sight of two armed soldiers on leaving town did nothing to aid my digestion, resurrecting the worries of bubonic plague. Out in the country that uneasiness soon waned when accurate map reading brought me to a loop of the Great Wall heading north toward Hengshan. It was, however, an all too brief reunion, as the Wall soon became broken and untraceable. The valley was an altered landscape. Gone too was the luxury of a 1:50,000 scale map. Now I was left to negotiate Shaanxi with a much less detailed piece of cartography—my familiar 1:1.6 million sheet which had successfully guided me through Gansu and Ningxia.

The track, surfaced with sharp limestone chippings, rode high above a precipitous gorge. Using my camera lens as a telescope, I peered cautiously over the edge of the chasm to focus on slabs of crystalline bedrock washed by the white waters of the Lu He. This bedrock was the solid foundation to a soft surface landscape some 425 feet above, a landscape that was so easily washed by desert downpours into gullies and so conveniently sculptured by man. Farther down in the valley, which widens out to hold a lake, the people of the loess lands tunnel their homes into the hillside to be safe from floodwaters and escape the heat of summer. I took a steep and crumbly path that zigzagged to one such *yao dong* and found an old man sitting at the archway entrance to his cave dwelling. We entered the cool dark home illuminated only by the light filtering through trellised wood windows backed with newspaper (used commonly before the availability of glass). The temperature within these chambers was markedly cooler than outside, enough, in fact, to chill me in my damp sweaty vest. We returned to the sunshine of the threshold to drink our tea. I had disturbed the man as he polished a long-barreled rifle. Admiring the filigree work upon its shoulder butt provided an excuse to feel the weight and balance of the weapon. Lifting the antique firearm to aim, I wondered what skirmishes this defender of Shaanxi had experienced.

The green-blue water of the lake was the home of two large birds. From a slow and labored flight they splash-landed upon the water. Stationary, they appeared larger than a man. I named these birds (without any ornithological expertise) giant cranes—for they were gargantuan, grey and aquatic. What puzzled me more was their survival. A single easy shot would provide a season's larder of good meat. And their feathers would doubtless fill a coat or two. The only reason to account for their preservation was their probable status as birds of good omen in the superstitious eyes of the Chinese.

The river resumed its course from the dammed lake through a valley wide enough to be farmed. For so much of my journey the people had merely survived around a ground well—static water. What life the flowing water nurtured here. The emerald green leaves of the *dao zi* peeped through the glassy surface of the paddy field. Under fierce sun I climbed the track up the valley side and plunged down again to the river's edge, through a level of *yao dongs*. Then there was plenty of company from peasants engaged in start-of-season work in the fields: building mud pathways between paddies, thinning out and planting *dao zi* from nursery beds, working knee deep (or worse for children) in the mud. I experienced a most suspicious and timid reception, especially from the women and children. News of an approaching "big nose" was soon spread by small gangs of urchins, terrified of me at close quarters even to the extent of removing their shoes to facilitate escape across the marshy ground at the side of the track. But from their preserved and safe distance they continued to shadow my progress for several miles.

I began to wonder if I would find a night's lodging but was cheered by the sight of what I took to be a small commune. It proved to be a home for the mentally and physically disabled. Driven out of the cookhouse to begin with, I found the leader, Hu Jun Shan, a calm man of fifty who saw I was fed. His room was well stocked with books. A photographic collage and some local maps adorned the walls. The photographs, a common sight in the Chinese home of whatever standard, were a collection of snaps from studios and peddlers who traded their skills at all of the country's scenic spots. Mr. Hu was pictured in Beijing, Xi'an, the capital of his province, in the army with his comrades, with his wife, sons, and grandchildren. Every significant and memorable event in his life was souvenired within the frame. It made me consider what a memento the photograph was, and how I wished my equipment allowance could have accommodated an instant camera, capable of delivering a print into the hands of my host.

> We, representing the people in the welfare home, warmly welcome our friend Comrade Will who contributes to the development of friendship between China and England.
>
> *President, Hu Jun Shan Caretaker, Guo Huai Jun*
> *Hengshan County Welfare Home,*
> *Shaanxi Province, 5/18/87*

The morning light was quite exquisite, reflecting off the rectangular paddy fields. Some advanced plots were vivid green, others were completely still mirrors awaiting plants, and those in between showed a faint green tint of sprouting. Peasants, antlike from the height of the track, made their way toward their current plot of work over the strands of mud.

At the head of the valley towered a pagoda, tapering skywards. Primarily of religious significance, it was ideally placed to command a clear view of the valley and, in such close proximity to the line of the Great Wall, would undoubtedly have been utilized for observation. So it was ironic that my own enemy should have crept up on me as I approached it. Two Gong An Ju officers passed me on an old motorcycle. I would soon be climbing out of the valley to cross a short stretch of tableland to Yulin. Perhaps they would ignore me. But around a corner I spotted the motorcycle parked. The officers proffered their red identity cards and demanded my passport. There was little point in refusing their request. Surprisingly, they returned it and I walked off. But the encounter had not finished. The motorcycle passed with only one officer; his comrade was tracking me. And just five minutes down the track there was a most unwelcome roadside reception. There was no escape back or front.

PART THREE

Forbidden

The three armies can be deprived of
their commanding officer but even a
common man cannot be deprived of
his purpose.

— *Confucius,*
The Analects

From the top, sentence of punishment stamp, Yulin County PSB; YellowRiver bridge-crossing stamp at Lamawan; postmark of Togtoh, Inner Mongolia; safely into Hebei Province.

11

Criticism

Criticize yourself—write more!
—*Zhou Ji Bin,*
Foreign Affairs interpreter in Yulin

Toddlers are often seen wearing a mock uniform of the Public Security Bureau, gold braid, red stars and metal buttons added to the universal green suit. That was the reason, I concluded, why the urchins outside this Gong An Ju office had no fear of the genuine uniforms of my arresting officers. Despite several admonitions, their retreat from the curtained window and bolted door was only temporary. Within seconds, the clamor and heaving commotion resumed. Eyeballs appeared at every nook and cranny. All openings were exploited, even the inch-wide gaps between the planks of the wooden door. As they competed for the cracks and keyhole, I could hear their deep breathing and snorting, their bubbling unwiped noses, and the commentaries from these "peeping Wangs" to the small boys behind. Our arrival called for a winding up of the telephone to get a line to the county town, Yulin. "*Wei. . . . Wei? Wei! . . . Yulin ma? Wo shi Heng Shan Gong An Ju. . . . Wai guo ren—Ying guo. . . . 041400B.*" The volume necessary to conduct a conversation on a Chinese telephone gave the eavesdropping urchins a continuing share in the proceedings. From my own piecemeal translation I knew that my nationality and passport number had been relayed to Yulin Gong An Ju, where

I would be taken for questioning. Now, sitting facing the two officers behind a locked door, I mustered a philosophical appraisal of my achievement to date. Considering I had run all the way from Jiayuguan, I could have no grounds for disappointment. Already I had accepted that this was the finish of the spring stage—and could only hope and pray that I would have the opportunity to resume the run in the autumn as planned.

At the risk of being regarded as insane, I decided to do something about the eavesdropping mob outside. I stealthily moved to the door. Inhaling the deepest of breaths I unleashed an unreserved roar with all the aggression of a martial arts strike, "GRRRggHhh!!! GRRRggHhh!!!!"

The eyeballs disappeared—and the deathly silence induced was only broken by the roars of laughter from my captors.

It was not until a car arrived, when we emerged from the shade of the room into dazzling sunlight, that I was to comprehend the drawing power of a "foreign spy" drama. There were two hundred or more villagers outside. The Shanghai-built "Hong Qi" (Red Flag) was a shining black piece of Soviet-inspired engineering from the 1960s. As a path through the crowd was forged, an angular bodywork trimmed with chrome fittings and reminiscent of the Ford Zephyr was revealed. Sandwiched between the two officers, I sank down into the soft leather upholstery, hidden from the glare of the throng by lace curtains. The driver jumped in, pulled on his white cotton gloves, fired the engine and, engaging gears with the stick on the steering column, drove quickly away.

When the Red Flag car has the red pennant flying, everything must yield to its passage. This car had no such pennant, yet the approach of these cadre class wheels cleared the road. We sped along in a trail of dust to Hengshan. A personnel change was carried out at the headquarters there, to be followed by a stop at a house in the town. It seemed that the leading Gong An Ju officer of Hengshan did not want his family to miss out on a chauffeur-driven luxury car trip to Yulin, nor the chance of seeing a rare animal in this part of the world. "*Ying guo ren,*" he pointed out to his wife and mother as they climbed aboard. First, I was a community service entertainer to a crowd of peasants. Now, I was the excuse for a family joyride.

It was ironic that ever since crossing the Yellow River some weeks before, the city of Yulin, in the middle of north Shaanxi, had been my oft-contemplated terminus for stage one of the journey. To be apprehended on its threshold was particularly aggravating—even though the shortfall was only eighteen miles. We arrived at a complex of buildings that formed the Gong An Ju *danwei*, a complete unit of working and residential blocks for the officers and their families, present and past.

All hopes of duping my interrogators evaporated the moment I entered the room. I was immediately drawn into eye contact with Gao Qingwen from the Dingbian Gong An Ju.

But first a young man, dressed in a Western-style shirt and jacket, sprang up from his seat. "Sit down, please," he ordered loudly.

Attempting to exhibit a good attitude from the start, I complimented him on his courteous English.

"That man is our Foreign Affairs leader in Yulin County." I looked towards the tall, thin, elderly man dressed in a high-collared jacket. "And I think you know this man. Is it true?"

"Yes, I know him."

"He told you to go to Yinchuan by bus! But you didn't go! Did you? Again—two times you've broken our law!"

He picked up a booklet—the bilingual law book concerned with the exit and entry of aliens—and shook it repeatedly.

"You know this, it's true?"

"Yes, I know it."

"But you don't keep our law, do you?" I remained silent. "What can you say for your crimes?"

"Only the Gong An Ju think they're crimes. The common people of China—peasants, miners, quarrymen, teachers, even county leaders—welcome me."

He only answered back when he had translated my beliefs to the other man.

"The Ministry of Public Security make the law to protect the people from the foreigner!"

"But I'm a friend of the Chinese." He ignored the comment.

"Bring your bag here—empty it on the table."

All the men, and a woman secretary taking notes, gathered around.

"What's this?" he said, prodding my sleeping bag. I opened it out. He held a bottle of tablets up to the light. "These are medicines, are they?"

"Put these clothes, this bed bag . . . and these water bottles back in the bag." The leader picked up the films. "Where's the other notebook?" he asked, holding the completed diary which recorded my journey up until Yanchi. "The book the policeman of Dingbian wrote something in."

"It's here." They chuckled as I delved into the front of my shorts, then ordered me to sit down again.

"The Shaanxi government in Xi'an city will decide what to do with you . . . We will examine your things—it's in our law. You've been very foolish."

The woman placed a pen and wad of paper on the table beside me.

"Now, you will write an article to criticize your crimes—you are a bad influence from the outside world coming to unopen places again and again."

Under these orders I proceeded to write a brief account, certainly less than a hundred words in length, about my fascination for China. Meanwhile, they chatted and smoked. Presenting my "self-criticism" to the interpreter, he translated it for his leader. Walking over towards me he shook the paper as he had done the law book.

"This isn't enough! Criticize yourself—write more! Look, those books of yours are full—so write more—and then we can proceed!"

Bearing in mind that they held my films and diaries, I deemed it wise to produce a more lengthy piece of writing, something that "would be good enough for now" according to the interpreter. Then I was ushered outside with my bag into the back of a green jeep.

My destination was a mystery until the interpreter announced, "Yulin hotel is open to the foreigner" as we drove into a forecourt. But walking to my room he warned, "Yulin is unopen, so you cannot leave your room—don't do anything else foolish."

Left alone in the room I felt mentally deflated. Sprawled out on the bed, I lay still, trying to predict what punishments would be meted out for this second offense in Shaanxi. For the first time ever I could not go outside and for that reason I yearned to. As I watched cyclists streaming along the street, I felt imprisoned—for how long I knew not. My gloom intensified at the thought of never seeing the records of my journey again. Those diaries were personal and private. But in China individual privacy does not exist. I remembered how their law provided for the confiscation of any materials which "endangered national security." And, for the first time since starting the run, my spirit, heart and mind were depressed. Turning to that "hymn" of retrospect I murmured, "Yesterday . . . all my troubles seemed so far away, now it seems . . . " There was a tap at the door. *"Chi fan,"* said the waitress. It was time for dinner.

The trouser-suited girl marched ahead of me to the dining room. I was served plenty of good food, a variety of which I had not seen since the day I left Beijing. Through the frosted windows of the room the blurred and distorted heads of inquisitive peasants could be seen. *"Wai guo ren kan yi kan!"* (Look, a foreigner!) they called—until a waitress cleared them off with a blast of abuse.

At first I lay splayed out on my bed, contemplating a wornout pair of shoes and feeling every bit as spent myself. I only got up to look out of the window when I heard a passing jeep that could be the Gong An Ju coming to tell me my fate. Then I borrowed a pen from the waitress and the room's calendar became my diary. On the third morning I was encouraged by a visit from the Foreign Affairs interpreter, Zhou Ji Bin.

"Mr. William," he said apologetically, "it is unfortunate that your great journey has been stopped; your strong spirit is something we can all learn from."

This was not the first personal tribute I had received from someone whose official duty was to speak in another voice and his words were a great boost. I was recovering. No wonder my shoes were dishevelled, they had carried me 944 miles! I recalled the words of my family mentors at home. "Go to China," they had said, "and find out what you can do." And later, "Six hundred miles would be a success." To my knowledge, I had already achieved the longest recorded journey by a foreigner on foot and alone in China . A good reason to keep fit for the autumn stage of the run, for with a background of 944 hardwon miles, I now possessed a hardness of mind that I felt sure would spur me on to my destiny. Opening my room door, I began to exercise by stretching and running on the spot. Going down for meals, I looked happy. When peasants gazed through the frosted glass, I got up to say *"Ni hao,"* and to the chagrin of the manager, I chatted to the waitresses to get them giggling. It all helped me to believe in myself again.

Diary, May 22nd: fourth day in Yulin

After breakfast (plenty of eggs, *mantou,* steamed bread with dates), I continue with my optimistic outlook by putting time to good use in writing an article about the first half of my journey—perhaps for the *China Daily?!* It's very hot outside—still. At 3:00 p.m. I'm having *xiu xi* and there's a knock at the door. It's the interpreter. Back to official tones though: "Come with me to see our leader." We drive by jeep in silence to the headquarters.

"Now we will tell you the result," said Mr. Zhou, as he picked up the familiar law booklet. "By coming to an unopen place you've broken our law—these laws—not once . . . again and again!" He continued with the well-prepared offensive. "My comrade fined you one hundred yuan in Dingbian—that's an expensive amount—but not enough to stop!" Neither would a million be enough, I considered. "Our government in Shaanxi has decided harder punishments to stop you—you cannot continue along the Great Wall. We know you are not a spy—but you have to stop . . . you will be fined 150 yuan this time . . . we will keep all your films—taking pictures in unopen places is not allowed." That blow was half-expected, but it was not the finish. "Finally, you will not enter an unopen place again—because we order you to leave our country within seven days of release from your detention." A killer blow!

"You can ask our leader questions if you wish."

"My films—only one of them is of Shaanxi. All I've photographed is the Great Wall, a Beijing opera and peasants working in the fields."

He relayed the question but answered, "You've been through so much unopen territory in China—Gansu, Ningxia, Nei Mongol, that we have to keep all—every one of your films."

To add insult to injury I learnt I had been detained at my own expense of sixty yuan a day. China is a country where the prisoner pays in time and money. I would need to telegraph the Midland Bank in Beijing for the cash.

In the more approachable surroundings of my hotel room, I questioned Mr. Zhou about the order to leave China within seven days. It was not deportation, he confirmed, "just a cancellation of your visa." He asked me about my plans.

"Go to Beijing—then home to England," I muttered sorrowfully.

"You can leave your room now and go outside into the hotel grounds—but please, Mr. William, don't go through the gates."

Already my overall strategy had been formulated. In Hong Kong I would attempt to get another visa, "clean up" my passport, even assume a false identity if necessary. I was in a vigorous fighting mood. Now I could hardly wait to receive my money, leave China and proceed about the required business to effect my return.

The treat of these days was the knock at the door by the waitress who escorted me down to eat three times a day. As I went from a state of exhaustion and undernourishment to one of rest and overnourishment, the sight of this cute little waitress clattering her high heels and waggling her backside was quite some pleasure.

On my final day in Yulin I spent the morning considering possible methods of getting my films returned. Writing a classic of kowtow and self-criticism was my only hope of bringing about a moderation of their rigid enforcement of the "Xi'an directive":

> To the Foreign Affairs leader of the Shaanxi government in Xian:
>
> Dear Comrade,
> I wish to apologize for the inconvenience that I have caused in entering an area closed to foreigners. Only now have I had time to realize how foolish I have been. As you know, it is my dream to make a journey on foot along your Great Wall, one of the wonders of the world. Relations between China and England are now good. Our countries have come to peaceful agreements over Hong Kong, and last year Queen Elizabeth came to China. We are friends and allies. I plead with you to allow me to take home the confiscated films. In that way I can show the people of my homeland photographs of your Great Wall and of the friendly people living close to it. My family and friends will be so disappointed if I have no photographs to show them.
>
> *William Lindesay*

The Beijing jeep arrived to take me to the headquarters for the last time to receive my belongings, which were laid out neatly on the table. I checked the camera and flicked through the two notebooks.

"We know that page seventy-three, where our Dingbian comrade wrote some things, has gone."

They missed nothing. I had removed it for security purposes. I handed the leader my letter, which the interpreter translated.

"He will telephone Xi'an now," declared Zhou Ji Bin.

The call was through all too quickly, for even I knew it was impossible to telephone long distance right away. The answer was going to be no.

Retrieving my passport from a safe, the secretary proceeded to frank a collection of black marks within its pages. My current visa, so generously extended by my good friends in Zhongwei, was replaced with "Bearer must leave China by June 6, 1987." Another stamp declared, "This visa will not be renewed."

.ıı 12 ıı.

Zou Le?[1]

We have friends all over the world.
— *Mao Zedong,*
proclaiming the foundation of the
People's Republic

Dawn is the exodus hour of long-distance buses from Yulin. Shortly before the mass departure, I crouched down on a tiny stool at a curbside snack vendor's. There was only a handful of seats crowded around this restaurant on wheels, which was stacked high with bowls, chopsticks, baskets and sauces. Simmering cauldrons of gruel sat atop oil-drum stoves. The smiles of the efficient woman who attended to my breakfast order, given in my best *Putonghua*, were every bit as warming as the toasting heat trom the makeshift stoves. She scalded me out a bowl with boiling water then ladled *xifan* into it, giving the bamboo chopsticks an extra vigorous wipe upon her rather soiled apron. I appreciated the gesture and proceeded to scoop and slurp the rice porridge down, demonstrating my acceptance by and familiarity with the Chinese people Mr. Zhou was supposed to be protecting from my baneful foreign influence. He and his comrade Mr. Liu frowned and patronizingly warned me about health hazards. Unperturbed, I ordered another ladleful.

---

[1] *Zou le*—I'm off; off I go!

I went from Yulin to Yan'an to Xi'an by bus, and from Xi'an to Beijing by train—each proved to be an overcrowded and uncomfortable ride. For the first stage I was under escort. Inside the bus station there were near-riot conditions at the ticket-office window, a mousehole of an opening, down to which the traveller stooped and strained his neck to yell to the clerk. Out in the yard the waiting throng was choking on the exhaust fumes that clogged the air as the drivers revved up their buses. Even before our Jiefang (Liberation) bus stopped, the stampede for the doors had begun. But those to the front of the crowd had largely wasted their efforts, since they were soon evicted by reserved seatholders.

A rest stop in the town of Suide gave me the chance to warm up, stretch my stiff legs and numbed backside. Hunger got the better of my escorts. We all sat eating *bingzi* at a stall where my friendliness attracted the attention of a dwarf, who seized upon my leg like a child in quest of his pittance. "Foolish boy!" remonstrated Mr. Zhou mildly. It was the first beggar I had seen in all my China travels.

We crossed the muddy Yan He River, which cut through the center of Yan'an, in late afternoon. Out on the misty hillsides above the town I caught glimpses of temple pagodas and pavilions floating upon the low clouds. At street level conditions were less romantic as we hurried to an hotel under dripping plane trees doused by a recent deluge. "A famous place," repeated Zhou Ji Bin. Indeed it was—the Communist capital for thirteen years, the cradle of Chinese Liberation and the stronghold of Mao. Nevertheless, my knowledge would stay restricted to recollections gleaned from Edgar Snow's *Red Star Over China*.

For, although Yan'an was an open place, the brief of my escorts was to see me out of town on the bus to Xi'an. At dinner they preferred to keep their distance, although they accepted an invitation to join me for a drink in my room afterwards. They called to find me looking over a selection of local postcards that provided my only positive memory of "the famous place." When I offered them a card each to write to their loved ones, they surprised me by penning a tribute.

> The spirit that you have shown in inspecting the Great Wall on foot is precious, and we should learn from your courage. It is unfortunate that you cannot finish your journey, but we would welcome you to return to China

in the hope you can pursue your ambition by other means and complete your travels along the Wall.

Your friends Zhou Ji Bin, 5/26/87, Yan'an
Mr. Liu—(signature undecipherable)

In Xi'an, caped cyclists pedalled through a warm downpour along streets that seemed to be almost enclosed by the French plane trees that edged them. Xi'an was another bit of history I would be missing out on. For close to the city is sited the terracotta army of the first Emperor, the original strategist of the Great Wall.

A student who came to the railway station every day to help foreigners and practice his English helped me buy my train ticket to Beijing and twenty hard-seat hours later I was back in the capital, being congratulated on my achievements by my friends in the Midland Bank and catching up on a wonderfully morale-boosting parcel of mail.

Although workers' days off are rotated between different units within the city, Sunday remains the day of leisure in Beijing. Two months before, the people had worn a padded cloak of winter; now the city looked a different place. Joining the pedalling column clad in flapping white shirts, billowing skirts and ribboned sunhats, I cycled into the city. From the small post office facility within the Beijing Hotel I telephoned home with news of my success. From these conversations I decided that my strategy before leaving for Hong Kong would involve feeding the success story (minus the skirmishes) to the correspondents based in the city. It would be a busy time—I had five days remaining in the People's Republic.

My weight was the lowest I had ever known it, just 147 pounds, and the whiteness of my fingernails suggested a calcium deficiency. These problems would be resolved over the coming weeks; meanwhile, I would begin my fitness program in the cool of the evening.

On the steps outside the hotel, spotlighted in the final warming rays of the evening sunshine, stood a young girl of such graceful posture and elegance that it was impossible for me not to look at her. I crouched down to fumble with the laces of my trainers and looked across: dainty feet, bare, shapely legs, a pencil waistline, black shining hair, clipped above her ears and cascading down her straight back, she seemed to me the perfect definition of oriental beauty! "Can you speak English?"

"Of course—I am English!" I managed to utter, still captivated.

In words that melted my heart, "What you do in China?"

I stuttered in my trance, "I'm . . . er . . . I am going to write about my journey along the Great Wall—that I'll finish in September."

"A book?" she asked. "What is it called?"

A title . . . A title . . . "*From the Desert to the Sea*—perhaps!" We laughed.

"Glad to meet you and welcome you stay China—my name Wu Qi."

"*Ni hao*, Wu Qi! I'm William."

"Oh, your Chinese good! Any more words?"

"Important ones . . . like . . . rice, egg. I'm hungry!"

She giggled girlishly, shielding her laughs with clasped hands. "This my taxi—I eat dinner with my company friends, Japanese Securities." Like a butterfly she skipped down the steps, her long hair flowing and green silk dress billowing. She was driven away. I had been struck with love at first sight. I could never forget Miss Wu Qi—she would always be Miss China to me.

* * *

As an act of confidence that somehow I would return to China, I left most of my baggage in the Midland Bank. The young secretary, Stephanie, escorted me to the taxi and asked the same question I was thinking. "When will you return?"

The Guangzhou train sliced through the heart of China, stopping infrequently on its 1,400-mile race south in just thirty-six hours. As we crossed the Yangzi River on the mighty bridge at Wuhan, "one of China's three furnaces," the temperature and humidity rose with every hour; it became wetter, the landscape greener and the people in the fields, on roads and in the stations wore fewer clothes. Even the style of straw hats changed, in shape, color and materials.

When I emerged into the humid atmosphere of Guangzhou on Friday, June 6 at eight o'clock, I had just sixteen hours left. Thankfully, it looked like I could meet that deadline: I procured the last available seat on the express train to Kowloon at eleven o'clock.

Like Beijing, Guangzhou (better known to foreigners as Canton) is now one of the country's most affluent cities and has a long history of international trade. It retains something of that foreign atmosphere—

there are plenty of Hong Kong and Macau businessmen here, and foreign advertisements around the station square, where China's home brand Seagull watches have to compete with Seiko and Sony.

The border development of Shenzhen shares this affluence, for it is designated a "Special Economic Zone" where conditions for international trade are made attractive by a reduced burden of red tape. Here, where Deng Xiaoping's per capita income targets for the year 2000 are already achieved by the workers of Shenzhen, the open-door policy is already well established. But the "go to Shenzhen, young man" spirit is selectively controlled by fencing off and is only accessible to those Chinese possessing the internal equivalent of the "Alien's Travel Permit."

Just miles ahead, "Xiang Gang" is still almost a decade out of reach. Until 1997 it is Hong Kong—and despite the high-rise architecture outside the train window, Shenzhen still manages to project the readily recognizable constitution of the People's Republic. This familiar constitution soon vanished as we edged through sidings where green antiquated rolling stock sat dormant, and passed the platform adorned with the words of Mao spoken as he proclaimed the existence of the PRC on October 1, 1949: "We have friends all over the world." Within a hundred yards the green and gold of the Gong An Ju was replaced by the royal blue and chrome of the Royal Hong Kong Police. The bare concrete of Shenzhen *Zhan* had become the bright blown plastic of Lo Wu station, and Mao's proud boast in Tiananmen Square had given way to advertising billboards, bombarding the people with the slogans of a Hong Kong dollar-fuelled philosophy. These two systems were separated by a modern Great Wall—a double defense of high barbed-wire fences patrolled by Alsatian dogs and British Army Gurkhas.

13

Friendships
and Strategies

> Is it not a pleasure to have friends come
> from afar?
>
> —*Confucius*,
> **The Analects**

They say you can buy anything in Hong Kong. Within six hours I had collected a new three-month visa for China. Now the pressure was off—temporarily. I was on my way back and intended to use my Beijing summer as constructively as possible.

As a temporary Beijinger, I rose early to exercise in the cool comfort of dawn. Longtan Park with its trails winding around the Dragon Pool was a training paradise for relaxing a mind and body wracked by the pressure of recent months. I delighted in the lapping of water on the lakeside path, the orange sunlight reflecting overhanging willows, the scent of the cypresses and cool shadow of the rockeries. At every glance, weird and wonderful sports were taking place: cloaked martial arts students grappled to throw their opponents; cries came from the strikes of karate and kung-fu followers; men swung swords and poles or engaged in mind games of meditation at the water's edge. Here there were circus acts; jugglers entertaining toddlers and babes bedded in bamboo and cane bassinets and pushed by their adoring grandparents; group and individual exercises; classes of *tai-ji*; shadow boxing in the shade. New sports abounded: jogging to breathlessness, old people's disco-group aerobics to music from a tape deck; badminton without a net. It was all here except walking the dog. They are not allowed in the city. But that's no reason to keep you indoors—take the caged birds instead!

Eating in local restaurants and snack stalls gave me the opportunity to use my latest phrases. Shopping at the free market was a chance to banter and haggle humorously over the price of a melon. Cycling on my hired "Flying Pigeon," I joined the bicycle commuters occupying half of Beijing's wide avenues. Now I felt quite at home within the populous maze of China.

In experiencing the broad spectrum of Chinese life, I was fully aware that the citadel of the Great Wall was an entirely different matter compared with the security of urban living. Reminding myself of the task half-completed I drew a line from Jiayuguan to Yulin on a wall map of China and pinned it above my bed in the room I shared with Oliver, an Austrian. He was a highly disciplined roommate, a fanatical launderer who polished his shoes religiously every morning. Occasionally, he accompanied me to the park to run a lap, then amazed an audience with situps and pushups. To the matchstick-limbed people gathered around he must have been the epitome of the foreign devil—six feet six inches tall, golden-haired and blue-eyed. His appearance, however, did not prevent the woman at the park gates from assaulting him both physically and verbally for failing to purchase an entrance ticket. The following morning he returned, reformed, to pay double.

Entering the Longtan Hotel dining hall one evening, I could not quite believe my luck for my eyes focused on Miss Wu Qi. "And you're Mr. William," she giggled in her embarrassment while introducing her cousins.

The Japanese Securities Company was not difficult to locate in the International building where Midland Bank was also housed. Using a collection of press cuttings as an excuse to call on her, I knocked on the door of Daiwa Securities. And there she was, seated at a word processor, tapping away, looking immaculate. Jumping up, she laughed and smiled, and stepping into privacy outside the office, I invited her to dinner. I had no idea how a Chinese girl would react or interpret such an approach. She looked unreservedly delighted. And I could barely think of much else until our date came around.

Miss Wu Qi emerged from her office bright and bouncy, wearing a dark blue silk dress and wielding a dictionary of encyclopedic proportions. "If cannot understand I can look—my English not very good," she explained; in fact her lack of fluency only added to the great humor of our evening as we dined at the Jianguo Hotel, serenaded by musicians playing traditional instruments. The atmosphere was quite romantic and I hoped a treat for her, since local Chinese were not admitted alone. But the food, though good, was not half the feast that Miss Wu looked. She was ravishing, with a personality and humor to match.

"Call me William—not Mr. William. Can I call you Qi?"

"Difficult, Chinese people only use one name if close relations!" she laughed. "Wu Qi is fine between us."

Seeing Wu Qi became the highlight of my days, which were crammed with training, learning Chinese and teaching English at a summer school run by the Beijing College of Tourism. Their enthusiasm for the English language was most impressive and touchingly archaic. "Welcome Sir" was chalked upon the blackboard as I lectured to a score of different students each morning. Not one of the hundred students had ever seen the Great Wall in the west. Lack of time and money to travel were the reasons given. But most of them had paid their own fee for this summer course, primarily to improve their English, the mastering of which would be a pathway to a good job in the tourist industry. They were pleasantly surprised by my ability to speak Chinese and particularly impressed by my use of colloquial phrases, something I could thank Wu Qi for.

We spent increasing amounts of time together. We met at lunchtimes to walk, in the evening to eat together, spending the hours until sunset strolling in the parks and cycling along the shaded avenues, eating watermelons and panda ice-creams, picking up Beijing beer and Coca Cola to drink in her room. To minimize gossip we would part a half mile from the hotel and meet up afterwards in her room, always leaving the door ajar, for only yards away sat the floor attendant. During these weeks I longed to hold her, kiss her and tell Wu Qi how much I loved her. Cycling along, her long hair and dresses blew tantalizingly in the breeze, and she would answer my compliments with attractively shy cordiality and "*Shi ma*?!" (Really?!)

Like an orchid in summer our love blossomed. A beautiful girl and a foreigner, we strolled at dusk in the magical landscape of Longtan Park through the jagged rockeries, along the water's edge, in the shade through the scented evening air, through groves of weeping willows and ornamental arbors, past beds of giant tiger lilies and rustling bamboo, across the pavilion-covered bridge to the tea house amongst the lotuses on the lake. "This park is magical," I told Qi. "I came here and wished to be successful on the Great Wall." The dragons of the pool had granted those requests, and now as Qi held my palm to read my future, I made another wish that somehow she would become a part of it.

Any outward showing of affection between the sexes is strictly taboo in China and this etiquette is largely respected by the courting generation until the sunset hour, when they make the park their own. Only then would couples be seen to hold hands, whisper sweet nothings, cuddle and kiss. Some undoubtedly used the bamboo as an effective curtain. Qi and I followed the rules, for apart from a streetful of Chinese mouths being agog, any obvious display of tenderness was tantamount to asking to be spied upon. Sex outside marriage is deemed improper and punishable by the Chinese. Between a Chinese and a foreigner such relations would be regarded as even more improper. In fact, the only acceptable relationship, beyond a business one, was marriage itself—no courting situation in between was safe. A foreigner would be fined and deported, but for a Chinese the axe would fall harder. A girl especially would be branded a promiscuous outcast with a black mark on her personal file.

Marriage between Chinese and foreigners had been permitted since 1984, but when I asked Qi she said it was difficult, even impossible. I could only cite my philosophy that after the Great Wall I would never use the word "cannot." In spite of the risks, she continued to give me her love and for that reason I believed the Wall within her mind would eventually crumble and she would take on the challenge. Ignorance works both ways. Some foreigners think oriental girls are easy pickings, subservient and willing to marry anyone for a passport. But I had faith in our love that blossomed in the most unlikely of nations—China, where the foreigners and natives are largely segregated and little opportunity exists for close relations. Our meeting was destiny.

After a couple of weeks, the Walls of doubt came tumbling down. "Running the Great Wall will make you strong enough to face all difficulties in our life—ask me again." I was ecstatic. "But I've got a secret to tell you—about my age." She was twenty-five, wasn't she? Was she

153

going to say she's younger? Often she looked twentyish. "Will, I'm twenty-nine. . . ." I laughed but couldn't believe it. "No problems—don't worry . . . I'm not twenty-eight—I'm thirty!" I had been fibbing, too. . . .

In the wonderful days that followed, we talked about circumstances leading to our happiness, how I had been guided to China, pursuing my goal in the face of incredible odds; how Qi had moved from Hebei Province to Xi'an as a child during the Great Famine, been cared for by her sister during the Cultural Revolution, when her father, a professor, had been punished; then her fortunate move to Beijing, and our incredibly lucky meeting on the steps of the hotel; her hilarious tales of introduced boyfriends and the pressure to marry from family and relatives. Matchmakers or "red mothers" were particularly concerned to find her a suitable partner, for, as a female graduate of history, she was not the average Chinese idea of good wife material—too well educated and likely not subservient enough. It was all laughable and our good fortune—fortune that would give me extra strength in stage two, when I would be running for my future wife.

Qi's wearing an engagement ring did not make our relationship acceptable or confer a recognized status; we were still judged as a Chinese and a foreigner flirting. We cycled together all round the city. Ritan Park became a favorite retreat in which to help Qi with her English studies. We walked in Tiananmen Square at sunset, and at Tian Tan, the Temple of Heaven, on a Sunday. We rode to the former residence of Soong Ching Ling, the wife of Sun Yat Sen, beyond the northern lakes district. Qi was always bright and fresh, like a breath of hope, gentle, comforting, playful, affectionate and tender. We discussed our future hopes, how Qi could help me on the run and how she would improve her English by enrolling at a college.

Like the countdown to an examination, the China map posted above my bed served as a constant reminder of the test to come. To return to Yulin seemed suicidal; it would involve a 125-mile "approach march" from Yan'an (since bus tickets to a closed place would not be sold to a foreigner without the necessary documentation—the Alien's Travel Permit). One consolation was that, according to my information, little or no Wall remained between Yulin and Fugu on the Yellow River border between Shaanxi and Shanxi. The previous year I had been shaken by reports of a British-born reporter on the *New York Times* being held on spying charges following his arrest as he attempted to depart from Beijing airport. He had toured Shaanxi on a motorbike with a Chinese student. The province would be a minefield of problems. Already the authorities had apprehended me twice there and a third offense would surely result in deportation and blacklisting. As my exploits had already been widely reported in the media, I decided to observe Mao's maxim "to be open and above board." The China Sports Services Company had even telephoned the Midland Bank inquiring, "Do you know the Great Wall runner?" The manager, Lance Browne, fluent in Mandarin, told them to bugger off and reminded them he was a banker, not a runner! At any stage, I could hardly be accused of being undercover, and for those reasons I had ruled out any idea of going into disguise for part two. It had been a consideration . . . for twelve yuan I had purchased a green "Mao suit"—it looked a little skimpy on me, and therefore I decided not to proceed any further by shelling out thirty yuan more for a pair of smoke ground glass spectacles. Nothing was sufficient to hide my big nose—or feet.

When faced with a problem, think sideways—or upwards! Inner Mongolia, the autonomous region to the north of Shaanxi, has over 6,200 miles of Walls of various ages! By departing from a point due north of Yulin I would be continuing my entire length exploration of the Great Wall, even enhancing interest by traversing a different terrain and ethnic region. Once across the Yellow River I could head south on the main line of Wall towards Datong. Accessibility would be the critical factor in the plan—fortunately the town of Dongsheng, about 105 miles north of Yulin, was, for some reason, open.

* * *

The searing heat and heavy humidity of August with its late afternoon downpours were now behind us. Qi and I had saved our day at Xiangshan, Fragrant Hills, until the freshness of the wind heralded September. We made our way up the rocky path, zigzagging to ease the climb, soon escaping the crowds. Perched on a hillside promontory peeping out of the thick woodland, we sat to get our breath upon red lacquered rails, looking down over evergreens and the flaming red of the smoke trees, the rich midtone browns of sycamores, maples and cedars.

As we continued, the path grew steeper, becoming a ladder of gnarled roots. I pulled Qi up this natural staircase to the sky until we fell laughing on the dry spongy carpet of pine needles. Now the forest was at its most fragrant in the hunting playground of the Qing! Out from this royal arbor on to the rolling summit ridges of Incense Mountain stretched a grassland of golden straw.

Qi collected a Xiangshan bouquet of flowers, grasses and seedpods. Under the basking radiance on a southern slope, we lay down on the golden carpet to love, looking up to the clouds, making faces and places, talking about life's most wonderful summer, which was inevitably drawing in. We knew its warmth would forever lift our hearts. Autumn was in the air, the fall of leaves in the forest below was the final curtain call. The golden season had arrived. It was time to run.

◨ 14 ◧

East Victory

> Go into the mountains knowing full
> well there are tigers there.
> —*Old Chinese saying*

The fact that Dongsheng meant East Victory had to be a good omen, and in the middle of Inner Mongolia I needed all the encouragement that I could get. Mongolia, together with its African counterpart of Timbuktu, has earned from its gazetteer's obscurity a popular definition as the heart of nowhere, famous for the possession of nothing.

On my two-stage journey to Dongsheng via Baotou, the local people had provided further food for thought about the region I was entering. One train passenger in particular, a Mr. Zhang, had voiced curious interest over my reasons for travelling to Dongsheng. "Why, oh why, should a foreigner want to go there?" he queried, inviting many of his fellow passengers to help him solve the mystery. "Nothing is there. No scenic places for sightseeing." He was certainly not in the employ of the Inner Mongolia Tourist Board. "We want you to see beautiful places in our homeland," he persisted, suggesting a tour of the northern grass-lands. "You can see nomads living in yurts there—and you could stay in a Yurt Hotel," he said, with all the zeal of a salesman trying to dispose of a Mongolian timeshare. Most of the passengers within earshot had now gathered around to join in the "*What's My Line?*" game. "That man lives

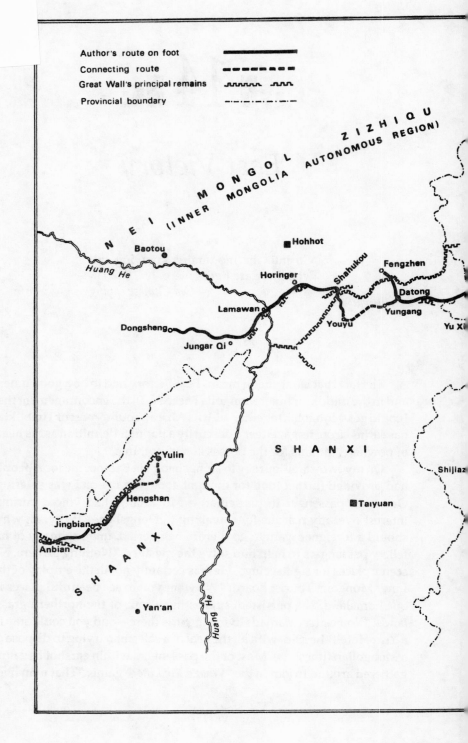

N E I   M O N G O L   Z I Z H I Q U

(INNER MONGOLIA AUTONOMOUS REGION)

Baotou

■ Hohhot

Shahukou

Fengzhen

Huang He

Horinger

Datong

Lamawan

Yungang

Dongsheng

Youyu

Yu Xi

Jungar Qi

S H A N X I

Yulin

Shijiaz

Hengshan

■ Taiyuan

Jingbian

S H A A N X I

Anbian

Yan'an

Huang He

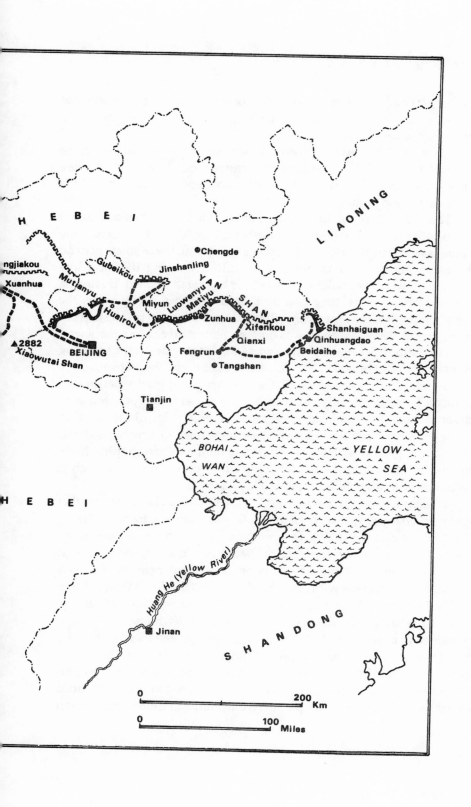

in Dongsheng," said Zhang, pointing to a Mongolian, "and he says that a foreigner would only visit Dongsheng to make business with the cashmere factory there."

"Not me," I answered, and not wanting to be subjected to the Mongolian inquisition any longer, I announced, "I'm a spy." They laughed hysterically and Zhang added his own punchline. "The British have such good humor."

Just a day later, having stopped to rest after the initial few uphill miles out of the shallow basin of Dongsheng, I could well have used some of the essential British humor. From this viewpoint, the desolate plateau appeared far worse than anticipated, fully deserving the local low opinion on what the roulette wheel of life had dealt to them. If Ningxia was the jackpot, then they had been landed with a booby prize, the wooden spoon of the Inner Mongolian Plateau. The train people had not exaggerated. They said there was nothing here. And nothing there was.

For the time being, the plateau was still, sleeping under the seducing serenity of a clear blue sky. This was a wrinkled domelike plateau, sandy on its surface, barely vegetated. There was hardly a single li of flat ground before a precipitous gully. Some of these were so wide and deep as to deserve the title of canyons. Each represented a colorful memorial to some catastrophic deluge occurring perhaps once in a man's lifetime. Slices through the sediments exposed a rainbow stratigraphy, highlighted by the clarity of the morning light: reds, greys, green-grey, purple, white and yellow. A Mongolian badland.

It was another arid region to add to the villainous list of deserts that had marked my progress along the Wall—the Gobi-like tracts of Gansu, the Tengger and the Ordos. Geographically, the latter was now to my southwest since the threat of Shaanxi had driven me some one hundred miles due north of Yulin. In terms of the ancient peoples and their boundaries, I was now with the nomads, beyond the Great Wall of Ming and Sui, which in those times had marked the northern limit of agriculture. To what extent the region had retained its nomadic heritage remained to be seen, but initial impressions suggested there were more Han (ethnic Chinese) than people of Mongolian nationality. There were herdsmen watching both sheep and horses, but wherever a pocket-settlement was situated, it was flanked by an apron of maize, terraced into the gully. Nothing is inseparable from politics in China, and the Han influx has likely been a combination of directives, incentives and sheer necessity to occupy land not under population pressure.

After a great deal of psychological kicking into gear, I had managed a good start covering perhaps twelve miles along the rough track that threaded a tortuous way across the gullied plateau. The first Mongolian farm I called upon proved the people were kinder than the unrelenting landscape. It seemed the cauldron was always simmering here, and they served me a local dish of mutton broth seasoned with fresh coriander.

No Chinese maps of Inner Mongolia had been available in Beijing, so I was forced to use an Operational Navigation Chart—which named just one town between Dongsheng and the Yellow River. However, it was not the town of Narin which was frequently mentioned by these peasants. The name they repeated was Jungar Qi. They spoke *Putonghua* but with a strong accent and we were forced to engage in cartographic communication by sketching in the sand outside the farm. Jungar Qi was "*dong nan*" (southeast) they repeated—and that concerned me because the Shaanxi border was less than sixty miles south of an eastern trek across the plateau from Dongsheng. At all costs I had to avoid setting foot in Shaanxi again.

Back on the run my concern increased as the track weaved its way around gullies, changing direction every mile. This made it difficult to ascertain my true progress east, both in terms of distance and direction. Occasionally the sight of dust in the wake of a distant vehicle allowed me to take a quick compass bearing to check the trend of the way ahead.

Fatigue and darkness came early. In Beijing, I had run for a maximum of ninety minutes in very high temperatures. Those hard and serious sessions had been interspersed with appearances at runs organized by the Beijing Hash House Harriers. Like paper chases, they were fun runs of between five and ten miles through the parks, *hutongs*, *dajies* and markets of the city. The varied athletic capability of the runners is evened out by frequent "hash house halts" (HHH) when the stragglers group again with the front runners. Only over the last stage of the run, the "on home," is there a race—although all the losers insist a race was never intended. Of all my hash runs I had only lost one of these "on homes"— the most memorable sprint out being under the portrait of Mao across Tiananmen to finish at the side of the Mausoleum. But in the context of running in Inner Mongolia, all my preparations, even the most diligent one hundred miles per week training phases, seemed like fun running. In a full day I had covered about twenty-five miles , and as the sun was setting behind me, casting a one hundred-foot shadow on the trail, I began to look for shelter. An hour and a half later the giveaway glow of fire in an empty landscape attracted my attention.

Most of the workers had gone to their homes, but a handful of men remained to keep the fires at this pottery kiln stoked up during the night. The biting cold of nightfall under the cloudless sky had chilled me for over an hour, so the bright and homely glow of the kiln was very welcome. Around the site, the stockpile of large-mouthed water pitchers was silhouetted like a giant honeycomb, but soon the eerie outline of their gaping rims faded with the last of the dusk. Guiding with a torch of flaming pitch, one of the men led me up a steep zigzagging path from the foot of the cleft to a derelict outbuilding. The kiln below created a giant *kang* system, for the floor and walls were hot, and the air within the room pleasantly warm. At the risk of being cremated should the giant "kiln-*kang*" collapse, I laid out my sleeping bag and lit a candle.

As eight o'clock approached, I prepared to keep two telepathic appointments: one to Britain, the other to Qi in Beijing. Inevitably, a vast proportion of both waking and dreaming moments were concerned with Qi and the pain of parting at Beijing railway station. Qi had looked so tearful that I had to turn, go, and not look back. Despite that departure, thoughts of her now gave me strength. How often, I thought, had the Great Wall forced lovers apart, whether soldiers, convicts or work-gangs, destined for the frontier of the Empire to be engaged in the back-breaking toil of Wall construction. Nevertheless, I could not hold any grudge against the Great Wall. I was here by choice, and, after all, the Great Wall had been our matchmaker.

At dawn the fireminders were already tucking into a bowl of meagre gruel, but my spirits sank once I had glimpsed there was none left in the pot. It took a great act of self-denial to be a good comrade and refuse the charitable offers of the men's own portions. But it was an even harder lesson in self-discipline not to look crestfallen by the reality of no breakfast. After a vigorous round of handshaking, they wished me well and advised me to "go slowly" ("*Man zou!*"). I had no intention of doing anything else, until some sustenance could be found.

As I made my way back up to the track, a shaft of golden sunlight was reflecting off the brown glazed pitchers piled up in the cleft outside the kiln. These first ten minutes or so on the move served as a warmup and parts check. Stiffness in the shoulders was the main problem, and the shins also felt a little sore. But given an empty stomach, such pains often appeared worse than they actually were. It had been some twenty hours since my introduction to Mongolian regional cooking. I envisaged that great cauldron like the original pot from the opening scene of Macbeth. All the sheep had been in there: legs, ribs, skull, and the steaming smell of mutton fats had filled the room with a slightly obnoxious and nauseating sweetness. Now that smell would be perfume. I was famished. Man has an inbuilt tolerance of hunger, I told myself sternly, that developed in primitive times when he was a hunter-gatherer. Days of feast were followed by days of famine until the next successful kill. Two hours of fasting brought me into a village called Fan Jia Qu. Phonetically *fan* means rice or more generally food, and I crammed it in, as much rice, pork and vegetable as I could manage.

Another day of weaving across the badlands ensued, the color of the strata changing with the rotation of the sun and the cloud cover. Some of the whiter levels had their mud washed out to appear like frozen waterfalls gushing into the gullies, and some of the fleshy-leaved flora clearly preferred soils of a particular stratum. Both north and south of my route, observation towers, their boxlike shape still intact, stood out. They were possibly remnants of Warring States Walls between the Qin and Wei kingdoms, or, more likely, solitary watchtowers built along supply roads leading north to the Great Wall, which during Qin and Han dynasty times followed a route across Inner Mongolia.

Although Walls served as sharp dividing lines between the ethnic Han Chinese (or occupying foreigners) and the barbarians outside the defense, a considerable amount of trade was conducted across the Wall. Reaching Ma Jia Qi Pu was a distinctive reminder of the importance of the horse—*ma*—of which the nomads were masters. Horse markets were set up throughout the border region, where the nomads traded livestock, hides and mares' milk for the salt and woven cloth of the Chinese.

There was little traffic on this track and therefore it came as quite a shock to find myself confronted with a dreaded Gong An Ju jeep. I was relieved to find they only wanted to engage in general chat. The officer and his driver were a reliable source of route information. In fact, I pushed my luck to inquire if they owned a map; they did. We spread out the chart upon the hot bonnet of the green jeep, examining my route ahead to a Yellow River crossing at Lamawan, having made it perfectly clear I wanted to stay in Inner Mongolia and not drift south into Shaanxi.

The friendliness of the local Gong An Ju inspired me to push hard in the afternoon, descending from the plateau into a river valley and the town of Narin (marked on the wrong side of the river on the ONC). My distance of over thirty hilly miles had been too much in the bright sun. Sunstroked and footsore, I almost collapsed on the threshold of a *luguan*, the humblest type of lodging house, and within minutes I was fast asleep, only to be woken up by the return of the Gong An Ju—the friendly and cooperative variety.

> Narin is located in the south of Nei Mongol near the borders with Shanxi and Shaanxi; in fact, most of the people have come from these two provinces. The town is old and is just ten miles to the government of the Qi of Jungar Qi. How do you do? I am a Public Security Bureau officer from the County Police Bureau.
>
> *Shi Jun Feng, 9/26/87*

Perhaps I was on to a good thing! The fact that the PSB jeep driver had signed the diary earlier in the day probably alleviated all this officer's suspicion of me. When he departed, proudly pocketing a signed photograph of me leaving Jiayuguan, the inn proprietor brought me a basin of mutton and potato stew, as near to Irish stew as you could get anywhere in the world! It had been my lucky day.

Running detects flaws in one's health long before the symptoms become fully developed. Immediately on awakening I felt hot and tired but persisted in leaving the *luguan* early, in case the Gong An Ju decided on paying further attention to me. As I struggled out of the valley back on to the plateau, the landscape became less desolate and some of the hillsides supported sizeable crops of maize, which was being harvested and piled high as golden yellow mounds on the dust.

Diary, September 27th: east of Narin

By midday I decided not to attempt a full day's running. I called in at a wayside farm where a young couple and their daughter were cooking in the kitchen. After having a little corn porridge and water, I asked to sleep—all afternoon, on and off, with face burning and head thumping. Took two Nurofen and drank plenty of water—thankfully undisturbed because of the farm's isolation. The little girl was called Wu Tai, so I told her mother, a kindly lady of twenty-eight, that I had a friend called Wu Qi in Beijing. Cold and rainy in the night but the heat of the *kang* kept us warm. Morning was clear. I felt recovered so made a move to the river.

The plateau generally became less incised and more cultivable the further eastwards, likely due to a different drainage system in proximity to the big river itself. Information provided to me by Mr. Li, the Yanchi schoolteacher, was still relevant. He had told me of one of China's largest open-cast coal mines to the north of Fugu, and although I was to the north of the field itself, convoys of trucks began to use the road. Fully laden vehicles crawled eastbound, overheating on the hills and jackknifing on the hairpins as empty trucks puttered westward. Perhaps one day a railway would be built; until then it was left to road and river haulage to transport the coal out. Inhabitants on the banks of the Yellow River had no complaints about this; they benefited from a seasonal deposit of coal when the waters receded in the dry winter, just when fuel was needed.

A more effective transport route was already under construction in the form of a new road being built by large groups of manual laborers using picks and shovels. For such a large scale civil engineering project there was a total absence of any machinery. Like so many of China's public works projects, this one was labor-intensive and slow.

Following an uneventful night in a truckers' stop, I continued a further seven miles through dunes to the Yellow River. From afar I stopped to view the single-span bridge across the muddy channel, instantly reminded of the security I had witnessed while crossing the Yangzi River bridge at Wuhan en route to Guangzhou in the summer. There were armed soldiers and sentry boxes there. What were my chances here? Surely better than at Qingtongxia in Ningxia, for now in my diary I possessed two entries from Gong An Ju officers of Jungar Qi.

The channel was perhaps 200 yards wide, and the concrete and metal bridge looked very new. Daring was the name of the game. I stopped thirty feet before the barriers and sentry boxes, at a mound of melons. This was a time to show confidence—and skill in choosing a good watermelon from the peddler. Picking up the giant green fruits, I slapped them gently—too high a pitch, unripe; a dull thud, overripe; too red. Let's try that one—perfect ripeness. He cut out a triangle for me to examine the flesh. Yes—nice pink flesh. "This foreigner knows a good melon," murmurs an old man, surveying the scene. The peddler attempts to place the melon in my rucksack. "No, no, too heavy. Cut it all up!" On to my haunches, gorging down huge chunks of the slices which spread from ear to ear. The crowd swells to twenty or more. Two guards included. Casually I pass one of the uniformed men my notebook, unconcerned with dripping melon juice—the pages are waterproof. Great excitement as the guard recites some tributes . . . one of them shouts . . . an idea perhaps? . . . he runs into the sentry's hut . . . oh, no . . . not a phone call . . . No! The frank of the bridge, red stars and all, in my notebook! "The Yellow River Bridge at Lamawan Sept. 29, 1987." And then an armed escort across the bridge to a *fandian* for some hot food!

With the second crossing of the mighty river now behind me, Shanhaiguan at long last appeared an assailable target. The menace of Shaanxi Province was behind me, and I ran long and hard, climbing away from the flat and verdant plain into foothills whose ridges were dotted with remains of watchtowers. This was likely the outer defense of the Exterior Great Wall, for to the east of the Yellow River the Great Wall was split by the Mings. As they strove to defend the arable farmlands of Shanxi and Hebei, and their capital Beijing, the Wall system proliferated into an entanglement of layers, loops and spurs.

In darkness, on the eve of National Day, I reached Horinger. On the edge of town my fortune continued in finding a quiet and homely *fandian* which served excellent food—fresh, hot and plenty of it. The hard day made me exhausted, achy and ill-tempered. I had gone too far, for although those symptoms would be cured by food and rest, the injury to my shins would not. Downhill walking, let alone running, was particularly painful and the prospect of facing the mountains en route to Datong filled me with trepidation.

There was already a carnival atmosphere brewing as I prepared to leave Horinger on Communist China's thirty-eighth birthday. Communism had rescued China and I knew it. A child born less than a century ago would have faced a bleak future. If it survived infancy, it faced a life of near-slavery under feudalism or even imperialist rule. Western traders had corrupted the Chinese peasantry with the evil temptation of opium addiction, sinking to any depths to rob the Middle Kingdom of her fabled wealth. A child born in 1949, however, entered a New China transformed by forty years of revolution and the repulsion of imperialist aggressors. But the turmoil was not yet over. Reaction and revolution had persisted into the sixties. Now, following a decade of reforms, China is approaching that milestone of middle age—forty years, perhaps set to experience stability and prosperity under her liberal new parentage.

Within this China of different systems, different nationalities, whether they be special economic zones or autonomous regions, the country as a whole is set to change fast. My proposed marriage to Qi, who on this special day would visit Tiananmen Square with her friend, Kang Hua, was symbolic of this. Slowly, China was realizing that, in the words of her own philosophers, "the essence of the city is in its people not its walls." If China is able to harness the momentous fervor and patriotism of her glorious youth to achieve the goals of current economic and foreign policy, then her many children are set to enjoy a middle-aged flowering.

In any town or city, or any day, one can see a plethora of red flags. Nationalism is a daily rather than an annual phenomenon. The "Internationale" blasts from the streets' loudspeakers, and in Horinger rows of silk pennants attracted passersby to take note of the current public education campaigns. Doctors in rather hideous cloth caps stood behind blackboard displays, colored and written in chalks, proclaiming the dangers of smoking or carrying too much on a bicycle (like a passenger). And of course there was the neverending family planning propaganda. Children, delighted with a day's holiday, played in the streets proudly wearing their Young Pioneer scarves. It was a day for family gatherings—that meant banquets, and banquets meant *jiaozi*. The peasants were into town early with the *jiu cai*—the vegetable for the dumpling. There were long queues for pork at the meat shop as it is a luxury food in short supply

Surprisingly, the post office was open, an opportunity for another franking in my diary. Inside, a student showed off to his fellows by conversing with me in a string of disconnected phrases. "Ger-lad to know you sir! Sitter down please!" In a post office queue there naturally wasn't a seat in sight.

Out in the country many of the farmers have become partially free from the yoke of state control, although they are still obliged to meet production quotas. After that they are free to sell off produce in the free market. A school of children came out from their village playground to watch me eat a watermelon which I split open by banging the fruit on a rock. The flesh was barely pink, almost white, it was so unripe. But it was the only refreshment available. The children laughed, admiring the audacity of the peasant for selling a bad melon. It was, however, the end of the season and becoming increasingly difficult to buy a good fruit.

Apart from the occasional irrigation canal in Gansu, the environment had rarely provided the opportunity for an impromptu bath. Now the time and place was perfect for such a luxury—a clear mountain stream, warm sunshine, no wind, and no peasants to be stunned at the sight of an old foreigner's backside.

Continuing upstream, I reached the watershed. A panoramic vista opened out: foothills dotted with beacon towers, a river and its flood-plains beneath a jagged range of mountains. The descent was long, steep and painful through remote communities nestled on southern slopes sheltered from the winds of the north. Shepherds already wore their huge sheepskins, snuggled down motionless in hollows for shelter, their necks stretching out from cover like that of a tortoise from its shell to watch me pass by. Around them on the crags and rocks their sheep and goats darted. Rare Asian breeds these, so surefooted and agile on the angles and boulders, their flowing fleeces momentarily alive in the wind as they scampered, defying gravity with the ease of drifting snow skimming over the hillside.

Diary, October 1st: Xin Dian Zi

I was surrounded by a ring of mountains where the hillsides were ploughed concentrically. Some of the people's dwellings are carved into the hillside like the Shaanxi *yao dong*. By the time I had descended to Xin Dian Zi, I was fully convinced, on the basis of sighting six towers, that an ancient Great Wall had existed on these very hills. Xin Dian Zi is a country village close to the Hun He River. A sandy and rocky road forms the main street, which has three *fandians* marked by red lanterns. Pigs, piglets, hens and dogs roam around, as do the usual urchins—who disappear down the *hutongs* to appear a minute later with their whole family. I'm at a *lüguan*; two women clean up the room. There's a sackful of cabbages under one bed and a huge string of garlic under the other. They sweep the floor and damp down the dust with water. Next door is the eating room. In it are tables with the usual plastic cloths, an ornate *mao tai* alcohol bottle holding plastic flowers, and on the walls are the first nine months of a 1987 calendar of pinups wearing regional dress.

Late last night there were murmurings about the Gong An Ju, so I was up and away at dawn. Getting off the bed, my shins ached so much I almost wished the worst would happen, but once on the road approaching a high ridge of mountains and spotting the Wall, I felt my spirits lift. Following a stream flowing through a valley exposing outcrops of basalt columns, I reached a mountain hamlet that immediately earned itself the title of "The Hamlet of Thick Walls." Small clay-baked bricks formed the interior walls and large stone blocks the outer—the latter looked very much like Great Wall material. The proximity of ramparts on the crags above provided a convenient source of ready-hewn building materials. Peasants have no interest in the conservation of their historical monuments, and more than that, they were positively encouraged to destroy the "four olds"—including relics—during the Cultural Revolution. According to one villager the main-line Great Wall, *da bian* (literally the big frontier), was further south, some three miles ahead. Was this the second frontier, "*er bian*?" I enquired. "*Shi de*," (Certainly) he replied.

And so it proved to be, for on the lower rolling hills beyond, the main element of the Ming's triple-layer defense of the Datong region came into view, the most serene view of the Wall I had yet seen. Smooth rounded hills were set to pasture. Stacks of baled grain dotted the landscape, drying in the bright autumn sun. Unless the locals had succeeded in a complete stripping of the Wall's stone, with the efficiency of vultures scavenging on the flesh of a carcass, then it had never been cased in this region. It was entirely of rammed earth construction—almost a dyke formed by the excavation of two parallel trenches. Farmers had plowed their land right up to the edge of the Wall, which made the going extremely rough over the clods of dry rocklike earth. I could only run uphill. Walking downhill was excruciating and so slow that an old woman laden with maize plants, looking like a bush on the move, kept ahead of me on the descent to the Cang tou He. On the valley slopes beyond the river, the Wall's condition was better preserved, angular in shape, slithering up the hill like a giant serpent of mud. At its sides, fields were plowed and crops harvested, and down in the valley bottom lay the small village of Shahukou.

> Shahukou is an important pass on the Great Wall where many battles during each dynastic age were fought. Perseverance is victory! Hope you can finish your great journey.
>
> *Zhang Cheng Ping, 10/2/87*

Shahukou, "the pass where the tiger is slain," became known as the "pass where barbarians are slain!"—hu is a phoneme for barbarians although the characters of the two words are entirely different. The sinister name of the pass seemed to cast a spell of despair upon me. Here I was, a barbarian from beyond the Great Wall passing through one of its gates—entering the Middle Kingdom after my run through Inner Mongolia. This was Shanxi Province, the fifth region of my route, for even today the Great Wall serves as a provincial boundary.

The wounded invader limped on, shins splitting with pain, walking on the outside of his feet, the injury eating away his morale. The ominous name of the pass, though a few miles behind, still had its revenge to vent on the helpless foreigner. Forced into a *lüguan* to eat, but seduced by its comfortable convenience, I remained there to sleep. And paid the price for the lapse in self-discipline. Was it a nightmare when my eyes strained against the glare from the torch thrust close to my face? No, it wasn't. Regaining my senses, I slowly recognized the familiar angularity of the peaked cap of the Gong An Ju.

A bedside interrogation of over an hour followed, using a school-teacher as an interpreter. "Don't think I'm a policeman like them—I'm a schoolteacher like yourself." (That was the safest profession to confess, I had always believed.) "They called for me and I must do what they say." It was nearly midnight but still the questions about the numerous visas persisted. Soon they grew tired themselves and decided to adjourn proceedings until morning. But they did not actually order me to stay put, nor confiscate my passport. I lay there, tired, lame, smelly and unwashed. The rules of continuing were the same as they had always been—go for the gap! Already I had been planning the escape for over an hour. Now it was time to do it!

Seemingly amplified by the dead silence of night, the door creaked hideously like a hinge on the lid of Dracula's coffin. Outside, guided by a full moon, I walked with a moon shadow. Frozen, I grappled blindly in my rucksack to get my gloves. My shins ached even more, for I could not see the undulations on the road. I plodded on. Datong was just forty miles away. "Da-tong-Da-tong-Da-tong," I murmured, like a pilgrim chanting a meditation. What were my chances? Perhaps two to one at best. If I were fit, the "dog-legs" would not have had a chance, but being injured, with shins feeling as though they were going to fracture, I was forced to stay on the road to Datong. A posse would surely be dispatched when they found only pillows under my quilt. I recalled a much-talked-about mischievous act of my early schooling. I was a fourth child and my parents had been burdened with school fees for far too long so at the age of six I was transferred from St. Aidan's Prep to St. George's state-run primary school. They were arch rivals. "Our class in—St. George's in the bin. Our class out—St. George's up the spout," we used to sing vociferously in the playground. And they could hear us, just around the corner. But I was a determined little boy, and even at that age, a very good runner. Once I was at St. George's a request to go to the toilet became a chance to escape. But as my toilet trickery became known, the mistress sent another boy with me—not a clever one, however, nor a good runner. While he was still pointing Percy at the porcelain, I would make a bullet start off the slimy floor of the outdoor lavatories, dart out into the playground and, leaping down the full flight of steps into the street, run for almost a full mile home. In the end I got my own way and returned to St. Aidan's. It also turned out to be good training for China.

I managed to reach Youyu county town before they caught me. It was an unequal contest. Tracking a lame foreigner on a Chinese road must have been an easier predatory strike than a shark sniffing out a bloody corpse in a swimming pool. The ensuing procedure was so familiar to me that I could have conducted it myself. An austere and robotic officer, extremely smart with shining black leather shoes, metal-clipped on their soles to give his authoritative gait added audible menace, conducted the interrogation swiftly. Within two hours they were putting me on the bus and warning me not to come to an unopen place again. As the bus started up, the teacher slapped me on the back and said, "You have a great spirit, Mr. William. Keep on this bus to Datong." "*Shi de*," (Certainly) I replied, after telling them I could speak no Chinese.

Thirty minutes later I got off the bus at Yungang, the site of the colossal Buddhist grottoes, hewn into the cliff during Northern Wei times (AD 386–534). A quick look was a mild consolation for the day's turn of events. Recovery and rest interested me more. By the time I had reached the drab streets of Datong, I had decided to postpone any decisions on strategy until after a morale-boosting bath. Two soaks were required to rid me of the smelly dog which had followed me since my river bath.

No matter how much my heart wanted me to continue, after a couple of days' rest my mind told me that I should formulate a long-term rather than temporary strategy. There were still at least 300 miles remaining to reach Old Dragon's Head, and now as my route would take me through the Beijing region and more populous Hebei Province, the going in terms of security would get tougher. To set off before my injured shins had recovered would be suicidal. I was just making myself easy prey, jeopardizing almost 1,250 hard-won miles. Also, my "dirty" passport was not helping me. That was the decisive factor, something the British Embassy in Beijing could help me with.

▪◣ 15 ◢▪

Towards Beijing

. . . Allow the bearer to pass freely
without let or hindrance . . .
—*The Secretary of State,*
wording in British passport

Passport L04I400B was cancelled. Long live C711350D! Three cheers for the British Embassy and my new alphanumeric identity!

Qi had been a constant source of encouragement during my stay in Beijing. Before I left she wrote a fresh introduction and request for comments on the diary's cover—my only reminder of her during the run. To carry a photograph might risk providing a juicy lead for investigation, even tailing, on my final return to Beijing. I was adamant that under no circumstances should I give the Gong An Ju any opportunity to employ their manpower in following up even a sniff.

Qi was unaware of the access difficulties with which I had to contend. Most foreigners, and even Chinese themselves, are quite ignorant of the cumbersome restrictions on free movement in China. The Chinese rarely harbor any desire, let alone the spare cash, to penetrate the remote and hostile heartland when the comparative attractions of the developing cities and perhaps the "gold-paved" streets of Shenzhen and golden sands of Beidaihe are accessible. A "them and us" superiority complex has divided the relatively well-off urban class from the peasants. To squander time and money on interior travel is an utter abhorrence for a generation that can recall bitter memories of enforced years spent in the countryside during the "wasted decade." However, the relative unawareness of the Chinese about access restrictions imposed on their "foreign friends" worked to my advantage. Peasants were unlikely to inform the Gong An Ju of my presence on purpose, but the villages and towns of China are the ultimate self-policing communities, where gossip spreads like wildfire by word of mouth. Back in the cities one will often hear the Chinese talk enviously of friends studying abroad, free to roam wherever they wish, and work and live unsegregated. Yet they fail to realize no similar situation exists for foreigners in China, nor anywhere near it.

It is not surprising people in the West have a misconception about the travel situation in China. Regular reports from the People's Republic are rare, for investigative journalism, like travel, is difficult in a country where 99.99 percent of the land is out of bounds. News policy is simple: the good is emphasized. Lead stories on CCTV National News are often portrayals of model workers, soldiers, cadres and Party members parading at the Great Hall of the People. Such ceremonies occur several times a week. Hard news is closely concealed. In the face of these odds it is perhaps not surprising that during the summer only two UK newspaper correspondents were based in Beijing to cover the activities of 22 percent of the world population. If investigative journalism is admitting defeat, the burden falls upon the adventurous traveller to conceive imaginative journeys and enter the forbidden zone. Perhaps Zhuang Zi, a follower of the Daoist faith, summed up this theory long ago in his belief that "a good traveller doesn't know where he's been, and a great traveller doesn't know where he's going." Either that or the statement was an early comment on the quality of Chinese maps.

Reminding myself of all this formed the cornerstone of self-motivation. It was a journey that was never supposed to be without problems; it required the ability, now well honed, to recognize and be spurred on by subtle pointers towards progress. At the outset it had been a fifty-five-hour chug westwards to Jiayuguan—now it took a trifling seven hours to return to Datong. Each hour towards the interior spelled greater elevation and distance from the sea; and that pronounced an earlier winter. Streets were gray and dusty. Autumn had come and gone. A cold dryness stretched and dried out the face. As though chemical warfare had broken out, the people wore white surgical face masks. Women went further, protecting themselves, beekeeper-style, with gauze scarves. It was difficult to tell a baby from a bedroll.

Faced with these bone-chilling conditions, I was grateful for Qi's advice and the provision we had made for my thermal well-being. It is no empty generalization that the Chinese feel the cold. Prompted by a calendar dotted with days titled "Great Cold" or "Beginning of Autumn," they change their wardrobe accordingly. Qi was typical of the seasonally induced fashion victim, putting her skirts and dresses into mothballs after National Day and sporting several layers of clothing. Now I carried three layers too—one of locally acquired silk, one of Lifa thermal and another layer provided by my Ultrafleece. Accessories for the extremities included two pairs of gloves and a balaclava.

Qi's concern for my survival in north China's bitter winter had a parallel in the well-known legend of Meng Jiang, who made warm clothes for her husband. He was conscripted by Qin Shi Huang's generals to travel from his Shaanxi home to work on the Great Wall. Winter came and he failed to return. Meng Jiang travelled across China to find his work camp but tragically heard of his death during construction work. So great was the storm of her grief that her tears caused the Wall nearby to collapse and reveal his bones. Less romantic scholars suggest an earthquake struck at that moment, for the Yanshan are in a high-incidence zone for tremors. The legend of Meng Jiang looking for her husband has become symbolic of the heartbreaking separation that the Chinese people are subjected to by their conscription to public works projects. The legend had a particularly sinister and poignant relevance for me, for I was subjecting Qi to a similar scenario. I might never be able to return—not through death, for despite the dangers I am a born survivor, but because of the unbearable prospect of banishment from the country. So I was determined that my eventual success should in some way recompense her for the uncertainty and pain that she endured.

* * *

The Wall divides into an exterior and interior line enveloping Datong, and of the several routes leading to the plethora of remains in the Beijing Municipal Region, I decided to chance my luck with the northern exterior line. That would lead me into the more desolate mountains of north

Hebei, away from the somewhat more densely populated area crowded with satellite towns and cities of the "home counties" further south. As I struggled to find a way north out of Datong's sprawl, I understood the gamble I was taking, especially in the Zhangjiakou region, the base of the PLA Beijing garrison. The endowment of that area with gold deposits also added to its sensitive status, even to the extent that representatives of foreign companies selling mining equipment were strictly prohibited from visiting there.

As I made my way out of the Datong basin, the sky grew brighter. Looking back south, I could see the enormous pall of smog hanging over the coal-burning city. Initial response from my legs was encouraging, and moving through the freezing air made running burdened with a rucksack much more bearable. Apart from sweating in the small of the back I was warm and dry, but whenever I stopped, I quickly became chilled. Soon the faint appearance of the Great Wall coming in from the west, with its watchtowers perched on top of hill summits, could be verified. This was the *da bian*, the big frontier. Here the grassy mound that had disappeared under pressure from the plow in the valley reappeared, regaining stature on the uncultivated slopes, then continuing in its full glory, watchtowers intact, into the hills eastward, still marking the border between Shanxi and Inner Mongolia. In the failing light I continued up this river gap and soon reached the town of Fengzhen. As I approached the town, I was blasted by an icy wind, the worst that Central Asia's cold heart could muster. Any hope of surviving such cold in the sleeping bag was imaginary. No matter what preconceived safety rules I held, they had to be shelved—or, more aptly, deep frozen. Reluctantly, I found myself making overtures for shelter in a mystery building, perhaps a depot. The caretaker was a kind-faced woman, and her two happy-go-lucky deputies fetched hot water to drink and wash with, then guided me to the cookhouse. I huddled between the coal-fired ovens enjoying the warmth radiated by their hot bricks. A dinner of potatoes, celery and steamed bread did something to quell my internal chill, but once back in the room I needed the cover of two quilts to keep warm.

Diary, October 21st: Fengzhen, Inner Mongolia

ANOTHER NIGHTMARE—"they" came last night, wrapped in big fur-collared coats and pointing at their cap badges. Early this morning, I tried to escape, but everything was locked and I was apprehended trying to force open rust-seized windows. The three wise men returned and in discussing my route the Gong An Ju officer analyzed my map upside down for a good twenty seconds. . . . It's Trafalgar Day, England expects every man to do his duty. . . . I shall take the southern route to Beijing! They did exactly as expected—and seventy yuan poorer, I arrived back in Datong.

A familiar and threatening challenge now confronted me. With my name already on the files of the Shanxi Gong An Ju for the Youyu skirmish, a second apprehension could be fatal. Faced with a similar problem in Gansu, I had reached the safety of a new province, Ningxia. In Shaanxi, I had been less successful and the consequence was harsh. Now the stakes were even higher. Leaving the drab Datong streets once again, themselves a strong incentive to make tracks, I fully understood that over sixty miles of Shanxi remained to be negotiated. A difficult target. No more underestimating anyone or anything—regardless of the pain or the weather.

The provenance of the traffic could be learned from each vehicle's number plate. Two Beijing truck drivers told me it was 235 miles to the capital, although my psychological target for peace of mind was Hebei Province, perhaps two days away. For the first time on the run I was less concerned with finding remains of the Wall, yet unexpected fortifications were in abundance. Huge watchtowers, almost small forts, pitted with large caves, were spaced out alongside the road. Such structures were built outside the Great Wall, as islands within a potentially hostile sea, enabling a small garrison to keep watch, safely and self-sufficiently, on activities in the border region. The seventh structure I sighted became my refuge for the night. As predicted, the human geography was changing. Isolated farms were fewer and farther apart; townships were centralized—that posed great threats.

Diary, October 22nd: beacon tower near Sun Qi Gong she

From a cave burrowed some fifteen feet into the body of the tower, I watched the sun set at 5:35, 235° W of N. The blue sky gave way to the pink dusk, the purple night chill and finally darkness. Still air and a starry sky threaten frost. At 6:40 I climb into the sleeping bag, eating one boiled egg, one *mantou* and two dry cakelike sponges.

Often frozen and curling up like a ball to minimize heat loss, I could only doze for five or ten minutes. Then I would awaken, shivering, repositioning, wafting the down bag to get air between the feathers, waggling my toes to get some circulation there, embedding frozen hands in my crotch, telling myself to hang on until morning. Time seemed switched to slow motion. Each minute seemed an hour, each hour, a day.

Breaking camp was agonizing; its comparative comfort seemed almost acceptable to the refrigerated dawn. The wind howled, almost gale force, from behind as I shuffled east partly wrapped in my foil insulating mat. I had survived the worst night of my life.

Diary, October 23rd: Sun Qi to Yang Yuan

After an hour I cannot run, I am feeling very weak and hungry. Immediately I become more chilled, the back of my head freezing in the strong wind. No more haircuts. Most cookhouses along the way have little to offer except hot water, which is painful on the frozen teeth and throat, like boiling water going down an icy drain. I reach a village with a main street market where I eat *mantou* and oranges from a jar, narrowly escaping injury when a madman swings his stick, banging the floor to attract the eyes of a thousand to my presence.

Late in the afternoon, entering a small village, I spotted the familiar dark green paintwork of the post office. Food was uppermost in my thoughts yet I slipped into the office. As an unexpected gift the clerk stamped the postmark of Yang Yuan, Hebei Province—the sixth region of my journey. For the time being, I was safe. Next I needed food. In the cookhouse of the *fandian*, I sat at the side of the fire-hole watching the hot oil sizzling and smoking in the grimy wok, overseeing the cracking and beating of eggs, the chopping of peppers and tomatoes and the slicing of *doufu* (bean curd). The latter food was a slimy, jellylike substance that I had found repulsive when I arrived in China but now I had become accustomed to its texture and taste. *"Gou?"* (Enough?) asked the startled chef, chopping with the efficiency of a human food processor. *"Bu gou, bu gou,"* I replied, encouraging him to throw in more ingredients, a dab of chili and splash of soy. Never did I eat a plateful of Chinese stir-fry so quickly!

Light was failing rapidly as I belched my way out of the village, eyes scanning the fields for suitable shelter. Often in summer, for both comfort and security of their crop, the peasants will sleep out under a straw canopy, fearful of thieves getting away with a free barrow of vegetables in the night. Most of these shelters were now derelict, wrecked by the wind or munched by mules. Fortunately, I spotted dark patches on the face of a cleft and discovered small narrow dugouts. Perhaps they were freshly hewn graves, but that did not concern me. I needed their shelter to survive. Compared to the previous night my entombment allowed me to rest in peace.

Diary, October 23rd–24th: freezing to death?

After a twelve-hour visit to the realm of the dead, I emerge from my grave into a frosted landscape. I'm on the road again at 6:45 after a few biscuits. The sun rises as a huge orange disc. It is too cold and creaky to run. These are the most dreadful days. My spirits lift marginally after a breakfast of fish, fruit and biscuits, but my digestion is not aided by the Gong An Ju ensuing roadside harassments. They are happening so frequently of late that I'm becoming blase about their danger. Taking evasive action after passport checks, I cross open fields. The final preparations of grain storage are underway—donkeys pull stone rollers on concrete circles to grind the wheat. Farm workers throw grain into the air, the waste husks being carried away on the breeze. Still, I incite incredible reactions from the children. They shadow my progress, steering bicycles far too big for them, their seats sliding off each side of the saddle as they pedal.

After sleeping rough for the last two nights, I was painfully aware of the discomfort and loneliness. Not only did the peasants offer shelter, they provided a boost to morale every evening, an opportunity to chat and entertain the children. Feeling terribly depressed and dishevelled, I desperately needed such comforts. So often the simplest encounters were the most memorable. Now following the river Hu Liu He southeast, I stopped to ask an old shepherd about food and where to buy it. From his quilted jacket he produced some eggs, insistent that I should eat one immediately. But all eggs are not quite what they seem in China. Once before I had bitten into what appeared to be a perfectly normal egg to find it was marbled green and black, incredibly salty and totally nauseating in taste and odor. For fear of offense I had continued to force it down, smiling to its salty end. When in China don't judge an egg by its shell.

A group of urchins led me to the village store, but it was hardly a larder. Filled with unidentifiable preserved foods, cigarettes, banana juice and alcohol and sunflower seeds, it stocked nothing substantial and convenient. Dejected, tired and ravenous, I marched two miles more. Then I found consolation. There was a workyard, filled with men chopping wood for a fire. They greeted me with smiles and shouts. We sat down around the stove as they plied me with questions and a huge mug of hot and heavily sugared jasmine tea—such comfort and pleasure in the wake of despair! But then I was distracted from speaking to a young worker (who registered his origins in my diary as Tacheng in Xinjiang, the most landlocked region in all Asia) by catching sight of the unit leader on the telephone. Obviously, my feet were not yet under the table. Was he speaking to his leader or the Gong An Ju? I could only assume it was the latter. Slamming the receiver down, he shouted, *"Zou, Zou!"* My "center of the earth" friend looked shocked and ashamed, yet he obeyed his leader's order to escort me off the premises. Outside, he pointed into the darkness, saying, *"Fandian shi er gong li."* (*Fandian* seven miles).

Undoubtedly that would be a trap, one that I was determined to avoid in spite of the perilous temperature. On I plodded, hoping the light of a smallholding would proffer an invitation of shelter. But there was only blackness, bitter cold and cutting wind. Flicking on my torch, I caught sight of a stack of drying plants—they turned out to be sunflowers. I rolled out my bed alongside, feeling for stones, then, slithering down into the comfort of my three-piece, I prepared a dinner of the egg—

thankfully an ordinary hard-boiled one! Zipping up the head flap of the Gore-tex sleeping bag I was now totally enclosed. I tightened the head cord of the mummy-form duck down sleeping bag. Soon the cold intensified and I began to shiver constantly. Curling up into the fetal position, I placed my head against my knees. With no roof, the heavy frost came down, stiffening the shell of the bag, with icicles forming from the moisture of my breath.

Another eight hours of this would be impossible, unbearable. I breathed hard into my hands to thaw my fingers and wriggled my toes continuously. Oh to be in Gansu, in the hot desert of the Tengger.

I imagined red sands and bright sun and felt my eyes squinting from the glare. I gasped the stuffy blasts of air billowing off the dunes, feeling the dryness in the mouth and throat. All my thoughts were focused on heat, the sweat seeping from my pores. Only later was I to learn that the willing of heat into one's body by such a method is termed *thumo reskiang* by Tibetan ascetics. Like many other phenomena that illustrate the power of the human mind, such acts have no essentially religious significance. Yet because the minds of holy men are trained on faith and intangibles, they are more likely to be successful in performing such supernatural tasks and hence are credited with being the only people with such talents.

Miraculously, I saw the light of day through the thickness of the sleeping bag. Quickly, I snaked out of my icebox into a hellish world of ice and hoar-frosted plant debris. The imposing snowy range of Taihang Shan with its prominent summit of Xiaowutai Shan loomed ahead. The sleeping bag would not pack: the inside, moistened with body and breath vapor, was frozen stiff. Grappling to reduce its size to fit into the bag made my already frozen hands feel like two ice blocks. A similarly excruciating task was tying shoe laces; my fingers were so numb I couldn't feel anything. Wrapping the down bag around my torso, I shuffled away, laces trailing, trying to generate some heat, shivering like a junkie, teeth chattering. Only once before had my hands been disabled like this. In my midteens I ran a fifteen-miler in the snow and arrived home unable to insert the key in the door. I was rescued by a neighbor as I tried to turn the key with my teeth. Afterwards, I sat in front of the gas fire, cocooned in a comforter, drinking gallons of hot coffee and dunking digestive biscuits. But this was the middle of China.

Suddenly, a green jeep carrying the veritable devils on wheels came sweeping round the corner. For several minutes I resisted and struggled at the back of the jeep, repeating that on no account would I enter. They treated me with some respect for I was unwashed and unshaven, a mysterious survivor of a bitter night. But eventually I was forced to climb aboard.

At the local bureau I was greeted enthusiastically with many thumbs-up gestures and handshakes. As an officer read out diary tributes, another reminded himself of the geography by studying a map hanging shabbily on the wall. From this reception came a fragile optimism, strengthened when one officer proudly produced a camera and organized a group photograph in the yard. These were personal gestures, as were the compliments and flattery from the two young girl schoolteachers brought in to act as interpreters. But as the questions were answered and phone calls were made, those familiar diversionary phrases—"After eating, you can go"—crept into the conversation, which finally subsided into a commentary over transport problems. "The jeep is being repaired," or "buses travel not often." My idea about walking back to my place of arrest was met with, "Would you like to meet our leader of Foreign Affairs?" The kiss of death. "No, I would not," I replied, picking up my rucksack. *"Wo men xian zai zou ba?"* (Are we going now?)

Signs that the situation would become drawn out came as we drove to the hotel in the walled county town of Yu. "Do you want a cheaper or expensive room?" asked one of the teachers. As two officers of the local force swelled the numbers of the interrogation panel, my hopes of a miraculous release shrank accordingly. Had I ever been to the British Embassy? Qinghua University? Did I have friends in China? "Yes—for my passport. I am a graduate of Liverpool University and I've got hundreds of friends all along the Great Wall." That was the cue to look on the map where I had been. "Where did you get this map?" *"Xinhua shu dian Wang fujing Beijing."* (The Xinhua book store, Wangfujing Street.) "Who taught you to speak Chinese like that?" "Mr Ling Gua Phone—a Liverpool teacher." The officer noted everything down. The usual lecture ensued, containing the usual criticism. Any altercation was useless. I simply wrote a brief account of my travels and listed many of the towns I had passed through along the way. But these officers had never learned any geography. Hebei was their world and I was obliged to educate them beyond the boundaries of that province.

After three nights of sleeping rough and a full day's interrogation, I could feel the escalating nastiness of the questions become demanding on my resource of patience. "Your photos please—give them to the officer." I flicked open the camera back, fogging the film and reeled it out. Unbelievably, one of them carefully rolled it up. That was the last straw. I felt totally wrecked, dejected and full of despair. On the verge of tears, I managed to hold back until they left the room. The people who at the start of the day had praised and respected me had ten hours later handed over a bilingual adjudication telling me that I had violated Article 29 of the Law on Exit and Entry of Aliens into the PRC. Hebei was geared up against the trespasser. It was proof that things were not going to become any easier. As I had always feared, the final miles looked to be the most hazardous. Regretfully, I had to tell the two schoolteachers that I could not return to the town's middle school to tell their students about my journey.

16

Blood on The Stones,
Writing on The Wall

Wind fills the tower before the coming
of mountain rain.
                    —*Xu Hun, poet c. 830*

I was accompanied on my trip to the railhead of Xuanhua by bus and then handed over to the railway station force. I was kept in the freezing cold station for eight hours while the paperwork necessary for my passage through the closed town was issued. Eventually I was put on a nonstop train to the capital and arrived at Beijing *Zhan* after midnight.

Between Jiayuguan and Yulin not an inch had been lost. Short of Datong, they deprived me of fifty li, and now I had been forced to concede about one hundred miles. The ladder's top rung, to cover every stride of the way, had never been the remotest possibility. The adventurer of the future, generations or centuries hence, inheriting a world without frontiers, might achieve such perfection. But I was faced with a walled world and barricaded China and had to perceive goals accordingly. Victory is never won in war without the loss of a battle or two. It just happened that my defeats had been in swift succession.

I was beginning to visualize an alarming scenario. Setting: the Ministry of Public Security in Beijing. Cast: a single clerk. Props: foreigners' files from Beijing, Yulin and points west. Action: scrutinizing and realizing a certain Briton headed a list—a hit list. The only kind of chart one didn't want to head. Fortunately I was in the Beijing Municipal Area, with no recorded "form" other than a three-yuan fine for riding two on a bicycle during the summer. In a final calculated risk I seized my last chance. The stakes were high: the journey's completion and my future wife. It was a case of both or nothing. My offenses were mounting up, and the weather was getting wintry. I had to get going fast, while my cold feet could still be comforted by two pairs of socks.

* * *

Getting initial access to the Great Wall was not too problematical. Taking a long-distance bus to Changping, I walked a few miles up to a road junction and hitchhiked southwest, then northwest beyond Hengling. Here was a convenient location to join an inner system of ramparts, well to the south of the Ming's main line of Great Wall some forty miles away. Nevertheless, this had been a defensive line of paramount importance to the protection of the capital and as such was built to a scale I had not before witnessed. A fearsome scramble on the broken stone-blocked ramparts, and I was climbing high on the snow ridges above the glassy Gaunting Shui ku, one of Beijing's enormous reservoirs. If ever an injection of inspiration and hope was needed it was now; and the sight of this solid stone dragon, its torso dotted with towers like fins and scales, was exactly that—the greatest Great Wall of China, the stupendous creation of the Ming, dipping and thrusting into the distance across multiple ridges a day's struggle away. I wanted to run fast and free.

First I had to tread slowly, climb, stretch for footholds, jump off the Wall, clamber back on, chimney down, balance low for fear of the strong wind blowing me to the ground some twenty feet below. The Wall was steep, its surface rough, loose and slippery, with crenellated ramparts in various stages of decay, weather-beaten and earth-shaken. Its overgrown pavement concealed holes where the core had been washed away. Beacons and watchtowers, for so long the providers of shelter to so many, rose like derelict ghost houses.

It was an awesome creation. In the afternoon sunshine its light-colored stone contrasted with the vegetation of the slopes, thinned by the approach of winter. It perched like a cardboard cutout upon mountains—not hills—undeterred by precipices. Cold stone blocks, rectangular lime facing bricks, bound by crumbly mortar, lay chalky white and friable at the side of the parapet, as if left by workmen just days ago. My feet were slipping on the gravel and slush; my fingernails were full of clay and mortar, my palms grazed, knuckles scraped, and my ankles banged and bruised between boulders and blocks. My lungs gasped for breath on the climbs and my teeth chattered in the bitter wind. Ice-cold inhalations stung my nostrils.

Certainly it was a Wonder of the World, arguably *the* Wonder. For I was aware that the Great Wall was not merely a single view—no more than a person's life is a single day. The Great Pyramid of Cheops had been a brisk scramble amid cries for *baksheesh*. Thebes and its Valley of the Kings was a morning's inspection; Pompeii, a sultry afternoon's walk; the Grand Canyon, a day's hiking. But the Great Wall was a wonder of a thousand vistas. A lifetime would be needed just to inspect every remaining rampart from the Warring States to the Qin, from Han to Ming. For when the feverlike fascination of the Great Wall takes hold of the imagination, one is drawn into studying the core millennia of China's wonderful civilization, uncovering inventions, discovering legends, analyzing the xenophobic mind, and paying respect to the laborers of countless generations who devoted their lives, somewhat reluctantly, to its construction. Beneath my feet was the world's longest cemetery. There was blood on every stone. The cannibalistic appetite of the Great Wall, perpetually in need of repair and extension, gave no dispensation from servitude to any Han generation.

No dynasty took the policy of Wall-building more seriously than the Ming (1368–1644). Their legacy was before me, a fitting climax to 2,000 years of building that resulted in thousands of miles of Walls all over north China, a creation of imaginative strategists and engineering innovators undeterred by scale. Four centuries later it still startles observers with its grandeur. Newly built it must surely have been regarded as a miraculous construction, the product of divine beings—gods on earth as the Emperors were believed to be.

For a century, the Mongols under the Yuan Dynasty had controlled China with their Khanate system of rule, governing all Asia from the Yellow to Black Sea, from Mongolia to Malaysia. To the cultured ethnic Chinese the Mongols, with their monstrous appearance and disgusting habits, were a definition of savagery and debauchery. Genghis Khan,

"Emperor of All Men," was a red-haired, green-eyed barbarian whose horsemen daubed animal grease on their faces as protection from the cold wind of their steppe homeland. They stank, since bathing was against their tribal rules, and made love to their women on horseback. Genghis Khan had instilled in his men the belief that "Victory over one's enemies is man's greatest pleasure—deprive them of their possessions, reduce their families to tears, ride their horses, and rape their wives and daughters."

Under this rule the indigenous Chinese became the lowest class rank in the Khanate system, and their eventual liberation from the yoke of oppression came Messiah-like in the form of a lowly peasant from Anhui Province, south China. Born in 1327, he was orphaned by plague and drought and resorted to begging for his survival. But Zhu Yuanzhang grew to lead a peasant uprising and then an army that just thirteen years later banished the enemy beyond the Great Wall. After centuries of foreign rule, he had restored some degree of brightness to the civilization of ancient China and aptly entitled his dynasty Ming, which means bright. Wall-building, to thwart any Mongol comeback, was in the very blood of the Mings from that day, and, first entrusted to General Xu Da, this most Chinese of activities continued during 267 years of their reign.

In the last hours of daylight I walked slowly, cautiously picking a path over the decrepit surface, slushy snow patches and low bushes. Often my passage was broken by the gaping chasms in the Wall, the results of explosive impact, landslip or earthquakes. These wounds on the body of the Dragon provided an anatomical cross-section. Huge blocks of fine crystalline rock, more than three feet in length, were so weighty that I could barely budge them an inch. Behind these was a fill of rubble rocks of various sizes—and likely some bones too—above paving blocks square in shape. The top facing bricks, composed of lime for the parapets, were quite small and surprisingly light for their size. Seeing, feeling, trying to lift these monumental stones, I pondered the most fascinating of questions: What were the methods of the Ming Wall-builders?

That they used locally available materials is evident from the quarries dotting the mountainside. At its most primitive, Wall-building was simply the digging of a trench to form a mound from the excavated earth. Construction, however, reached technical complexity with the Mings—

these huge blocks fitted together perfectly and millions of lime bricks were turned out in a consistent quality. Likely the smoke of the lime kilns and the ring of chisels on stones could be seen and heard from the ramparts. Nevertheless, even short-distance transport of such weighty materials would have been difficult. Handcarts, or wheelbarrows, were invented by the Chinese. I could imagine the frantic cries of mule drivers coaxing their overloaded animals on steep slopes, the animal's legs buckling under the strain, their hooves scrabbling on the gravel paths. Then the convict element of the workforce was left to heave the stones, the weight of several men, over the crags to their final destination. This Great Wall has thus evolved from the very mountain which it traverses, emplaced by the muscles of a million, the opposite to a river, which exploits the easy course, exposing the softness and faults in the rocks. A truly Great Wall must stride proudly across the loftiest peaks, scaling the sheerest slopes, plunging in and out of the most precipitous gorges to jump back again and ride the highest ridge.

Dangerous work in a hostile environment made the Great Wall bloodthirsty. During Qin times most labor was pooled from conscripts and convicts—but in Ming times the bulk of the workforce was the army itself, although there were still over two hundred offenses that carried the dreaded sentence of labor on the Great Wall—either for life or "perpetually." The latter penalty meant that the crime not only punished the criminal, but also his family, relatives and even his neighbors. For if a man was sentenced to "perpetual labor," upon his death a son was required to replace him. If no direct offspring were available, officials would select another relation or a neighbor. Such threats helped to enforce a strict Confucian code of virtuous behavior amongst the population. Even to this day it is the resulting stigma that falls upon the convict's family, *hutong* or *danwei*, that remains a major deterrent to crime.

The temperature plummeted as the sun dipped below the hills, plunging the mountainside into a cold shadow. This was a night I had prepared well for—with extra clothing and food. Within a beacon tower, its roof still intact, I hastily cleared a site and blocked up an arched lookout to lessen the draft. In all of my clothing, I had sufficient protection to be unconcerned about the night's temperature. I wore an extra layer on my legs, a beagle-eared hat made from rabbit fur as headgear and a down jacket. Thus, my imagination was left free to interpret the howling wind filling the tower and picture the ghosts of the men who rode upon its bloody breeze.

Having finally discovered a system to master the elements, I was not forced by discomfort to move off at dawn and could wait for daylight. However, when I continued on my way, I was confronted by a deadly frozen surface. Self-preservation frequently necessitated crawling on all fours since the mortar binding the parapets was so crumbly. The threat of ice made even the block-strewn surfaces safe in comparison.

For most visitors to China, Badaling is the Great Wall. It is almost an artist's impression, located in a stunning location made real by the "Mao Dynasty" of the 1960s and one of the four "olds" that even the Red Guards, contemporary barbarians in every sense, could not eradicate. The first tourists of the day tread gingerly on its icy surface, heaving themselves by the handrail up the wavelike rampart. Millions have trodden here: Chinese and foreign tourists, delegations and dignitaries, Presidents, Prime Ministers and royalty, Nixon, Carter, Heath, Macmillan and Elizabeth. Some walked west, others east, and, according to the observing press corps, from that choice their character could be ascertained.

As I veered south toward the Juyong Pass, the grey stone ramparts seemed all around. I was on the Wall but surrounded by it—on the ridges to the northwest, across the valley, on the next hill spur. Isolated blockhouse structures sat separate from the ramparts themselves. Stopping to try and unravel the strategic thinking behind such a maze, I counted four lines of Great Wall, one enclosure, and four separate towers—likely used as storehouses for ammunitions. This narrow and precipitous valley was the key to Beijing and the Mings knew well that every invader that had breached this stronghold had continued south to take all China and establish dynastic control.

On the steepest slopes the Wall became narrower. Before it was a width of five or six paces; now it was down to only three. Progress was pitifully slow as I scrambled over sharp fragile screes that were bound together by frost and broke up under my weight. On the ramparts it was a constant fight through the branches of birch and other shrubs. Below, a mile of green train snaked along a railway line that tunnelled under the mountains to avoid the gradient of the pass.

It took me five or six hours to negotiate this most difficult and troublesome terrain. Then the Wall vanished, leaving no trace anywhere except behind me and across the pass to the west. Dropping down out of sunshine to the valley floor where winter rays are rationed by towering peaks, I grew concerned about shelter for the night. Already the pass was filling with bone-chilling damp air, a breeze funnelled down its path from the north, and the dismal hollows were distinctly uninviting. I had lost all confidence in communes and instead sought out an isolated family home with bicycles outside and children playing. I wondered what effect proximity to the capital and familiarity with foreign faces peering out of taxis and buses en route to the Wall would have on my reception. But it was a fear unfounded. I was lapped in immediate heart-warming benevolence and placed in front of a glowing stove munching on crisp apples grown behind the homestead.

It was a farm typical of the many in which I had been welcomed along the whole route: calendars on the wall, shell-style giant thermos flasks, bedrolls neatly folded, enamel basins with spray-painted peonies. But here was something different—boxlike under a fondant pink nylon cover embroidered with appliquéd cats sat a black and white television. "The March of the Volunteers" stirs the nation's newswatchers at seven o'clock with a big report on the Thirteenth Communist Party Conference in the Great Hall of the People. But of more immediate interest is the preceding weather forecast. Guangzhou will be sunny—seventy to eighty degrees F. Beijing clear—below thirty degrees F. One nation: different climates.

Cold is cold. And when the wind is blowing it's best not to think about it. The palms of Guangzhou were the length of China away. At least the wind was from behind and I was running downhill. Soon I emerged at the valley's southern entrance, or mouth —"*Nan kou*"—where the Yanshan abruptly give way to the flat North China Plain. Behind me the mountains seemed to form a natural wall. The Ming surveyors of defense must have agreed, for they never tried to continue their Wall eastward, without breaks, on this southern line. Hence the next section of Wall in Huairou County could be reached by skirting Changping, along the edge of the plain.

A motorcade of black Red Flag limos zoomed past under the boisterous escort of blue and white Gong An Ju jeeps, the VIPs inside retaining anonymity behind tinted windows. Ahead I was approaching some Ming VIPs who, despite their elaborate efforts, have failed to RIP. Their fatal mistake was attempting to take riches from one world to the next. The Yongle Emperor even tried to provide for next worldly pleasures by rewarding his sixteen concubines with live burials around his own chamber within the Ming mortuary of Shisanling—the thirteen tombs. After four centuries the funeral procession in stone remains as a loyal vanguard to the Emperor and represents some of the few statues undesecrated in the whole of China. There are beasts, realistic, extinct and mythical, from all over Asia: elephants, camels, tigers in pairs and facing each other. How fitting a burial site the Ming Emperors chose—the men who rescued China from the hated rule of the Khan and built the Greatest of Walls to inhibit his return were entombed directly behind the most securely bolted door in all the country—almost within sight of the Wall.

Diary, November 4th: beyond Changling

As the road climbs back into the foothills, the view reveals the Shisanling landscape of mounds, large-circumference red walls, yellow tiled pagodas and bright red pillars, all amidst an auburn forest that holds its leaf a little longer in the lee of the Yanshan. On the edge of Changling there is a road sign stating in three languages, Chinese, English and Russian: "Entrance is forbidden to foreigners without special permits." Why in Russian? They left in 1960. Unperturbed, I continue. After a long climb I reach the top of Shisanling Pass from where I can see the Great Wall (leading on to Mutianyu?) shows itself beyond a jagged ridge. Peasants are harvesting lentils and peas—I could do with a good thick "pea wack" (soup) right now. They scatter their grain crops on the roads for passing vehicles, carts and bicycles to separate the grains from the stalks. A young and fresh-faced military man cycles by—but then swings back to criticize me. "*Bu xing . . . wai guo ren . . . bu xing.*" (Not allowed . . . foreigner . . . not allowed.) "*Mei guanxi; wo hao le.*" (No problem, I'm good.), I assure him smiling, but he persists in his shouting. "Bugger off, comrade!" I shout. He cannot comprehend but a gentle push—I think that's the only language he might understand— and he's off, freewheeling downhill.

With the young soldier riding pillion, the Gong An Ju motorcycle spluttered slowly to a halt right before me. As the boy grinned, continuing his "*bu xing*" chorus, the officer pulled out his red identity card and grabbed me by the arm. We went past the parked motorcycle, walked thirty yards along the road, stopped and turned. Another trilingual sign stared me in the eye. It was the writing on the wall, deep trouble for my journey and a handful of points for the boy soldier, who will doubtless be the model of the month in his unit.

It was a statement by the interrogating Foreign Affairs officer from Beijing city that brought home both the severity and humor of my predicament. With my passport in their hands, they had telephoned the city several times. I feared the worst.

"We have made our investigation." My heart thumped. "Because this is your first offense you will pay a fine of fifty yuan." I let out a sigh of monumental relief. "Another trespass and you will be made to leave China—you crossed twenty-five miles of forbidden territory."

I could have laughed and cried.

PART FOUR

Reforms

It doesn't matter whether the cat is black or white so long as it catches mice.

—*Deng Xiaoping*

17

Qing Ming— The Dragon Slain

No path exists until one man makes his
way by walking.
—*Lu Xun 1881–1936*

Retreating to Beijing yet again, bearing the scars of another defeat, I
felt my predicament to be hopeless. Had I travelled thousands of miles
only to be defeated by bureaucracy when the end was in sight? The
prospect of running to Shanhaiguan via the Tianjin highway was totally
unappealing—mere mile-collecting—nor could I stomach the thought of
taking the train to Shanhaiguan to cover the final miles down to the
Yellow Sea on foot. Then I happened to be browsing through *China
Reconstructs*—not a journal of civil engineering, but a magazine concerned with the unexpected Chinese activity of building bridges of
friendship. In it there was an article by a State Tourism Bureau guide
describing a journey with a group of French athletes along the Great Wall
between Beijing and Shanhaiguan. The thought struck me that if I could
secure the services of that guide, I might obtain the necessary travel
permits for the Wall in Hebei Province.

My good friends at Midland Bank and Thomas Cook got busy on my
behalf interpreting my request for permits, guide and a support vehicle
between Mutianyu and Shanhaiguan. It was not easy. In winter, we were
told, the guides and drivers were laid off to learn languages. The weather

195

would be terrible, the costs a prohibitive five thousand dollars (Thomas Cook gallantly reaffirmed its commitment in underwriting this expense by telephone at 7:00 a.m.). But when my fascination with the Great Wall and intention to write a book about it were stressed, the State Tourism Bureau suddenly agreed, subject to obtaining an Alien's Travel Permit on my behalf. Moreover, because I would be telling the world, the price of their services was slashed to fifteen hundred dollars. My passport details were forwarded and an anxious wait ensued while the Public Security Bureaus of counties bordering the Wall were contacted. Then, incredibly, we learned we could leave for the Wall the following week. Fifteen hundred dollars wasn't much of an entrance fee to complete the task. I owed China a great deal more.

* * *

Mr. Zhang, my guide, managed to gain access to a string of classic locations which were duly listed on the permit—places ending with the three characters of *kou, guan* and *yu*—meaning mouth, pass and valley. The validity of the permit was ten days, the method of travel, by foot on the Great Wall and by private vehicle to *binguans* each evening. For reasons clearly instituted to lessen the likelihood of document fraud, I was never even allowed to look at my own permit. Any hope of adding an ironic trophy to my collection of Gong An Ju adjudication memorabilia never presented itself.

Soon the taxi-clogged and bicycle-bulging daisies of central Beijing were behind us and we were cruising along the road to Mutianyu. Barring some disastrous injury on the Wall, reaching Shanhaiguan now depended largely on the ability of our drivers, Mr. Wei and Mr. Sui, to avoid providing the local Gong An Ju with gory illustrative material for their road safety campaigns. Driving was crazy. Jiefang trucks sped past as though the nation's economy depended on it.

Appropriately, we started on the section of Wall at Mutianyu, only miles to the east of my unfortunate apprehension, compliments of the "model soldier." Only now was I to learn of the reason for that arrest and for the classification of the Changping region as "forbidden." My trespass there had clearly been given the benefit of the doubt. I was fortunate to remain in China after having strayed close to Qin Cheng No. 1—or simply Q1, as the country's top political prison is referred to. One inmate is thought to be Jiang Qing, the evil widow of Chairman Mao and leader of the Gang of Four. Few of the "reeducated" detainees have ever been able to give detailed accounts of conditions in the "living hell" of Q1, though one Chinese proverbial saying is believed to sum up the establishment's policy: "force is the tactic of the petty man; psychology the way of the adept. . . ."

Only miles away from Q1, standing on the ramparts of Mutianyu, I became aware that the judicial policy of the Ming favored the forceful alternative. It was good to learn that the laborers who had recently rebuilt this section had been paid the going rate of approximately seventy yuan a month (about twenty dollars) for their efforts. But before them the pioneer builders had surveyed these mountains and set off from scratch with the singular aim of capturing the ridges of the Yanshan closest to heaven for their divine Emperor. Like Wren in St. Paul's, these men were architects at their acme, skillfully surmounting the problems of weight, bulk and gravity. They succeeded to the extent of making solid stones flexible, able to cross the most closely crammed contours, nonchalantly slide down slopes and climb over crags, a backbone of segmented discs. Within minutes smoke signal messages could be transmitted via the infinite number of towers that dotted each bend and summit all the way to the Yellow Sea. Chemical powders were able to produce color-coded communication on the relays of this telephone line of the Middle Ages, smoke by day, fire by night. No more a skeleton, the wall was now fleshed with newly quarried facing blocks bound by white mortar, fit for an inspection tour by the Emperor himself, with the banners raised from the watchtowers and soldiers at every parapet!

Bright sunlight, which had cast a perfect piano keyboard shadow on the Wall's paving flags during the morning, was challenged by an ever-clouding sky, heavy with rain that eventually turned into sleet. As darkness fell in our *fandian* at Miyun, the temperature plummeted and heavy wet sleet became light and dry sticking snow. . . .

It was the start of a big freezeup that would set a pattern for our whole journey. Beijing's Walls were now done with and we made our way north toward Gubeikou in blizzard conditions. Roadside checks were frequent at most junctions, with traffic Gong An Ju staying put in sentry boxes while passing drivers reported to them with fists full of papers. Driving licenses, identity cards, vehicle books—and, of course, my Alien's Travel Permit and passport—were all presented. Such security only emphasized the extreme difficulty of unrestricted movement for the Chinese themselves, let alone the near impossibility of hassle-free travel for the foreigner. Never before had I seen so many monitoring stops and checkpoints. It made me realize how crucial keeping off the beaten track had been for my unaccompanied success up to this point.

Over the following eight wintry days we edged our way along various passes and ridges of Hebei's spectacular Great Wall. Mr. Wei and Mr. Sui were engaged in the support role, priming the van to start in freezing temperatures at 7:00 a.m. Each morning, my guide Mr. Zhang and I, having donned every item of clothing that we possessed, were dropped at a section of Wall to climb on over the icy ruins. Sometimes a midday rendezvous was possible at the pass or valley to the east, where we could be welcomed by the steaming cauldron of noodles on the boil. Our rations were simple: sixty packets of *fangbian mian*—convenient noodles, flavored with chicken stock and monosodium glutamate. But more often we ate field rations of *mantou* or *baozi* and met up with our support in late afternoon. At Shangguan, however, the ever-shorter hours of daylight fooled us and we were forced into an emergency descent, missing the boat that would have ferried us to the others across the lake. How close we had come to perishing on the freezing Yanshan.

The splendor of the Wall in Jinshanling was unsurpassable for scale, complexity and dominance of its surroundings. In comparison, the Wall of Luowenyu was toylike, reminiscent of Hadrian's Wall. South towards Zunhua the plain was a smooth blanket of snow dotted with villages rebuilt after the devastating earthquake of 1976, which had centered on Tangshan just forty miles away. Hunger forced us off the Wall at Matiyu, into a village to buy poor man's meat—*doufu*—bean curd from a basket coddled by steaming rags and resting on the back of a peasant's bicycle. There are over a hundred varieties made in China; not surprisingly, I had never tasted this one before. Below Hengshoukou, children played on a frozen stream. Zhang asked if I could photograph them—"but we have no money" they replied, thinking I was a peddler. Into the final days, the final miles, China continued to show the unexpected, whether it be discovering details like holes for flag poles on the parapets, or being attracted like children to the music of a midwinter's fair in the village.

Crowded in the stone-walled courtyard of a mountain hamlet below Xifenkou, the peasants watched a performance of shadow puppets. Such a show is especially weather-dependent; it was midday and the sun shone down the narrow valley through the translucent sheet which formed the screen. Behind this screen the puppeteers held their metal marionettes flush against the sheet to thrill the children of the hamlet with the antics of their familiar characters.

* * *

It was the beginning of December and time to go down to the sea. Just two years ago I had been planning this journey in all my optimistic ignorance. Since then, amusing evenings, whole weeks in provinces and months on the Great Wall had all added up to two China years. The footprints on gobi sands had long since been covered. The most agonizing blisters had healed. The chill was out of my bones. A warmth of gladness filled my heart. Understanding had conquered ignorance, and friendship had won over fear. Many peasants had watched me pass by. The Chinese had extended their hands, and Qi had given me her heart.

The strides were counting down, reduced over the weeks from the order of millions now into the final thousands. Down Jioshan I ran, on to the plain, a route trodden before in my distant China apprenticeship. On the seventy-eighth day the Yellow Sea appeared on the horizon, although reaching it had consumed two years of my life. Two years, however, were not much in the history of the Wall. I was first to realize my inadequacies.

Running down to the sea seemed instinctively correct. From the Han to the Ming was a journey in time. The tail to the head was a journey in space. Old Dragon's Head is the end of the Great Wall—the end of *all* Great Walls. Breaching the seven-mile-wide "throat" of Shanhaiguan gave access to the wealth of the interior that had been sought by the Qing horsemen and archers who streamed through in 1644 towards Beijing. China went by the neck to the Manchu. The last Ming Emperor went by his own neck from a tree behind the Forbidden City. I too had conquered the Great Wall. The Dragon was slain. It seemed the only way to go, from the desert to the sea.

◼◼ 18 ◼◼

Beautiful
Jade

"China in Your Hands"
—*Popular song title by T'Pau*
(chart-topper in Britain
during December 1987)

Classical music over the loudspeakers heralded the start of lunch-time at Beijing Foreign Language Teachers' College where Qi studied. As a foreigner I was denied access to her hostel and telephone calls there were highly impractical via the overstretched city exchanges. The wait-ing and worrying were now over. This was our longed-for moment. Running towards me, Qi flung out her arms, all inhibitions forgotten. We held each other, embracing and jumping with delight—then laughed with embarrassment at the faces of shocked students. Oblivious, Qi continued with her welcome by presenting me with a scroll of Anhui calligraphic paper—carried expectantly for some days—on which she had written her own fitting tribute: Mao's "A Journey of a Thousand Miles begins with a Single Step." It would be a treasure to hang upon a wall of our future home.

From Midland Bank Mission Control, I telephoned my family and telexed my sponsors. Soon David, Nicholas and his wife Elizabeth were able to come out to Beijing to meet Qi and share our celebrations. The most amazing news from home was that after I had been harried across the breadth of China by the Gong An Ju, Thomas Cook had organized for me to be given a media reception at the Chinese Embassy in London when I got home. It was an irony I was to savor in due course.

* * *

Our Western New Year's Day in 1988 was the first opportunity for the public to walk upon the balcony of the Gate of Heavenly Peace on Tiananmen Square, which forms the principal entrance to the Forbidden City. Appropriately, this historical hinge stands at the southern end of China's Ming and Qing imperial past, facing south, as Mao's portrait still does, looking over a New China across the flagstones on the square. All buildings in the forward view postdate 1949: the Great Hall of the People, the Museum of the Revolution and the Mao Zedong Memorial Hall. For ten yuan one can stand at the very spot upon this rostrum from where the Great Leader himself proclaimed the foundation of the People's Republic. Later, Mao reviewed military parades from here, and inspected his Red Guards. Now foreign film crews were coaxing the Chinese to salute the cameras threateningly with their identity cards, mimicking the action of the guards waving their *Little Red Books*. At the entrance we had been given badges instead of tickets.

"Maybe twenty years ago as a little girl I collected Chairman Mao badges just like this—some as big as saucers!" recalled Qi. "And my sister, Wu Xiaoping, saw him here at the fourth Red Guard rally." I wondered what fate might have befallen foreign correspondents in those days. "Now, let's go to Longtan Park," I suggested. "I want to make a wish there." Qi looked out across the square. "I wish that you come back to Beijing soon." My recent and successful past had relied fully upon the benevolence of Chinese people I had not seen before, nor shall ever see again. But my future depended entirely on Qi, whom I was determined to come back for and marry.

* * *

Armed with a plethora of bilingual legalized documents that had been ratified by the Home Office and Chinese Embassy, I returned to Beijing in April. Qi produced her necessary quota of paperwork too: *danwei* permissions, personal files and citizenship certificates. After we were thoroughly evaluated by interviews and examined by doctors, we had our blood tested at a laboratory. With everything in order we crammed on to a bus to Xi'an, Qi's home city, and proceeded to the Shaanxi Provincial People's government office in the city center. Cleared to enter the main gate, I was prohibited from proceeding inside the actual building itself by a plainclothed security guard. Qi went upstairs to bring down the leader of the People's Affairs Bureau in order for him to verify the nature of our business there.

Inside the office, we sat opposite the marriage counselor, Mr. Teng, and penned "letters" to him describing the circumstances of our meeting, and our desire to marry. He approved of our relationship as being genuine and acceptable, commenting: "You love and know each other very well." Qi paid the requested fee of twenty yuan and we made our fingerprints in red ink upon a document that would be kept in the Provincial government files. In return, Mr. Teng presented us with our marriage certificates of glorious gold and red.

Over the ensuing weeks we travelled on a "honey month." This was Qi's first big tour of China. We went to Shanghai by train—a place I had often dreamed of taking her to. Then we spent a week aboard a Yangzi River steamer floating through the magnificent gorges to Chongqing, the hilly city devoid of bicycles. Later, we proceeded on to Kunming, a place of eternal springtime, then to secluded Dali on the Burma Road in deepest Yunnan, and finally into steamy Sichuan.

In early July the Xi'an city Gong An Ju issued Qi with a passport, and on the fourteenth of that month—surely our lucky number for we were engaged and married on those dates—we flew to England.

Seven months have passed since then. Qi is sitting across the room, planning her autobiography, while I write these final words on the eve of Spring Festival—the Year of the Snake. Another auspicious year dawns as a new animal brings fresh challenges and walls to face—together.

EPILOGUE

With the book written, we were happy to resume a more conventional way of life. Now I had the time to show Qi the British Isles. We visited Hadrian's Wall, where the whole China experience was rooted; the sights of London, which her English studies had convinced her was a foggy city; and Devon, where she tasted the delights of cream teas in a sleepy seaside resort.

Improving language skills, in particular a mastery of the Merseyside "Scouse" dialect, allowed Qi to return to a financial career, albeit without the abacus, for the Midland Bank in Liverpool. Most aspects of daily life were new experiences. Shopping, which offered self-service and huge choices, was a great adventure for Qi. Packaging often bewildered her. It was difficult for her to distinguish prepackaged chicken from other poultry, since in China she was used to buying a live feathered bird to slaughter at home.

Cycling proved to be too hazardous because of the hills, winding narrow roads and heavy traffic. Unaccustomed to seeing so many vacant seats on buses and trains, Qi preferred to use these types of public transport, which in Beijing had involved something of a gymnastic workout. Walking on uncrowded streets was a hit, and after reestablishing the good British tradition of taking a long stroll to work off the Sunday roast beef lunch, we soon graduated to tackling the 95-mile-long West Highland Way National Trail through Scotland. Qi showed herself a worthy comrade of the Long Marchers, coping with the distance without developing a single blister, unlike the feet of this out-of-condition author. Soon after, I reintroduced the daily training regime of runs along the Wirral coastline and began renewing old friendships again as I competed with athletes on the cross-country and road-racing circuit of Northwest England.

Meanwhile, my income was derived from lecturing at societies and dinners. However, my strategy of promoting China's increasing attractions as a tourist destination was soon scuttled by the political unrest that broke out in Beijing after the death of Hu Yaobang. Although China's domination of the world's news was quite unforeseen, the Chinese tactic of transforming an occasion of mourning into an opportunity for political protest was an age-old practice. Yet I did not share the predictions of those foreign correspondents who watched the tanks besieged by people and predicted that the days of the old revolutionary leaders were numbered. In defense of my scepticism, I offered the simple evidence of how bureaucrats had viewed my "crimes" in China. As individuals they had wholeheartedly welcomed me and sympathized with my philosophy of trespass, even praising my revolutionary spirit. But as the inevitable interrogations progressed, these small cogs in the labyrinthine machinery of China's public security had no qualms about dealing out the necessary punishment, whether it was a fine, detention, confiscation or expulsion. It seems quite clear to any student of modern Chinese history that the battle-hardy octogenarians would cling onto their power whatever the cost. Thus the events dubbed the Prodemocracy Movement by the Western press became the defeated Counterrevolution. The rest is history and unforgettable images. In China, however, the words of history are often rewritten.

The UK publication of *Alone on the Great Wall* in the autumn of 1989 coincided with the nationwide crackdown and hunt of the counterrevolutionaries throughout China. Criticism and questioning, reminiscent of the Counterrevolution, had returned. Against this background one critic of the book voiced concern that my decision to retain genuine names of Chinese people had incriminated scores of people who had played such a vital role in my journey. This accusation coincided with two replies to letters written by Qi on my behalf to friends along the Great Wall. The Wang family of Qingshui in the Gansu Province told us of their delight in receiving a print to mount on the wall of their remote farmhouse. Li Dong, the teacher of English from Yanchi in Ningxia, confirmed one of my highest hopes. The reports made by the Xinhua (New China) News

Agency in China's press and media after they had examined my four diaries had filtered through to the very people who had made my journey along the Great Wall a reality.

As I write this postscript, Qi and I are once again in China, residing in Xi'an. Soon I will be setting off once again to travel in remote regions, attempting to retrace the revolutionary transformation of China in the footsteps of Mao Zedong. I somehow sense that the final episode of this story still rests in the minds of the Chinese people, waiting to be played. That is the future.

Wu Qi and William Lindesay

CHRONOLOGY

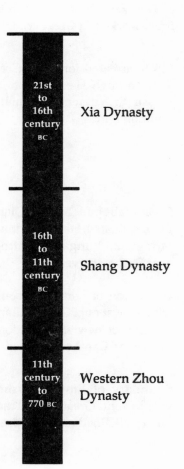

21st to 16th century BC	Xia Dynasty
16th to 11th century BC	Shang Dynasty
11th century to 770 BC	Western Zhou Dynasty

If we define Great Wall as any defensive fortification built by a dynastic ruler at the boundary of their empire, then there are the remnants of thousands of miles of Great Wall all over north China and the present-day People's Republic of Mongolia. This legacy of some two millennia of Wall-building is tabulated in the following chronology.

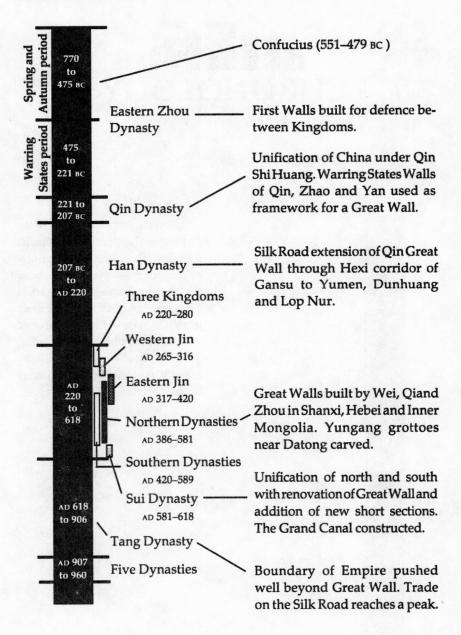

Spring and Autumn period	770 to 475 BC	
		Confucius (551–479 BC)
	Eastern Zhou Dynasty	First Walls built for defence between Kingdoms.
Warring States period	475 to 221 BC	Unification of China under Qin Shi Huang. Warring States Walls of Qin, Zhao and Yan used as framework for a Great Wall.
	221 to 207 BC	Qin Dynasty
	207 BC to AD 220	Han Dynasty
		Silk Road extension of Qin Great Wall through Hexi corridor of Gansu to Yumen, Dunhuang and Lop Nur.

Three Kingdoms
AD 220–280

Western Jin
AD 265–316

Eastern Jin
AD 317–420

Great Walls built by Wei, Qiand Zhou in Shanxi, Hebei and Inner Mongolia. Yungang grottoes near Datong carved.

Northern Dynasties
AD 386–581

Southern Dynasties
AD 420–589

Unification of north and south with renovation of Great Wall and addition of new short sections. The Grand Canal constructed.

Sui Dynasty
AD 581–618

Tang Dynasty

Five Dynasties

Boundary of Empire pushed well beyond Great Wall. Trade on the Silk Road reaches a peak.

AD 220 to 618

AD 618 to 906

AD 907 to 960

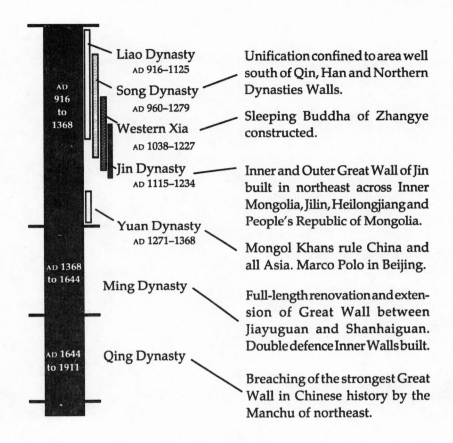

AD 916 to 1368	**Liao Dynasty** AD 916–1125	Unification confined to area well south of Qin, Han and Northern Dynasties Walls.
	Song Dynasty AD 960–1279	
	Western Xia AD 1038–1227	Sleeping Buddha of Zhangye constructed.
	Jin Dynasty AD 1115–1234	Inner and Outer Great Wall of Jin built in northeast across Inner Mongolia, Jilin, Heilongjiang and People's Republic of Mongolia.
	Yuan Dynasty AD 1271–1368	Mongol Khans rule China and all Asia. Marco Polo in Beijing.
AD 1368 to 1644	**Ming Dynasty**	Full-length renovation and extension of Great Wall between Jiayuguan and Shanhaiguan. Double defence Inner Walls built.
AD 1644 to 1911	**Qing Dynasty**	Breaching of the strongest Great Wall in Chinese history by the Manchu of northeast.

NB Overlapping dates are the result of long-drawn-out changes of rule and regional variations due to Internal strife.

GLOSSARY OF
MANDARIN WORDS

bian	border, frontier
binguan	hotel
bu xing	prohibited, not allowed
Chang Cheng	the Great Wall
Chang Zheng	the Long March
chi fan	to eat food
dajie	main street
danwei	work unit
dao zi	rice plants in paddies
dui	yes, correct
fandian	rice house, i.e., hotel or restaurant
ganbei	bottoms up (cheers)
Gong An Ju	Public Security Bureau (police)
gongli	kilometers
gong she	commune
guan	pass
hao	good
he	river
he shui	drink water
hao peng you	good friends
hutong	alleyway
jiaozi	dumpling of pork and vegetable
kou	mouth, entrance, pass
kuai	spoken form of renminbi (Chinese currency)
lao wai	old foreigner

li	Chinese unit of distance, equal to one third of a mile on the flat
ling	hills
lu	road
lüguan	small resting house
mantou	steamed bread
mianbao	baked bread
mian tiao	noodles
nei Mongol	inner Mongolia
ni hao	"you good" i.e., hello
Putonghua	"understandable language," i.e., Mandarin Chinese
renminbi	Chinese currency, lit. "people's money"
Ribao (Renmin)	Daily Newspaper (People's)
shan	mountains
shamo	"sand sea," i.e., desert
shangdian	general store
shu ku	reservoir
wai guo ren	foreigner
Xiang gang	"fragrant harbor," i.e., Hong Kong
xi gua	West Melon, i.e., watermelon
xifan	rice porridge
xiu xi	rest awhile, especially during the afternoon
Ying guo	Britain
yu	valley
zaijian	see you again (goodbye)
zhan	station
Zhong guo	China
zou le	I'm going

INDEX